Rainforest Corridors

Rainforest Corridors

The Transamazon Colonization Scheme

Nigel J. H. Smith

University of California Press
Berkeley · Los Angeles · London

University of California Press
Berkeley and Los Angeles, California

University of California Press, Ltd.
London, England

© 1982 by
The Regents of the University of California

1 2 3 4 5 6 7 8 9

Library of Congress Cataloging in Publication Data

Smith, Nigel J. H., 1949–
Rainforest corridors. The Transamazon colonization scheme.

Revision of the author's thesis (Ph. D.)—University of California, Berkeley.
Bibliography: p
Includes index.
1. Agricultural colonies—Amazon Valley. 2. Public health—Amazon Valley. 3. Rain forest ecology—Amazon Valley. 4. Rodovia Transamazônica (Brazil) I. Title.
HD1516.B8S63 1982 333.75 81-7478
ISBN 0-520-04497-5 AACR2

To Lisa

Contents

Illustrations

Tables

Preface

In 1970 I had the good fortune to be a student on Professor Hilgard Sternberg's field course to the Brazilian Amazon when the government decision to construct the 3,000-km Transamazon highway was announced. The region, still largely a wilderness, was on the threshold of major changes. Professor Sternberg, my major advisor while I was a student at Berkeley, actively encouraged me to pursue studies on the pioneer rainforest highway. I am immensely indebted to Professor Sternberg for his patience, enthusiasm, and help as I prepared a dissertation on the colonization scheme. My dissertation, finished in 1976, provides the foundation for this book. I am also very grateful to Professors James Parsons, Charles Bennett, and Jonathan Sauer for their advice and valuable criticisms during my training as a geographer.

I am indebted to Dr. Ralph Lainson for his comments on the health chapters of this book while they were in a preliminary stage. Dr. Lainson's long experience with public health problems in Amazonia, particularly with leishmaniasis, was extremely helpful. Several anonymous reviewers also made helpful suggestions on an early version of this study.

In Brazil I was honored to be linked with NAEA (Nucleo de Altos Estudos Amazônicos) of the Federal University at Belém. NAEA, particularly through the offices of its coordinator, Professor José Marcelino Monteiro da Costa, and Dr. Samuel Sá, enabled me to conduct research on the Transamazon and provided a stimulating atmosphere for the exchange of ideas on development of Amazonia. During my visits to the Brazilian Amazon in 1970, 1971, and 1972, letters of recommendation from Professor Aloysio da Costa Chaves, former Chancellor of the Federal University, Belém, and from Professor Maria Annunciada Chaves, Vice-Chancellor for student matters at the same University, were very helpful in my gaining the support of other institutions. Professor Antonio Vizeu da Costa Lima, former Vice-Chancellor at the Federal University in Belém, has provided unfailing assistance since I first went to Brazil.

Grants from the Center For Latin American Studies, Berkeley, and fellowships from National Defense Foreign Language and the Dean, University of California, Berkeley, have enabled me to make four trips to Amazonia as both undergraduate and graduate student. I am also grateful to INPA (Instituto Nacional de Pesquisas da Amazônia), Manaus, for providing research grants to conduct follow-up work along the Transamazon. I should also like to thank the Museu Goeldi, Belém, IPEAN (Instituto de Pesquisa Agropecuária do Norte), INCRA (Instituto Nacional de Colonização e Reforma Agrária), DNER (Departamento Nacional de Estradas de Rodagem), DER-PA (Departamento de Estradas de Rodagem-Pará), and the Brazilian Air Force for their cooperation and logistical support. A grant from the Ford Foundation in 1979 allowed me to conduct library research for this book at the University of California, Berkeley.

My wife, Lisa, joined me on several field trips to the Transamazon. Although she did not always share my enthusiasm for the jungle, Lisa's companionship was of immense psychological benefit during my field work. I am indebted to her courage and good humor during our rustic excursions. My appreciation for peasant culture has been enhanced by discussions with Emilio and Millie Moran and Michael Goulding. Along the Transamazon, the warm hospitality of the Morans, Keith and Paul Cornell, and John and Flo Lawson helped make field work an enjoyable experience. Finally, the highway colonists themselves provided close friendship. I found their forthright observations on pioneer life refreshing. I am very glad to have had the opportunity of sharing with them the drama of a frontier life.

Final appreciation belongs to the reviewers and editors of *Rainforest Corridors*. Dr. Robert Goodland, Dr. Emilio Moran, and an anonymous referee made many helpful suggestions on the book manuscript. Dr. Karen Reeds, sponsoring editor with the University of California Press, successfully and enthusiastically steered the book through the review process. Her courteous and efficient work is much appreciated. Dr. Herbert Baker improved my spelling of the scientific names of some of the plants mentioned in the text. And Mrs. Gladys Castor's copy-editing enhanced the flow of the text.

Abbreviations

BASA Banco da Amazônia
CAMNOF Cooperativa Agropecuária Mista Nova Fronteira
CEPLAC Comissão Executiva do Plano de Lavoura Cacaueira
CIBRAZEM Companhia Brasileira de Armazenagem
CIRA Cooperativa Integral de Reforma Agrária
COBAL Companhia Brasileira de Alimentos
COMACI Cooperativa Mista Agropecuária Colonial de Itaituba
COOPERFRON Cooperativa Nova Fronteira
COPEMBA Cooperativa de Marabá
COTRIJUI Cooperativa Regional Tritícola Serrana
DNER Departamento Nacional de Estradas de Rodagem
EMATER Empresa de Assistência Técnica e Extensão Rural
EMBRAPA Empresa Brasileira de Pesquisa Agropecuária
FSESP Fundação Serviços de Saúde Pública
FUNAI Fundação Nacional do Indio
FUNRURAL Fundo de Assistência e Previdência do Trabalhador Rural
HSA Hemorrhagic Syndrome of Altamira
IBDF Instituto Brasileiro de Desenvolvimento Florestal
INCRA Instituto Nacional de Colonização e Reforma Agrária
INPA Instituto Nacional de Pesquisas da Amazônia
INPS Instituto Nacional de Previdência Social

IPEAN Instituto de Pesquisa Agropecuária do Norte
PIN Programa de Integração Nacional
POLAMAZÔNIA Pólos Agropecuários e Agrominerais da Amazônia
SUCAM Superintendência de Campanhas de Saúde Pública
SUDAM Superintendência de Desenvolvimento da Amazônia
SUDENE Superintendência de Desenvolvimento do Nordeste

chapter

1 Introduction

A seemingly endless sea of undulating forest unfolds to the horizon. The rasping, hollow call of toucans announces dawn. The patchy mist slowly dissolves under the steady warm glow of the rising sun. A pair of brilliant scarlet macaws cruises effortlessly over the trees in search of fruit. A chattery band of parakeets explodes from a forest giant and then quickly melts back into the canopy. Suddenly, a new sound in the distance: the mournful whine of motor saws and the rumble of bulldozers and earth-scrapers announce the arrival of the Transamazon work crews. Soon, extensive corridors are torn through the canopy, irrevocably altering the landscape. A large-scale effort to colonize Amazonia is under way.

In 1970 the Brazilian government made a commitment to integrate the Amazon region to the rest of the country by clearing 15,000 km of pioneer highways (Fig. 1). The 3,300-km east-west Transamazon, also known as BR-230, slices across the forest that blankets the southern interfluves of Amazonia (Fig. 2). The government planned to settle 100,000 families along the Transamazon by 1976, and 1 million by 1980 (INCRA, n.d.). The most ambitious colonization scheme ever attempted in the humid tropics sparked a great deal of controversy in both the Brazilian and the international press. Concern was expressed that the highway would destroy Indian cultures, upset the ecological balance of the region, and create a scrub desert. Colonists, it was argued, would be exposed to debilitating new diseases and bring others with them. Others claimed that the highway marked a new age for Amazonia: the Transamazon would unmask natural resources and provide a catalyst for regional development.

This book takes a decade-long look at the Transamazon. It assesses the accomplishments and failures of the scheme and focuses on the factors that retard agricultural development in the environment of a frontier rainforest. The political and economic forces behind the decision to build the highway are explored. The logistical problems associated with such a far-flung project are described, and the sources of funding are identified. A major theme of the research is the viability of the Amazonian uplands for large-scale settlement.

The chapter on the ecological setting emphasizes the relevance of plants, animals, soils, geomorphology, and climate to the livelihood of settlers. The chapter on agro-ecosystem productivity investigates the cropping pattern and yields. The crops promoted by the government are analyzed with respect to their ecological, economic, and cultural suitability in a pioneer environment far removed from large markets. Factors responsible for the generally depressed yields are examined, ranging from ecological causes, such as poor soils, weed invasion, pest damage, and inclement weather, to socioeconomic aspects, such as inadequate credit, fiscal incentives, and poor farm management.

The health of settlers is also considered within the context of agricultural productivity. The amount of production from essentially unmechanized farm plots depends largely on the ability of the settlers to provide the necessary work. Theoretical estimates

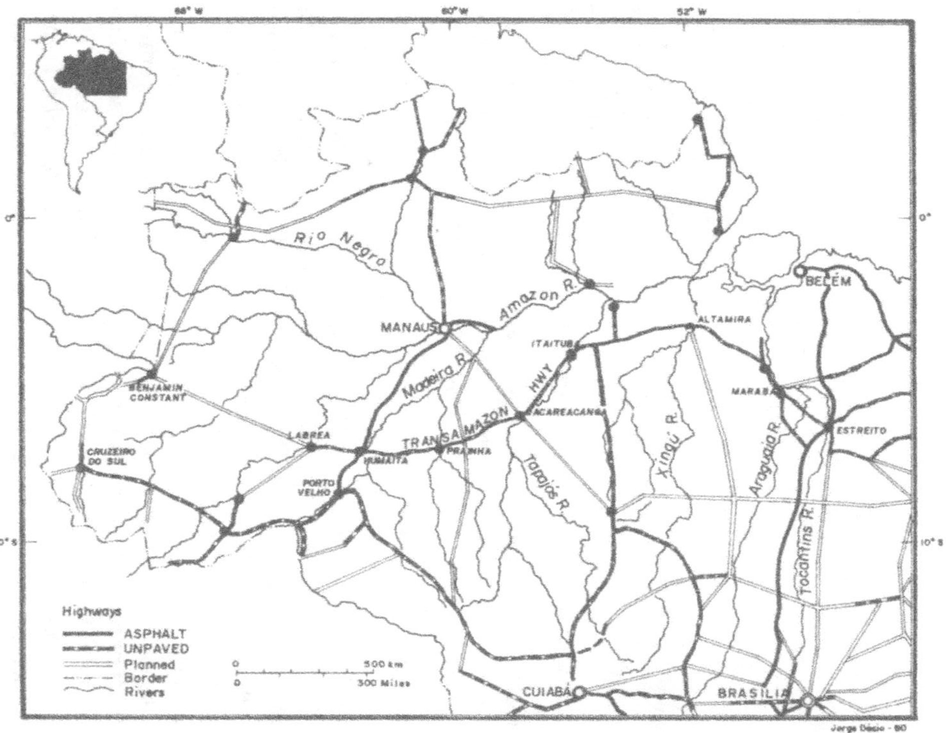

Figure 1. The Brazilian Amazon highway system

Figure 2. The Transamazon at km 12 of the Marabá–Estreito stretch in 1971. Note the remnants of forest trees, such as Brazil nut (*Bertholletia excelsa*), and escaped pasture grass, jaragua (*Hyparrhenia rufa*), along the roadside.

on crop yields are of little practical concern if the colonists are suffering from incapacitating disease. The chapter on public health problems begins with a description of the zoonoses that exist in the forest and of how settlers become involved in sylvan epidemiological cycles. The impact of malaria, injuries, gastroenteritis, respiratory complaints, helminthiasis, and the hemorrhagic syndrome of Altamira on the working capacity of settlers is then discussed. For each health challenge, the cultural and ecological factors involved in transmission are explored. Particular attention is paid to man-made alterations of the landscape and to cultural habits that increase the incidence of disease. The chapter on the possible future health problems along the Transamazon emphasizes the dynamic nature of disease transmission.

To better understand why the incidence of several infectious diseases remains high, the distribution and adequacy of public health services are analyzed. Deficiencies in the government-operated medical posts, clinics, and hospitals create a substantial market for private medical practice. The financial burden and health hazards associated with the two complementary health service systems are examined. Settlers often resort to alternative medicine by preparing home remedies from plants and by consulting spiritual healers. The sources of medicinal plants, methods of preparation, and pharmaceutical value are investigated. The Transamazon provides a particularly interesting stage for an ethnobotanical survey because of the cultural diversity of settlers. The study explores supernatural notions on the causation of disease in order to explain apparently irrational behavior by some colonists.

The final chapter discusses the Transamazon within the framework of development pressures on the earth's largest remaining tropical forest. Brazil's swelling population and ever-increasing appetite for raw materials have created a momentum for opening up Amazonia for settlement and exploitation. Much of the desire to gain access to untapped resources stems from multinational corporations and Brazilian firms. The Transamazon was an attempt to encourage small-scale farms under the auspices of the federal government; the apparent demise of the scheme has triggered a shift in official settlement policy for the region. Lessons from the Transamazon experience are discussed, and a model for modest settlement of Amazonia is proposed.

Duration of field work

I have spent two and half years on the Transamazon, stretched over a ten-year period. I was introduced to the Marabá area of the proposed highway in 1970, and returned there as well as to Altamira and Itaituba between July and September of 1971. My first two field seasons in Amazonia gave me the opportunity to learn Portuguese and to witness the construction phase of the monumental project. One month was spent with an advance party of FUNAI (Fundação Nacional do Indio), the Federal Indian Service, in search of natives along the highway transect 80 km east of Prainha on the Aripuanã River. During my first two years along the highway, I walked through closed-canopy jungle that is now replaced by weed-choked pastures, tangled second growth, open fields, or bustling settlements. A skyline of skeleton forest has given me a vivid impression of the rapid changes in the landscape.

I returned to the Transamazon in October and November of

1972, and from September 1973 to November 1974. Further visits were made in July 1977, December 1978, and April, June, and September of 1979. My experience on the highway spans several wet and dry seasons, which has enabled me to gain an appreciation of the ecological and cultural significance of the amount and distribution of rainfall. Follow-up visits have given me the opportunity to better understand biophysical and socioeconomic processes operating along the highway. Much of the research conducted in the neotropics takes place in the Northern Hemisphere summer, which in the case of most of Amazonia is the dry season.

The advantages of an in-depth study of just one area were weighed against a desire to attain a broader understanding of settlement conditions. Thus, most of my field work was conducted in three well-separated study sites along the settled 1,266-km stretch of the Transamazon between Estreito and Itaituba. In addition, two road trips were made along the same stretch. In this manner, it was possible to cross-check research findings and to verify the ecological and cultural heterogeneity of the highway transect.

To serve as operational bases, I selected three government-built settlements (*agrovilas*) along the main axis of the highway. None of the *agrovilas* are close to large towns, so conditions there are reasonably representative of a pioneer zone. Coco Chato,[1] the first *agrovila* encountered as one travels from east to west along the highway, rests on the crest of a hill, 42 km northwest of Marabá. The *agrovila* contains sixty-six houses and is unique in that the homes have cement floors and red-tiled roofs. The second community, Leonardo da Vinci, is located 18 km east of Altamira and 440 km from Coco Chato. The sixty-six wooden houses, with plank floors and gray asbestos roofs, are aligned

1. Government officials used to call the *agrovila* Coco Chato, after a small community of palm-thatch houses that once clung to the edges of a nearby stream. Coco Chato translates roughly as the "annoying coconut," and refers to the large number of babaçu palms (*Orbygnia martiana*) that grow in the area. The preexisting settlement was bulldozed by the government in 1973, and the inhabitants were required to move to the *agrovila*, if they had been given lots, or encouraged to move on. Officials now refer to the *agrovila* as Castelo Branco, in honor of the first president after the military coup in March 1964.

along the slope of a gentle hill. The third main study site, *agrovila* Nova Fronteira, contains forty-eight houses similar to those of Leonardo da Vinci.

Soil type was one of the principal criteria used in selecting the intensive study areas. The three study communities rest on different soils; thus it was possible to determine whether agricultural yields were significantly affected by soil fertility, or whether other factors were more important. Another factor considered in selecting the study sites was the degree of prior modification of the forest by man. The vegetation encompassing Leonardo da Vinci and Nova Fronteira has not been much disturbed in recent times, though the forest differs at the two locations. For close to a century, the vicinity of Coco Chato has been drastically altered by swidden farmers living in, or near, the Tocantins town of Itupiranga. A mosaic of second-growth patches and forest thus characterizes the surroundings of Coco Chato. I wanted to examine settlement in a variety of vegetation types in order to see how game and gathering yields differ according to habitat.

By selecting three communities, I was able to observe a larger sample of settlers from different regional backgrounds interacting with their new environment. The *agrovilas* chosen for intensive study contain a mix of settlers from several states. In 1974, 40 percent of the residents of the three study *agrovilas* came from Pará state, 25 percent from the Northeast, 19 percent from the South, 11 percent from Goias, and 5 percent from Minas Gerais and São Paulo. The 155 families surveyed in 1979 also came from varied regional backgrounds. A third had migrated from the southern states of Paraná, Rio Grande do Sul, and Santa Catarina. Northeasterners accounted for 28 percent of the sample, and Paraenses for 21 percent. Goias, Brasília, and Mato Grosso were the source for 12 percent of the colonists interviewed that year, while the remainder had traveled from the southeastern states of Minas Gerais, Espirito Santo, and São Paulo.

The 1979 sample was made along the 986-km Marabá–Itaituba stretch of the highway and includes only families who have resided on the Transamazon for a minimum of two years. The highway provides an unusually good setting for examining the role of culture in the adaptation of pioneers to a rainforest environment.

Two other books based on extensive field work have been written about the Transamazon, and readers are urged to consult them for additional information and perspectives on the highway scheme. The lengthy work by Emilio Moran (1981), an anthropologist, focuses on the potential for agricultural development on the Amazon uplands. Moran's excellent study differs from mine in that more emphasis is placed on aboriginal farming patterns, the history of natural resource use in Amazonia, and levels of analysis and methodological aspects of research in the region. Philip Fearnside (1981), an ecologist, uses carrying-capacity models to discuss agricultural productivity along the Transamazon. His stochastic models, based on a rich collection of data, attempt to identify bottlenecks to agricultural production and ultimately to the capacity of the land to support settlers.

chapter

2

Genesis of the Transamazon Scheme

For most of Brazilian history, the Amazon region, 3.5 million square kilometers, has remained isolated and largely ignored by the national society.[1] Although Amazonia accounts for 42 percent of the national territory, it contains only 5 million people, just 4 percent of Brazil's population. The economy of the region is largely a legacy of boom-and-bust cycles based on extractive industries, such as drugs and spices in the colonial period, the rubber boom at the end of the nineteenth century and the beginning of the present century, and more recently minerals, timber, and Brazil nuts. None of the industries has had a lasting effect on the

1. The text follows the regional division of Brazil according to IBGE (1978). The Amazon, or Northern region, comprises the states of Acre, Amazonas, Pará, and the territories of Rondônia, Roraima, and Amapá.

development of the region. Amazonia accounts for an insignificant 2 percent of the gross national product (Costa, J., 1979; Skillings and Tcheyan, 1979).

Only in 1964, with the inauguration of the Belém–Brasília, was the North connected by road with the rest of the country. Then in 1970, President Medici announced plans to build 15,000 km of National Integration Highways (PIN)[2] in the region. The Transamazon is envisaged as the east-west axis and backbone of the new road network.

The Transamazon was seen as a means of spanning South America at its broadest section. The western section of BR-230 was to extend from Humaitá to Labrea, Boca do Acre, Rio Branco, and Cruzeiro do Sul. The Brazilians hoped that Peru would cooperate with them in connecting Cruzeiro do Sul with Pucallpa, on the Ucayali. Pucallpa in turn would be linked with the Andean Perimeter Highway (Carretera Marginal de la Selva), thereby gaining access to the Pacific. The eastern terminus of the Transamazon at Estreito connects with roads to the Northeast and the Atlantic. The Peruvians never forged a road across the forest to Acre, probably because they feared that by so doing, they would facilitate the flow of products from the Peruvian Amazon to Brazil. The Carretera Marginal de la Selva is incomplete. Consequently, in 1973 the Brazilian government changed the trajectory of the Transamazon from Humaitá to Benjamin Constant (Fig. 1).

The Federal highway department, DNER (Departamento Nacional de Estradas de Rodagem), contracted private Brazilian firms to build the 3,300-km Transamazon. The two-lane road would be 8.6 m wide with a surface of compacted earth or, whenever possible, plinthite pebbles. Six companies were responsible for the formidable task of contracting labor and bringing in supplies, from as far as 2,000 km, to the various workfronts (Table 1).[3] The job of cutting a swath 70 m wide through

2. PIN (Programa de Integração Nacional) was created by decree 1.106 on 16 June 1970 to provide for new highway construction in the Amazon region as well as the irrigation of 40,000 ha in the Northeast (INCRA, 1972a).

3. Originally, Paulista S.A. was to build the Marabá–Rio Repartimento stretch of the highway, but the firm soon fell behind schedule because of logistical problems. Mendes Junior, a large construction company from Minas Gerais, then took over the contract.

Table 1. Companies Responsible for Building the Transamazon Highway between Estreito and Humaitá

Stretch	Kilometers	Company
Estreito–Marabá	280	Mendes Junior
Marabá–Rio Repartimento	160	Mendes Junior
Rio Repartimento–Altamira	340	Mendes Junior
Altamira–54°W 4°S	256	Queiroz Galvão
54°W 4°S–Itaituba	230	Empresa Industrial Técnica
Itaituba–Jacareacanga	300	Rabello
Jacareacanga–Prainha	406	Camargo Corrêa
Prainha–Humaitá	350	Paranapanema
Total	2,322	

Source: Departamento Nacional de Estradas de Rodagem, Belém and Manaus.

the imposing forest, some 23,000 ha of timber, was subcontracted by the firms to individuals known as *gatos*. The "cats" recruited work crews by seeking unemployed single men in run-down boarding houses and hotels in Pará and Maranhão. In this manner the large companies avoided the responsibility for the health and safety of the tree cutters.

Life for the axe hands was not easy. The *gatos* organized their employees into groups of three or four and paid them a set fee per area cleared. The work crews usually made camp by a small stream. Workers quickly erected a crude palm-thatch roof for cover and slung their hammocks from cross poles. Food, cooking utensils, machetes, and axe-heads were acquired from the middleman at exorbitant prices, to be discounted later from wages. The diet of the woodcutters was woefully deficient in vitamins and protein. Manioc flour, rice, sugar, and coffee were the main provisions. Little time or energy remained after work to hunt or collect forest fruits. Vegetables, except for the occasional palm heart, were absent from the daily fare. Wild honey, stolen from nests of stingless meliponid bees, was a rare treat.

Because of the meager diet and absence of medical facilities, the health of woodcutters suffered. Malaria was a common ailment; I saw pallid men shivering under sacks in their hammocks during the midday heat, their bodies wracked by alternating fever and chills. I do not know how many men expired in the forest. Grave-sites are prohibited along the Transamazon. Gruesome publicity might have interrupted the labor flow urgently needed for the construction tasks.

The balance of wages of the survivors was usually squandered on marathon binges and on whores, a release after months of hard labor with few diversionary outlets. Most of the money gone, the majority of wood cutters moved on to clear more forest for ranches, to hunt spotted cats, or to pan for gold or diamonds.

In the wake of the forest cutters, large bulldozers, made in Brazil and brought from São Paulo, pushed aside the charred logs. As early as September 1970, the machines were cleaning parts of the highway transect. The throaty roar of the diesel engines echoed through the forest day and night, under the harsh glare of headlights and the smoldering glow of embers. Giant earth-scrapers then began the task of shaving off the tops of hills and filling in small valleys.

The private companies generally treated their employees well. Lodging, food, and the services of a male nurse or a doctor were provided free of charge. Meals contained generous portions of rice, manioc flour, beans, and dried beef or game. Air taxis sometimes flew fresh beef in from Santarém, Belém, or Manaus. All workers were given paid leave, with free transportation, ranging from a week to a month, depending on job rank.

The first stretch of the Transamazon between Estreito and Itaituba (1,266 km) was completed in 1972. The portion between Itaituba and Humaitá (1,056 km) was finished in 1974. The expertise gained from construction of the Transamazon is now being used by some companies, such as Empresa Industrial Técnica, to build portions of other National Integration Highways. Camargo Corrêa and Mendes Junior profited handsomely from the Transamazon and have been contracted to build roads and railways across deserts of the Middle East and the Sahara.[4]

Reasons for Transamazon scheme

Geopolitical considerations were paramount in the decision to build the Transamazon and associated National Integration

4. Mendes Junior is building a highway in Mauritania and a $1.2 billion railroad in Iraq (*Veja*, 23 Janurary 1980).

Highways. Brazilians are nervous about leaving such a huge chunk of national territory virtually abandoned. A. F. Reis, a prominent Brazilian historian and political figure, has repeatedly stressed the dangers of international covetousness of Amazonia (1960). In 1970, Brazil began plans to inventory the mineral, soil, and timber resources of the river basin with the aid of side-looking radar (Hammond, 1977). The soon-to-be discovered natural resources would surely kindle outside interest. Published reports, such as the one by the United Nations Food and Agricultural Organization (Pawley, 1971), which suggest that the world could support as many as 36 billion people if the Amazon region was intensively farmed, have fed Brazilian fears of foreign intervention.

The Transamazon served as a dramatic demonstration that the Brazilian government was determined to effectively incorporate Amazonia into national society. New army garrisons on the outskirts of Marabá, Altamira, and Itaituba emphasize the military objectives of the highway. An extensive road network through the rainforest, coupled with improved airport facilities, would greatly facilitate logistical support in the event of military operations in the North.

A concern for national security has also prompted other governments to accelerate settlement of underdeveloped regions. After the disastrous Chaco war with Paraguay between 1932 and 1935, the Bolivian government promoted settlement schemes in its sparsely populated jungle territory north of Santa Cruz (Hiraoka, 1980). Uneasiness over the burgeoning population of Asia prompted the Australian government to sponsor agricultural development schemes in its tropical North (Davidson, 1972). The Russians built the Trans-Siberian railroad in a similar attempt to place a stamp of sovereignty on their northern territory.

The 1970 drought, which seared the backlands of the Northeast and uprooted 3.5 million people, was the triggering factor behind the decision to build the Transamazon (Hall, 1978:10). Periodic droughts exacerbate social unrest in the region, which accounts for 30 percent of the national population but occupies only 18 percent of the country. The Transamazon was perceived as a safety valve for the densely settled region, by creating access to the well-watered demographic void of Amazonia. The Northeast, one of the most volatile regions of Brazil, has a long history of peasant insurrections (Cunha, 1976).

The third major reason for the decision to build the Transamazon was a desire to reach natural resources. The forest masked soils to be farmed and minerals to be extracted. Advertisements appeared in Brazilian magazines depicting the Transamazon paved with glistening tin; the road would lead to El Dorado. The immense timber reserves of the southern interfluves of Amazonia would also be unlocked.

Funds for construction of the Transamazon were drawn from PIN and USAID (United States Agency for International Development). The National Integration Program was provided with a budget of $450 million (U.S., throughout the book) obtained by tapping 30 percent of the funds of SUDAM (Superintendência de Desenvolvimento da Amazônia)[5] and SUDENE (Superintendência de Desenvolvimento do Nordeste), agencies responsible for promoting development projects in Amazonia and the Northeast respectively. The siphoning of funds from SUDENE provoked considerable dissatisfaction in the Northeast: Why, it was argued, should a poor region make financial sacrifices for a scheme for which no cost-benefit analyses had been performed, and for which there was no assurance of success? A total of $100 million was drawn from the PIN fund for building the Transamazon (Pereira, 1971). USAID donated $10 million to Brazil in the form of PL-480 wheat, the proceeds of sale to be used on the highway project.[6]

Although Brazil has not received financing from foreign banks for the Transamazon, World Bank has loaned Brazil $629 million for construction or improvement of highways between 1970 and 1979. In addition, $132 million have been made available to Brazil

5. SUDAM was created by decree 5.174 on 27 October 1966 to coordinate development schemes in the Amazon region. Fiscal incentives permit companies to invest 50 percent of their taxes in projects approved by SUDAM. Authorized projects are exempt from taxation until 1982, and may import machinery and other supplies free of duty. Investment capital is deposited with BASA (Banco da Amazônia), a state-run bank established to service SUDAM-approved schemes.

6. W. Ellis (pers. comm.), USAID, Brasília. The PL-480 program is designed to provide a means for the United States to export surplus agricultural produce and thereby extend long-term loans to developing nations. DNER must repay the loan over twenty years at 3 percent annual interest, with a two-year grace period (L. Nobrega, pers. comm.).

by the same bank for integrated development projects which include the building or recuperation of roads.[7] The loans carry an annual interest of between 7 and 8.5 percent and are payable over fifteen or sixteen years, with a three- or five-year grace period. These generous allocations of money have allowed the Brazilian government to shift road construction funds to Amazonia that would have been spent in other regions.

The settlement plan

To attract settlers to the Transamazon, a large-scale propaganda campaign was launched on radio, television, and in the press. Officials feared that a common perception of Amazonia as an uncomfortably hot and humid region, full of hostile Indians and dangerous tropical diseases, might render the Transamazon a white elephant. The government recruited colonists in minifundia areas of Rio Grande do Sul and Paraná as well as from latifundia zones of the Northeast. It was hoped that southerners, many descendants of Germans and Italians (Fig. 3), would introduce more capital-intensive and sophisticated farming methods to Amazonia. During the first three years of colonization, the government flew southerners to Belém on chartered jets, then transferred the aspiring settlers to Air Force C-47s for the flight to Altamira. Drought victims from the Northeast were flown by the air force to Altamira, or sent by boat to the port of Vitoria, 20 km north of the town. Many settlers arrived on their own accord on the back of trucks (*pau de arara*), in rented pickups, or by bus.

To accommodate the influx of land seekers, INCRA (Instituto Nacional de Colonização e Reforma Agrária), an agency of the Ministry of Agriculture, erected wooden huts and large tents at various locations along the highway. INCRA's administration was not able to process the large number of applications for lots very quickly; consequently, settlers often lingered for months in living quarters with precarious standards of hygiene while waiting to be placed. The bureaucratic delays also prevented some colonists from clearing a field before the onset of the rainy

7. Source: World Bank (International Bank for Reconstruction and Development), Washington, D.C., *Statement of Loans*, 30 September 1974, p. 2, and *Bank News Releases*, 75/5, 76/11, 78/79, 78/108, 79/99, and 79/111.

Figure 3. Family of mixed German and Italian descent from Rio Grande do Sul on their lot near *agrovila* Nova Fronteira, 1978

season. As a result, they remained dependent on INCRA for subsistence needs for a year if they were unable to find jobs.

In an attempt to prevent land speculation, INCRA expropriated a zone 100 km wide along both sides of the pioneer highways. The government decree (1.164/71) brought 2.2 million sq. km into the public domain along the PIN highways, an area exceeded by only ten countries in the world. INCRA divided a 20-km-wide strip along the Transamazon into 100-ha lots for distribution to incoming colonists. Along the main axis of the Transamazon, a lot extends for 500 m along the road and for 2 km inland. Every 5 km, a side road was to be cut through the forest for 10 to 20 km (Fig. 4). Lots along side roads have 400 m of frontage and extend back 2.5 km.

Beyond the narrow strip of 100-ha lots, but still within the 200-km expropriated zone, INCRA has set aside large tracts of land (*glebas*) to be subdivided into lots of 500 or 3,000 ha for medium-sized farms and cattle ranches (Fig. 5). Although the Transamazon was designed ostensibly to provide a livelihood

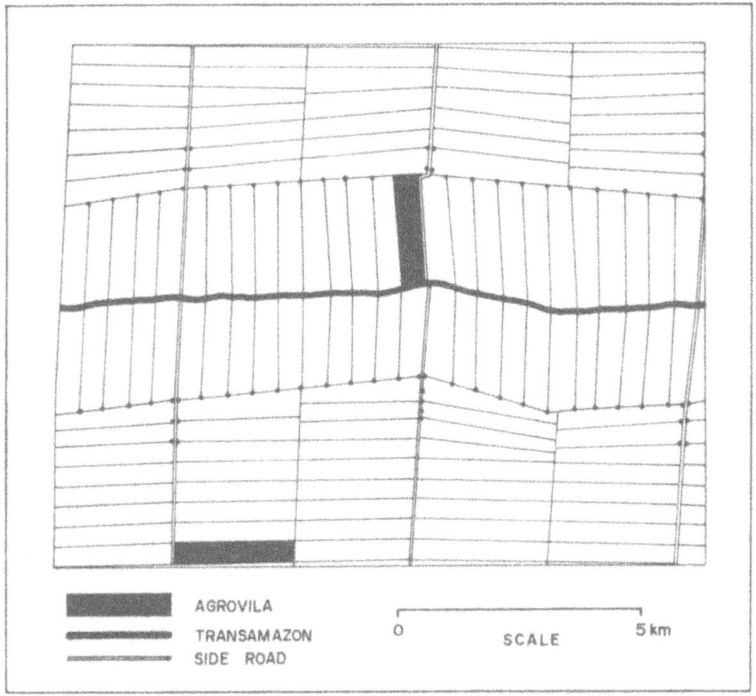

Figure 4. The pattern of lots along the Transamazon

for uprooted drought victims and the landless, medium and large-scale operators may benefit most by tapping the pool of labor in the strip of smaller lots. Along the Marabá–Itaituba stretch of the highway, *glebas* occupy 2.7 million ha, an area almost the size of Belgium.

To encourage small-scale settlers, INCRA offered the 100-ha lots for $700, payable over twenty years with a four-year grace period. Some settlers were also provided with a four-room wooden house at an additional cost of $100, under the same repayment terms. During the first three years of colonization, settlers received six payments averaging $30 a month for a large family to buy provisions and agricultural implements. INCRA stopped providing the six-month loans in 1974 because of the overwhelming flood of potential colonists.

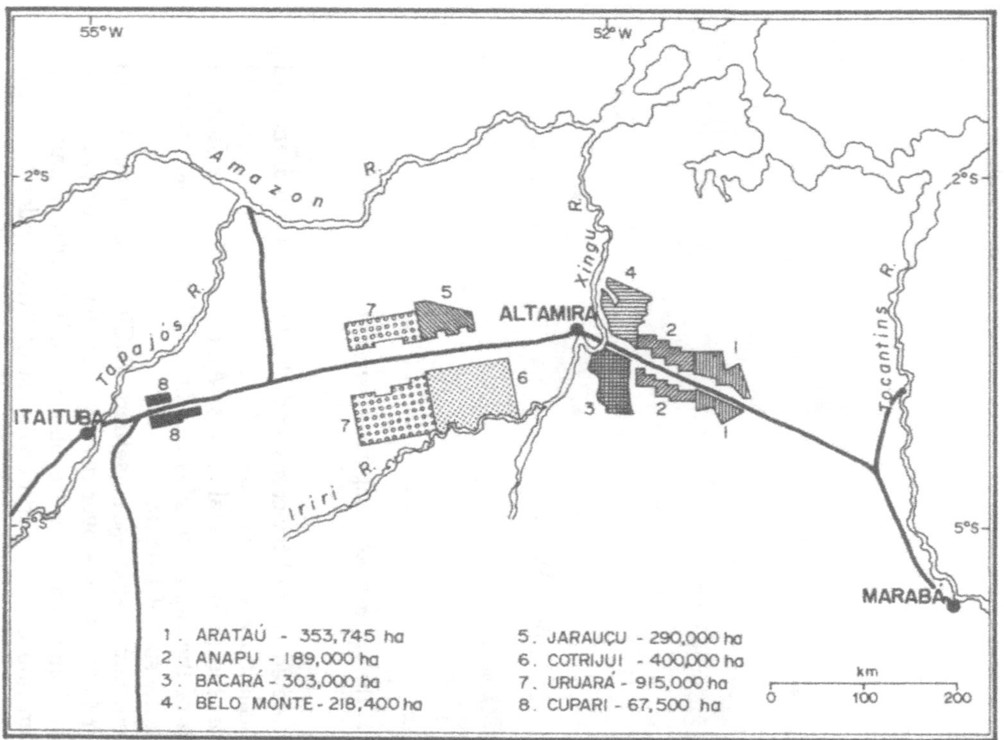

Figure 5. *Glebas* along the Marabá–Itaituba stretch of the Transamazon

Figure 6. *Agrovila* Abraham Lincoln, km 90 of the Altamira–Itaituba stretch of the Transamazon, in 1972

According to the original plan, the settlement pattern was to be dominated by *agrovilas,* INCRA-built communities containing forty-eight or sixty-six houses each, located every 10 km along the main axis and side roads (Fig. 6). The whitewashed *agrovila* houses are arranged along straight lines around a commons (*praça*), which is used for football matches and for grazing livestock. Each community is designed to contain a medical post, a primary school, a general store run by COBAL (Companhia Brasileira de Alimentos), an agency of the Ministry of Agriculture, as well as offices of INCRA and the agricultural extension service, EMATER (Empresa de Assistência Técnica e Extensão Rural).[8] Colonists were encouraged to build their own ecumenical churches and social centers. The underlying philosophy of the *agrovila* plan is that the settlements will foster cultural activities and facilitate administration. If a colonist lives more than 5 km from a community, he is entitled to a government-built, four-room wooden house on his lot.

8. In 1977 the name of ACAR (Associação de Crédito e Assistência Rural) was changed to EMATER.

The *agrópolis,* an urban center for up to six hundred families, is next in the rural-urban hierarchy (Fig. 7). *Agrópoli* were to be built every 20 km along the main axis of the highway and are designed as intermediate administrative centers equipped with a mini-hospital, a dentist, stores, administrative offices, and a police station (INCRA, 1973a). Homes for administrators are larger and more comfortable than *agrovila* houses (Fig. 8). The *rurópolis,* at the apex of the hierarchy, serves as administrative headquarters for the population living within a radius of 140 km. The small towns are projected to house up to 20,000 inhabitants and to offer such amenities as trade schools, banks, hotels, restaurants, a post office, a fully equipped hospital, an airport, and telephone service.

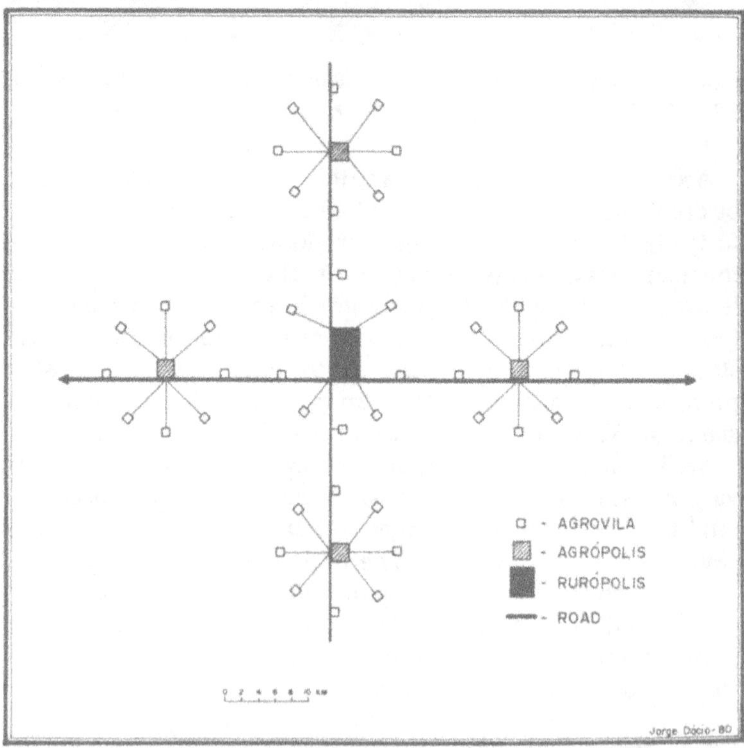

Figure 7. INCRA's plan for a rural-urban settlement hierarchy along the Transamazon

Figure 8. INCRA-built house in *agrópolis* Brasil Novo occupied by a government employee, 1978

Progress of colonization

The Transamazon colonization rate has been much slower than was anticipated. By December 1974 INCRA had settled 5,717 families along the highway, and as of December 1978 the number had increased to only 7,674 households (Table 2). No attempt has been made to colonize the 1,056-km Itaituba–Humaitá stretch of the highway, which is in very poor condition with deep ruts and rotten bridges. Spontaneous settlers along the stretch are given an occupation permit (Licença de Ocupação) after living on the land for at least one year. If after four years the settler has increased the cleared area by four times, he is awarded a property title (Titulo Definitivo). Work has not begun on the final Labrea–Benjamin Constant leg of the Transamazon. As the official colonization program for the highway terminates, less than 8 percent of the original target has been reached.

The total highway population, excluding preexisting river towns, is about 20 percent higher than official statistics reveal. Many families have impatiently invaded forest at the end of side roads, penetrating as many as 45 km from the Transamazon.

Table 2. Origin of Transamazon Families Settled by INCRA by Region of Last Residence, December 1978

Region	Marabá area	Altamira area	Itaituba area	Total	% Total families
Northeast	1,195	1,520	410	3,125	41
North	416	725	260	1,401	18
Center-West	888	267	66	1,221	16
South	46	766	234	1,046	14
Southeast	490	317	74	881	11
Totals	3,035	3,595	1,044	7,674	100

Source: INCRA

Most of the side roads have been extended by mule trails beyond the zone of 100-ha lots. Since most settlers have large families, the population of the Estreito–Itaituba stretch of the highway is approximately 62,000.

The spontaneous settlers are provoking disputes over land claims, since in some cases they are squatting in *glebas* that are destined for entrepreneurs. INCRA is slow in approving the purchase of the *gleba* lots because substantial quantities of documents are required. Furthermore, candidates must await a decision from Brasília. In the meantime, land seekers arrive daily at the INCRA offices in Marabá, Altamira, and Itaituba; there they are turned away, since all the 100-ha lots have been distributed. A late arrival may then occupy forested land at the end of a side road and clear a plot, knowing that it will be difficult for the owner to dislodge him. In order to evict unlawful tenants, the owner must seek a court order and pay squatters for any improvements to the land, such as crops and buildings.

In other areas of Amazonia, such as in southern Pará, violent conflicts have erupted between squatters and alleged landowners (Ianni, 1978). Guerrillas exploited the discontent among uprooted squatters in the region of Conceição do Araguaia for several years until they were crushed by the army in 1975. In most of the region, the land-title situation is extremely confused. False titles abound. A plot of land may have several claimants, each armed with a title supplied by different municipal or state governments. The Transamazon was supposed to provide an orderly environment for settling the land. The expropriated zone created the opportunity for a fresh start. So far, the strategic

Figure 9. Part of a family of sixteen children from Ceará at *agrovila* Coco Chato, 1979

presence of the army garrisons along the highway has discouraged hasty solutions to conflicting land claims.

The Transamazon scheme was originally devised to create small homesteads, but in 1973 INCRA began promoting the sale of large *glebas*. The policy shift was termed a second phase (INCRA, 1973b). In 1974, the new INCRA president, Lourenço Vieira da Silva, announced a further refinement of colonization plans. The maximum size of ranches permitted on land ceded by INCRA was raised to 66,000 ha. The president of INCRA explained the modification thus:

> There has not been a change, rather a natural evolution, already foreseen in the dynamic colonization plan for Amazonia. At first, we were concerned with the settling of farmers on their land. Today, the situation is different and we feel that large companies, exploiting extensive areas, are called for.[9]

The total area of the *glebas* along the Transamazon is 2.7 million ha, three and a half times the area set aside for 100-ha lots.

Plans called for 75 percent of the colonists to be northeasterners (Fig. 9). In December 1972, 67 percent of the Trans-

9. Author's translation from *O Liberal*, Belém, 5 October 1974, p. 1.

amazon settlers were Nordestinos (Smith, 1976a : 26), but by December of 1978 the proportion had declined to 41 percent (Table 2). The Transamazon has absorbed an insignificant portion of the Northeast's burgeoning population.

In the early 1970s the population of the Northeast was growing by 2.4 percent per annum, a yearly increase of 700,000 people. As of December 1978 INCRA had settled 3,125 Nordestino families along the highway. Since the Transamazon scheme began in 1970, the population of the Northeast has grown by at least 6 million. The Transamazon has accommodated only 23,000 Nordestinos, including spontaneous settlers, a mere 0.3 percent of the region's population increase. It is clear that the highway has done little to relieve the social problems of the Northeast (Kohlhepp, 1976). The safety-valve concept has not worked. In 1980 another drought seared the interior of the region, disrupting the lives of 9 million people. Driven by hunger, desperate mobs ransacked food stores in several small towns in Paraíba, reminiscent of the food riots in Fortaleza, the capital of Ceará, after the drought of 1877.[10]

The rural-urban settlement plan has not succeeded on the Transamazon and will not be adopted along other pioneer highways in the region. A total of sixty-six *agrovilas* were to be built by 1973 between km 20 and km 170 west of Altamira (INCRA, 1972b), but only twenty-five are in existence. A total of twenty-seven *agrovilas* have been erected along the entire Transamazon. No more are slated for construction. Houses in several of the communities have fallen into disuse and are being claimed by second growth.

Colonists generally prefer to live on their lots, where they are close to their fields and domestic animals (Wesche, 1974; Smith, 1976b). Few settlers are prepared to walk up to a 20-km round trip a day to work in their fields. Instead, the *agrovila* house may be rented, used for storage, or locked up. Chickens, ducks, pigs, mules, and cattle can be much more easily fed on the lot. In the first few years of colonization, officials discouraged the raising of domestic animals in *agrovilas* in the interests of community har-

10. *O Liberal*, Belém, 3 May 1980, p. 8; *Jornal de Brasília*, Brasília, 4 May 1980, p. 5; and *Jornal do Brasil*, Rio, 3 June 1980, p. 1.

mony. None of the *agrovila* homes were built with fences; poultry and pigs have taken advantage of their free range to dismantle backyard vegetable and herb gardens. Colonists are reluctant to confine their livestock, since the animals derive a considerable portion of their diet from scavenging. Chickens and ducks cannot be left unattended on the lot, because of predators, such as common opossums (*Didelphis marsupialis*), margays (*Felis wiedii*), and ocelots (*Felis pardalis*).

Few of the *agrovilas* boast the amenities that were promised. The government-run COBAL stores have ceased to operate in the communities. When the COBAL stores functioned their prices were cheaper than privately owned stores, but their stocks were very limited and they were frequently out of basic staples such as rice and beans. Family-owned shops, usually established in the front room of an *agrovila* house, have taken the place of COBAL. Whereas the private stores are better stocked, their prices are high. Primary schools have started along the main axis and side roads, so there is little incentive to move to *agrovilas* to educate children. Two of the *agrovilas*, Coco Chato and Nova Fronteira, had an electric-light grid erected by INCRA. But within a few months the generators burned out. They have not been replaced. Settlers use kerosene refrigerators to keep food and drinks cool, if they are wealthy enough, and kerosene or propane-gas lamps for lighting.

Of the fifteen *agrópoli* slated for construction by 1973 along the Marabá–Itaituba stretch of the highway, only three have been built. *Agrópolis* Amapá in Marabá serves almost exclusively as an administrative center for INCRA. *Agrópolis* Brasil Novo, at km 46 of the Altamira–Itaituba stretch of the Transamazon, has not prospered. In 1971, when the intermediate-sized community was built, it contained a first-class motel, telephone service, and a regular supply of water and electricity. Several federal agencies installed offices there, such as the forest and wildlife service, IBDF (Instituto Brasileiro de Desenvolvimento Florestal), and the agricultural research program, EMBRAPA (Empresa Brasileira de Pesquisa Agropecuária). But by 1974, most of the government agencies, except for INCRA, had moved to Altamira. Social amenities at the *agrópolis* were apparently too limited to attract middle-class Brazilians. The motel, used mostly by INCRA to accommodate visitors to the project, soon fell into disrepair when the spotlight of national and world attention shifted from the Transamazon. It is now leased to a cooperative. The water and electricity flow in Brasil Novo is now sporadic, and the telephone service has ceased.

The third *agrópolis*, Miritituba, on the right bank of the Tapajós opposite Itaituba, is virtually abandoned. Only about ten houses are occupied; the shells of others are cloaked with creepers. VARIG, Brazil's largest airline, was to build a tourist hotel in Miritituba with a commanding view of the Tapajós. But the hotel, as well as other amenities, never materialized. Two small offices, occupied by INCRA and EMATER, provide limited employment opportunities.

Only one *rurópolis* has been built, Medicilandia, at the junction of the Transamazon and the northern section of the Cuiabá–Santarém. Because of its strategic location, the community is relatively busy. Buses from Itaituba, Santarém, Cuiabá, and Altamira make frequent stops to take on fuel and passengers. Several noisy bars, fifteen general stores, and four modest restaurants compete for customers. Services include a well-run small hospital, a post office, the state telephone company, an agency of the Banco da Amazônia, and a government-operated warehouse, CIBRAZEM (Companhia Brasileira de Armazenagem).

Although Medicilandia is a relatively lively urban nucleus, it has not grown as was anticipated. The *rurópolis* contains only ninety-four houses with a population of about 600, well below the projected 1,000 families. The INCRA motel at Medicilandia illustrates the gap between the plan and reality. At first glance, the building is impressive, with swimming pool, bar, fully equipped kitchen, large dining room, and air-conditioned suites. Upon closer inspection, the deficiencies soon become apparent. There is rarely enough water for the pool. The freezers in the kitchens do not work, as broken parts have not been replaced, and most of the air-conditioners have burned out because of the erratic voltage. The shortcomings of the motel service are primarily a source of irritation to the occasional visitor and are hardly important in terms of the overall colonization project. The appropriateness of an enclave of luxury in a pioneer zone is open to question. But the motel situation provides a good illustration of the importance of probing beneath the veneer of public relations while doing surveys. A question concerning the existence of a service or a machine should be followed up with enquiries as to whether it functions, preferably with a field check. Few people care to admit that their house is not in order.

A suburb, containing about a hundred huts and seven hundred inhabitants, has sprung up on the eastern perimeter of the *rurópolis* since 1973. The slum dwellers do not receive electricity or piped water, and seek employment in Medicilandia as menial labor. The mud-walled, palm-thatched hovels stand in stark contrast to the spacious and well-kept homes of doctors and administrators. A parallel can be drawn between Medicilandia and Brasília. Both are futuristic, geometrically laid out urban centers in the wilderness. Brasília was built a decade earlier in the sparsely inhabited campo-cerrado of Goias. Both are symbols of Brazil's emergence as a modern nation and of its determination to conquer the interior. Medicilandia and Brasília spawned slums, a symptom of the failure to spread the benefits of development more equitably.

The malaise of the rural-urban settlement plan is due in part to the rigid nature of its design. Planners assumed they were dealing with a homogeneous, flat surface. Some of the *agrovilas* cannot be reached during the rainy season, because of the precarious condition of the side roads. The location of the communities does not always coincide with an unbroken surface or the close proximity of water. The settlements were not based on local needs; they are the fruits of an architect's imagination, conceived thousands of kilometers away.

A phlegmatic and highly centralized bureaucracy has been partly responsible for the stagnation of most of the rural-urban nodules. The communities were built by the federal government, so the facilities cannot be used for profit. If a water pump or an electric motor breaks down, colonists are not permitted to use their own initiative to repair the machinery. The parts must be ordered and replaced by federal agencies, a process that can take months or years. Diesel-fuel quotas have been cut back, so water is only pumped for a short time each day; colonists are not allowed to contribute fuel. Residents are prohibited from building private structures for commerce, such as stores, bakeries, or butcher shops. Settlers are discouraged from erecting their own homes in *agrovilas,* lest the structures offend the façade of equality.

Whereas the INCRA settlements are virtually paralyzed, the preexisting river towns of Marabá, Altamira, and Itaituba have grown spectacularly. In 1970 the 14,585 residents of Marabá were engaged in a modest commerce of Brazil nuts, wild animal skins, diamonds, and cattle (IDESP, 1977a : 88). I estimate that by the end of the decade the population had swollen to at least 40,000, distributed in the town center and four new suburbs. Marabá has emerged from a quiet Tocantins River trading center to one of Pará's leading towns. Regular jet service and daily buses link the town with Brasília and Belém.

Before the arrival of the Transamazon, Altamira was a relatively isolated hamlet of 5,734 inhabitants nestled on the left bank of the Xingu (IDESP, 1977b : 68). Rubber was the mainstay of the local economy. A handful of stores, concentrated along the first three streets parallel to the river, supplied goods to town dwellers and to people living along the Xingu. By 1980 Altamira's population had increased to an estimated 30,000, living mostly in slums surrounding the town. The main center of commerce, conducted by dozens of stores and five banks, has shifted from the riverside to the area of the Transamazon exit to Itaituba, at the southwest corner of the town.

In 1970 Itaituba was a village of 3,782 inhabitants (IDESP, 1977c : 64). A local fishing industry and alluvial gold strikes in the vicinity provided the main employment. Within a decade the population had spurted to some 15,000, confined mostly to small huts on old terraces of the Tapajós. In all three towns urban growth has been chaotic. The rapid influx of highway workers, builders, mechanics, settlers, and shopkeepers has severely taxed the municipal services. Few of the inhabitants have access to piped water. Garbage accumulates in the streets and provides food and breeding grounds for rats and flies.

Only two settlements have grown along the highway itself, both free of INCRA control. Repartimento, at km 160 of the Marabá–Altamira stretch of the Transamazon, has grown into a modest village of some 1,000 inhabitants. In 1972 it contained only a few palm-thatch huts on the perimeter of the DNER camp. Repartimento has grown because it is at the junction of the road to Tucuruí, the construction site for the 3,900 Mw hydroelectric dam across the Tocantins. Drugstores, wooden boardinghouses, bars, brothels, and small restaurants cater to the considerable stream of workers traveling to and from Tucuruí.

Pacajá, at km 212 of the Marabá–Altamira section of the Transamazon, was a cluster of huts occupied mostly by hunters after cat skins when I passed through in 1972. Upon my return in 1979, I found a bustling town of 1,500 residents. A gasoline station, two-storey wooden hotels, and closely packed brick stores line the main thoroughfare. A privately operated generator supplies electricity to many of the establishments and homes, already extending along five streets parallel to the Transamazon. Ice cream and a cacaphony from competing juke boxes lend a different flavor to Pacajá than the atmosphere found in *agrovilas* and *agrópoli*. Pacajá and Repartimento thrive because they sprang from a spontaneous need and are characterized by a minimum of bureaucratic control.

The Transamazon colonization scheme has fallen far short of expectations. The defects in the rural-urban settlement plan have been examined, but other factors are behind the general dissatisfaction with the progress of colonization. It soon became apparent that the considerable federal investment in the scheme was not nurturing the growth of urban foci or producing high agricultural yields. Before exploring the reasons for the low agricultural production, it is necessary to describe the biophysical environment along the highway so that ecological factors affecting farm yields can be brought into sharper focus.

chapter

3 The Ecological Setting

Geology and geomorphology

The Transamazon, slicing across a little over half of the broad beam of South America, traverses a great variety of terrain and rock substrates. For the most part, the highway crosses ancient surfaces, beveled by millions of years of weathering and erosion. The study communities, for example, are built on geologic substrates of Mesozoic age or older (Fig. 10). A salient feature of the geology of the Transamazon is that there has been no history of volcanic activity to provide rich soils. The highway does not accompany any rivers with fertile floodplains. The underlying rocks are generally acidic with few nutrients for plant growth. Furthermore, the weathering front of the substrate, where the few minerals are being liberated into the soil, is usually too deep to be tapped by plant roots.

Agrovila Coco Chato rests on a Pre-Cambrian granitic shield. Road cuts in the vicinity of the community reveal that the bedrock has been weathered to a depth of at least 10 meters. Small tors occasionally protrude from the soil along the Marabá–Altamira stretch of the highway between km 70 and km 400. Light-gray rocks, scattered on the surface of lots along the Transamazon between Medicilandia and Itaituba, also indicate the presence of the northern fringe of the Brazilian shield.

Leonardo da Vinci is built on the contact zone between Devonian and Tertiary sandstones. Nova Fronteira is located on a diabase dike, which, in a molten phase, squeezed through a fracture between Silurian and Devonian sandstones during the Jurassic (DNPM, 1974a). Rounded, dark-gray boulders commonly jut above the surface in the vicinity of Nova Fronteira.

When flying over the Amazon basin at jet cruising altitude, one gains the impression that most of the terrain must be monotonously flat. In the literature the region is often referred to as a plain, and development planners often assume so. Some of the *agrovilas* were thus built on the slopes of steep hills, for the forest conceals a generally undulating topography along the Transamazon.

The relief of the Brazilian shield, where close to half of the colonists have settled, varies from sharply to moderately undulating (Fig. 11). Based on field observations and discussions with highway engineers, extremes of relief attain 40 meters from trough to hill crest within half a kilometer in some areas. Ab'-Sáber (1966a, 1973) and Journaux (1975a) characterize the relief of the shield as a sea of hills or half oranges. DNPM (1974b) classifies the Pre-Cambrian basement as a dissected pediplain.

Relatively flat plateaus and terraces are occasionally encountered along the Transamazon, such as along the Estreito–Araguaia River stretch of the highway, but most of the Transamazon is a seemingly endless sequence of hills, which considerably slows traffic. A bus normally takes twelve hours in the dry season to complete the 500-km trip between Marabá and Altamira.

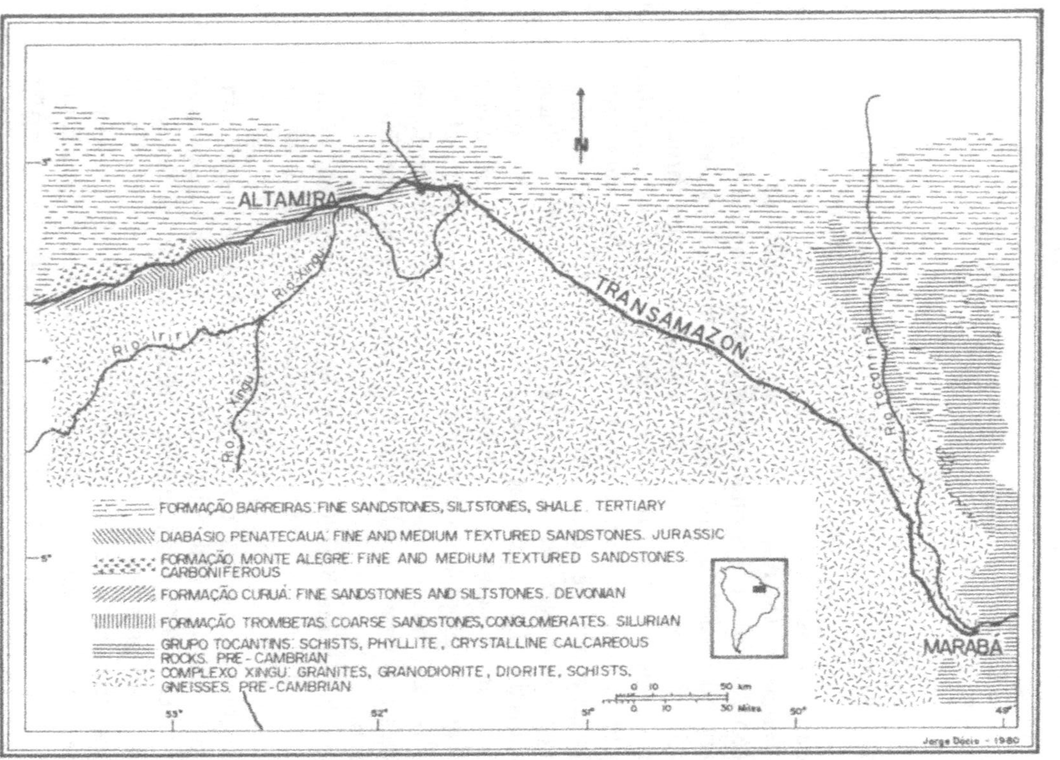

Figure 10. Geologic substrate of Transamazon highway from Marabá to km 175 west of Altamira

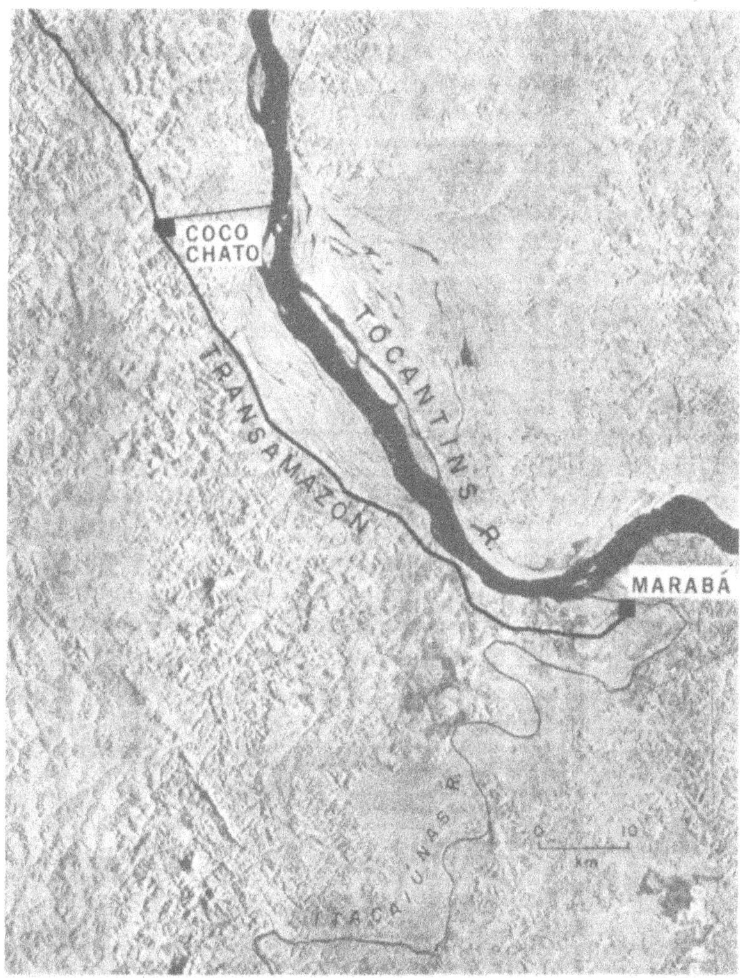

Figure 11. Transamazon highway in vicinity of Coco Chato; Projeto RADAM image taken in 1972, scale of 1:250,000

Although no criteria are indicated, Wozniewicz (1974) estimates that 53 percent of the highway between Estreito and Humaita is moderately to sharply undulating.

It seems unlikely that the broken relief along the Transamazon, and other areas of the region, could have originated under a protective cloak of rainforest (Colinvaux, 1979). The poor erosive power of streams in closed-canopy tropical forests is generally recognized (Douglas, 1969; Moss, 1969; Thomas, 1969, 1974:119; Tricart, 1974, 1975; Zonneveld, 1975). None of the forest streams along the highway were observed carrying a sediment load, even in the rainy season. Water courses become murky only in cleared areas. Forest streams generally flow over a bed of sand or rock and do not carry very abrasive material such as gravel.

The crumpled topography of the highway was probably inherited from alternating wet and dry climatic cycles that reportedly affected Amazonia during the Quaternary. During Pleistocene glaciations, the climate of the region was apparently considerably drier than at present. The retreat of the forest into enclaves would have exposed the soil to erosion.[1] During the arid periods, attributed to a northward shift of the South Atlantic high-pressure cell, the glacio-eustatic lowering of the sea level by up to 135 m along the Brazilian coast (Fairbridge, 1976) rejuvenated stream gradients, resulting in deep entrenchment (Sakamoto, 1960; Tricart, 1974; Journaux, 1975b; Sternberg, 1975; Tricart, 1975). It is not clear how many dry periods affected Amazonia, but at least three have been postulated for Brazil during the Quaternary (Bigarella, 1971).

Pollen samples from cores taken in Rondônia and Roraima suggest at least one dry cycle in the Amazon during the Quaternary (Van der Hammen, 1974; Absy and Van der Hammen, 1976). Absy (1979:77) hypothesizes that a strong dry climatic phase occurred in the Brazilian Amazon from 2,700 to 2,000

1. The theory of Pleistocene forest enclaves, or refugia, has been proposed by several botanists and zoologists to account partly for the distribution of plants and animals and the rich species diversity in the Amazon basin. During dry periods the forest shrunk into islands, thereby isolating gene pools. When the forest refuges spread and merged again during wet climatic cycles, some populations had differentiated in response to local ecological conditions such that they no longer interbred. The exact number, locations, and size of the refugia is still in dispute. Morley (1975) asserts there is strong evidence for only one refuge among the Memecyleae. Prance (1973) criticizes the refugia proposed by zoologists as being too small to sustain a forest ecosystem with its complex animal-plant interactions. For a discussion of forest enclaves proposed by zoologists, see Haffer (1969) on birds, Vanzolini (1970) on lizards, K. Brown (1977) and K. Brown, et al. (1974) on butterflies.

Figure 12. Soil erosion in *agrovila* Abraham Lincoln, situated on a weathered diabase dike at km 90 of the Altamira–Itaituba stretch of the Transamazon, 1972

years before the present, based on pollen analyses from lake cores. Arkose sands in marine sediments off the mouth of the Amazon indicate a former dry climate in the region during the Pleistocene (Damuth and Fairbridge, 1970). Corroborating geomorphological evidence, such as pediments, lateritic plateaus and stone lines have been found in various parts of the region (Pimienta, 1958; Barbosa and Ramos, 1959; Ab'Sáber, 1966b, 1970b; Journaux, 1975a,b).[2]

The uneven terrain along the Transamazon exacerbates soil erosion when the forest is removed (Fig. 12). Most of the fertility in field soils is concentrated in the top five centimeters; nutrient-rich ash is particularly vulnerable to removal by run-off after showers. During the rainy season, fill that was bulldozed across swales is frequently washed out, thereby closing certain sections of the highway. Some of the side roads are cut off for the entire

2. Although stone lines in soil profiles may be due to termite activity in some cases, they are generally attributed to pediment gravel that has subsequently been covered with a mantle of soil (Ab'Sáber, 1970a; Thomas, 1974:130). I observed stone lines in road cuts along various sections of the Transamazon, particularly in the vicinity of *agrovila* Coco Chato.

rainy season, resulting in considerable economic loss to farmers.

The cost of regrading the Transamazon after the wet season is substantial. No official statistics on the maintenance costs of the highway are available, but Pinto (1973) estimates the annual cost from 3 to 10 percent of the initial expense of building the road. Asphalting would reduce the erosion problem, but it is considered too costly for a pioneer road. Ten years passed before the Belém–Brasília was asphalted in 1974. The undulating topography of the Transamazon transect should surely have justified its immediate paving.

Soils

The great diversity of underlying rocks along the highway, combined with differences in topography, plant associations, and a dynamic history of paleo-climates and human agency, have produced a complex mosaic of soil types. No detailed soil maps have been compiled for the Transamazon, so only a provisional classification of the main soil types and their occurrence is possible.[3] Along the Estreito–Itaituba stretch of the highway, podzolic soils (ultisols) account for roughly 41 percent of the soils, latosols for 40 percent, sandy and miscellaneous soils for 8 percent each of the earth surface, and *terra roxa* for 3 percent of the highway soils (Falesi, 1972; DNPM, 1974a,b).

Podzolic soils, usually well drained with an accumulation of clay in the B horizon, are particularly common on the Pre-Cambrian granitic shield and account for 41 percent of the soils in the colonized zone. The soils are generally strongly acid with a low cation exchange capacity (Falesi, 1972). The relatively sandy texture of the topsoil exacerbates the moisture deficit during the dry season, a factor which has been responsible for the demise of some cacao plantations in the vicinity of Coco Chato. In the *agrovila* area, the granitic basement has disintegrated into a red-yellow podzolic soil.

3. Transamazon soil surveys conducted by Falesi (1972) and Ranzani (1978) are based on sampling at very few sites along the roadside during the construction phase of the highway. The soil maps of DNPM (1974a, b) are approximations, based mostly on the extrapolation of the geologic substrate.

Latosols (oxisols) are primarily associated with the Tertiary *barreiras* formation and are characterized by poor horizon development, low cation exchange capacity, and a pH generally under 5. They account for some 40 percent of the settlement area. Latosols have a much heavier texture than podzolic soils and along the highway range in color from yellow to reddish-yellow, depending on the iron oxide content.

Diabase dikes are responsible for the eutrophic oxisols known as *terra roxa estruturada eutrófica* in Brazil. Because the weathering front of the parent material is at or close to the surface, nutrients lost to leaching are constantly being replenished. Another factor accounting for the relatively high fertility of *terra roxa* is that diabase is basic and rich in ferro-magnesian minerals. Unfortunately, the dark-red eutrophic clays account for only 3 percent of the highway soils. *Terra roxa* is restricted to a few patches along the Transamazon, mainly between Altamira and Itaituba. In southern Brazil, molten diabase flooded huge areas of São Paulo, Paraná, and Rio Grande do Sul, thereby producing some of the most agriculturally productive soils of the country. Along the Transamazon, limited quantities of basalt leaked to the surface through narrow veins. The largest area of *terra roxa* along the highway occurs between km 75 and km 105 of the Altamira–Itaituba stretch, but it averages only 10 km in width.

The outstanding feature of Transamazon soils is their generally low fertility. The sandy soils, found mostly between Estreito and the Araguaia River, account for an estimated 8 percent of the highway soils. Sandy soils, because of their extreme paucity of nutrients and low moisture-retention capacity, are particularly inept for agriculture. According to the potential-land-use classification of Projeto RADAM (Radar da Amazônia) (DNPM, 1974a, b), most of the soils along the colonized stretch of the highway are of limited agricultural value, especially for annual crops. Only the restricted areas of *terra roxa* are considered naturally fertile and promising for peasant farmers (Camargo and Falesi, 1975). No known *terra roxa* patches occur along the 2,000-km uncolonized portion of the highway between Itaituba and Benjamin Constant. The Transamazon was clearly not designed to provide access to the best soils of Amazonia.

Climate

Meteorological data are too few and discontinuous to permit an accurate characterization of the climate of the Transamazon, but most of the highway probably falls within an Aw zone, according to the Köppen system. There are no thirty-year periods of uninterrupted observation of the weather for any of the Transamazon towns, or for most stations in Amazonia. Ephemeral budgets and problems with personnel account for the gaps in data collection. In the case of Altamira, for example, complete data for the year on mean monthly temperature, minimum and maximum temperatures, rainfall, and relative humidity are only available for 1934, 1937, 1939, 1948, 1968, 1969, and 1973 to the present. Whereas the recording of meteorological information along the Transamazon has been more consistent since 1973, there are still lapses. In March of 1978, for example, no recordings were made at the Itaituba station, because the employee left on vacation.

Rainfall

The seasonal distribution of rainfall is the pulse of the ecosystem; it strongly influences the phenological cycle of plants as well as animal and cultural activities. The onset of the rainy season is highly variable, but usually occurs in October or November in the Marabá region (Appendix 1), and November or December in the Altamira area (Appendix 2). The rainy season normally lasts until May or June and is associated with the southward migration of the Inter-Tropical Convergence Zone (ITCZ) to at least lat. 10° S over the ocean (Caviedes, 1975) and as far as lat. 20° S over Brazil during the Southern Hemisphere summer (Flohn, 1969; Hubert et al., 1969). The Altamira area of the highway seems to be slightly wetter than the Marabá region; the annual rainfall for the former averaged 2,352 mm (s = 227) from 1973 to 1978, whereas the mean was 2,104 mm (s = 158) for the Marabá area during the same period.

As soon as the rainy season ends, settlers begin clearing underbrush (*brocar*) prior to felling trees (*derrubar*) in July or August. The slash is left to dry for a couple of months before it is fired in September or October. During the burning season, smoke taints the sky with a characteristic whiskey-colored haze. The time of the burns is always a tense period; early rains can soak the slash and render a good burn impossible. Unusually heavy rain in October 1976, for example, reduced the effective planting space in the Marabá area.

Settlers normally opt for an early-burn strategy in order to be assured of a thorough fire. Poorly burned logs and branches are stacked and fired again (*coivara*). Second growth proliferates during the two-month wait for the arrival of the rains. The task of weeding just before the crops are planted is considered preferable to the risk of a late burn.

The fertility gains obtained by burning slash are vulnerable to erosion when the rains come. Storms can be very intense; a total of 157 mm of water fell within a few hours in February 1974 in the Marabá area (Appendix 1). Neither terraces nor contour ploughing are employed to check erosion along the Transamazon. Deluges at the beginning of the rainy season, when there is little plant cover in fields, account for most of the topsoil loss. Up to 2 cm of soil may be lost annually on 15° slopes planted to annual crops along the Transamazon (Smith, 1976a : 111), the equivalent to the stripping of 100 tons of topsoil per hectare every year. Near Ibadan, Nigeria, with a similar climate, soil erosion on cleared slopes of 15% can attain 120 tons/ha within a year (Lal, 1974).

Spencer (1966 : 33) has argued that erosion removes the highly leached mantle of tropical soils and thereby exposes more fertile earth closer to the weathering zone. But the loss of topsoil in latosols and podzolic soils is serious because most of the fertility is concentrated near the surface (Falesi, 1972; Smith, 1976a : 111). The heavy rains also provoke chaos for traffic. Some hills become too slippery for heavy traffic to climb, while other stretches of the road become a quagmire and trap cars, buses, and trucks.

The accentuated dry season creates a severe moisture deficit in the soil. Sometimes no rain falls for a month, as happened in August 1978, in the vicinity of Marabá. Or an entire month's rain falls in one day. The moisture soon evaporates from exposed soils, leaving a parched surface. The evergreen forest is well adapted to withstand the five- to six-month dry season, but the damp microclimate is destroyed when colonists clear the trees for their fields. Root and tree crops, established during the wet season, can survive the dry period, but shallow-rooted annuals, such as maize and rice, wither. Only a few settlers of Japanese origin employ crude irrigation systems along the Transamazon, and then only for vegetables. The gasoline-powered pumps and plastic pipes are too expensive for most farmers.

Annual crops are planted at the onset of the rains and are harvested in May or June. Beans are put in after the rice harvest at the close of the wet season. Soil moisture storage and the occasional shower are sufficient to enable the pulses to grow. If beans are planted during the rainy season, fungi destroy the crop.

The seasonal distribution of rainfall strongly influences hunting methods and yields. In the wet period, white-lipped peccaries (*Tayassu pecari*), one of the most important game animals, roam in bands of up to a hundred through the hunting zone of *agrovilas* in search of fallen fruit. The arrival of the rains swells ephemeral streams, thereby permitting the wide dispersal of *T. pecari*. White-lipped pecarries are usually shot during the rainy season and account for 40 percent of the game take in forested areas (Smith, 1976c).

In the dry season, hunters employ the *espera* method to capture game. A hunter waits in a hammock, or pole platform, some three meters above ground close to a tree with falling fruit or flowers, such as those of the Brazil-nut tree (*Bertholletia excelsa*). The rustle of crisp leaves or the snap of a brittle twig alerts the hunter to the approach of game, such as succulent paca (*Agouti paca*), tapir (*Tapirus terrestris*), or brocket deer (*Mazama americana*). When the animal is judged to be in range, the hunter switches on his flashlight and shoots the mesmerized quarry with a shotgun. Hunters do not normally use the *espera* method in the wet season, to avoid becoming drenched and because the soaked litter makes little noise when disturbed.

Fruit-gathering trips into the forest during the rainy season are more rewarding (Tables 3 and 4). The increase in number of fruiting trees in the wet part of the year occurs throughout Amazonia (Ducke and Black, 1953) and is related to the generally short period of seed viability and the need of propagules for a

Table 3. Wild Fruits and Nuts Eaten by Settlers along the Transamazon

Local name	Scientific name	Family	Habitat
Babaçu, coco	*Orbygnia martiana*	Palmae	Forest, second growth, fields
Açaí	*Euterpe oleracea*	Palmae	Forest streams
Tucumã	*Astrocaryum vulgare*	Palmae	Forest, second growth, fields
Najá	*Maximilliana regia*	Palmae	Forest, second growth, fields
Bacaba	*Oenocarpus distichus*	Palmae	Forest, second growth, fields
Frutão	*Pouteria pariri*	Sapotaceae	Forest
Cajá	*Spondias lutea*	Anacardiaceae	Forest
Uxi	*Endopleura uchi*	Humiriaceae	Forest
Cupuaçu	*Theobroma grandiflorum*	Sterculiaceae	Forest
Cacau bravo	*Theobroma speciosum*	Sterculiaceae	Forest
Castanha do Pará	*Bertholletia excelsa*	Lecythidaceae	Forest
Genipapo	*Genipa americana*	Rubiaceae	Forest
Piquí	*Caryocar villosum*	Cariocaraceae	Forest

Table 4. Monthly Availability of Wild Fruits and Nuts Eaten by Transamazon Settlers

Local Name	J	F	M	A	M	J	J	A	S	O	N	D
Babaçu	X	X	X	X	X	X	X	X	X	X	X	X
Açaí						X	X	X	X	X	X	X
Tucumã	X							X	X	X	X	X
Najá	X	X							X	X	X	X
Bacaba										X	X	X
Frutão	X	X	X									X
Cajá		X	X	X								
Uxi	X	X	X								X	X
Cupuaçu	X	X	X	X								X
Cacau bravo	X											X
Castanha do Pará	X	X	X									X
Genipapo	X	X										
Piquí	X											X

Note: For scientific names of trees, see Table 3.

moist environment for germination. Settlers collect Brazil nuts, cupuaçu (*Theobroma grandiflorum*), cacau bravo (*T. speciosum*), and the canon-ball-sized frutão (*Pouteria pariri*) only during the wet season.

The arrival of the heavy and prolonged rains has an important impact on the epidemiology of human diseases along the Transamazon. The morbidity of malaria, a major public health problem along the highway, is closely related to rainfall. After the rains have subsided, conditions at breeding places become more stable, so malaria vectors increase. During the rainy months, black flies, deemed responsible for the hemorrhagic syndrome of Altamira, proliferate along certain stretches of the highway and aggravate the lives of settlers.

Temperature

No cold season restricts vegetative growth. The mean annual temperature along the highway is close to 26°C, with less than 2° C monthly variation (Appendixes 1 and 2). The diurnal range of temperature can be considerable; at night temperatures may drop sufficiently to require a blanket for comfortable sleep. Temperatures can climb to 38° C in the shade in the dry season. Settlers are usually at work in their fields by 6:30 A.M. to take advantage of the coolness of the early morning. By 10 A.M. the sun is often beating fiercely, so the family and workers retire for lunch to the forest or their home. Work normally resumes in mid-afternoon and continues until sundown.

Most of the government-designed buildings along the Transamazon offer poor respite from the midday heat. *Agrovila* houses are like ovens. The roofs are low and covered with asbestos panels, which efficiently absorb solar energy and reradiate it onto occupants below. Settlers who build their own houses on their lots usually cover the roof with either palm fronds or shingles, thereby producing a much more refreshing interior. The coolest home I visited had a high, palm-thatch roof and open sides. Welcome breezes passed through the house without obstruction.

Southerners prefer to use wooden shingles for the roofs of their homes. A ceiling is often added to create an attic. Two barriers are thus erected against the sun; rooms are cooler and the additional storage area is kept dry. The Arara Indians, a group of about two hundred who once lived in the vicinity of Nova Fronteira, built a large communal house of babaçu palm fronds. The high-roof design of the dwelling, some 8 m above ground, effectively reduced heat radiation. A palm-thatch roof requires replacement every four to five years, whereas asbestos lasts at least fifteen years, hence the preference for the latter by most architects.

Vegetation

The Transamazon transects a variety of vegetation types determined by such factors as topography, soils, and human activities. No inventory of all plant associations is attempted here. Rather, I describe briefly the five main categories—forest, second growth, cerrado, grassland, and campina—encountered along the highway and focus on their relevance to settlers. The system I use for classifying vegetation is modified from Pires (1974), who emphasizes morphological aspects easily recognized in the field. The plant formations designated by Projeto RADAM (DNPM, 1974a, b) are based primarily on geomorphological features rather than botanical variation.

Forest

At least 90 percent of the highway transect cuts through forested areas on uplands (*terra firme*). During the construction phase of the highway, the forest walled in the road, dwarfing the workers and their machines. The forest canopy varies in height from 25 to 35 meters. Two principal *terra firme* forest types are distinguished: mature upland forest (*mata pesada*) and liana forest (*mata de cipó*). These broad categories simplify a complex picture. The composition of the forest constantly changes along environmental gradients, sometimes abruptly, at other times subtly. Palms are especially useful indicators of shifts in the makeup of plant communities.

Mature upland forest is one of the richest biomes on earth. There are at least 50,000 species of higher plants and as many as one million plant and animal species in Amazonia, most of them concentrated in forest environments (Myers, 1979:23). The bewildering variety of life humbles the naturalist and makes it difficult to adequately characterize the plant communities. The diversity of plant species in the forest along the Transamazon has not been measured, but figures can be drawn from studies of mature upland forest in other areas of the basin. In a *terra firme* forest near Belém, Black et al. (1950) report an average of 75 species of trees per hectare with a diameter at breast height (DBH) of at least 10 centimeters. In a 175-sq.-m plot of *terra firme* forest near Manaus, Aubréville (1961) found 107 species of woody and herbaceous species in 37 families. Prance et al. (1976) encountered 179 plant species with a DBH at least 15 centimeters in one hectare of mature upland forest near Manaus.

Forest giants, such as the majestic Brazil-nut tree and angelim pedra (*Dinizia excelsa*), tower conspicuously above the canopy to a height of 40 or 50 meters. *Dinizia excelsa* has been known to reach 67 meters (Scaff, 1979). In the *terra roxa* zone of Nova Fronteira, sumauma (*Ceiba pentandra*) also puncture the canopy. The latter tree is usually associated with floodplain areas, but the high fertility and moisture-holding capacity of the red clay provide a favorable environment for sumauma in *terra firme*. Light gaps, torn open by falling trees, create wells of dense second growth that are a source of weed seeds when settlers clear the forest. No discernible layers of vegetation were noted in *mata;* forest storeys are an artifact of those attempting to impose order on nature's profusion. Epiphytes are rare, probably because of the pronounced dry season.

A tangle of lianas and vines, and a generally lower and more uneven canopy, characterize *mata de cipó*. Liana forest grows in extensive patches along the Marabá–Altamira stretch of the Transamazon, and is particularly evident in the vicinity of *agrovila* Leonardo da Vinci. Sombroek (1966:196) suggests that *mata de cipó* grows on heavily textured soils with a compacted subsoil which prevents the penetration of deep roots. But I have seen liana forest on sandy podzolic soils with no detectable subsurface hardpan. There appears to be no correlation with soil type or topography (Pires, 1974). Liana forest may be a disclimax caused by millennia of felling and burning by aborigines. The pre-contact Indian population of Amazonia has been considered too small, especially in interfluvial areas, to have triggered any significant ecological impact. But recent evidence, in the form of anthropogenic black earth, strongly suggests that the *terra firme* was relatively densely settled in the past (Smith, 1980a).

Whereas Brazil-nut trees still protrude above the canopy, emergents are less common in *mata de cipó*. Thickets of bamboo (*Guadua* sp.) flourish in the frequent light gaps. Although plant biomass and species diversity are reduced, there is no discernible drop in game yield from liana forest (Smith, 1976c). Farmers regard *mata de cipó* favorably, since the abundant undergrowth provides kindle for a good burn.

Forest is the preferred vegetation to clear for fields. The nutrients locked up in the generous plant biomass are quickly released in the form of ash and gases during the burn. Nitrogen and sulphur are lost to the atmosphere, but calcium, phosphorus, and potash enrich the topsoil and provide the fertilizer for most of the colonists. Rice yields, for example, are higher in fields cut from forest, averaging 1,742 kg/ha (s = 717, n = 56), compared with a mean of 1,391 kg/ha (s = 571, n = 41) in plots cleared from second growth (Appendix 3).

Mature upland forest and *mata de cipó* are the principal sources of fruits and nuts for colonists (Table 3). Palms figure prominently in the diet of settlers. The grape-sized fruits of açaí (*Euterpe oleracea*) are rubbed in water to make a savory drink rich in vitamin A. The purple mesocarp is also stirred into manioc flour and sugar to make a satisfying dish. Groves of the slender palm are often destroyed when settlers clear their fields up to the margin of streams and rivers. Fruits of bacaba (*Oenocarpus distichus*), the size of plump olives, are prepared in the same manner as açaí. The prickly tucumã (*Astrocaryum vulgare*) provide green-skinned fruits, shaped like golf balls, that contain three times as much vitamin A as carrots. The oily, orange pulp of tucumã fruit is also rich in vitamins B and C (Pechnik et al., 1947; Cavalcante, 1974). The oily fruits of the majestic najá palm (*Maximilliana regia*) are eaten raw and are given to pigs. Fruits of urucuri (*Scheelea martiana*), observed growing in small stands on poorly drained podzolic soils in the Altamira region, are fed to pigs.

The bright orange fruits of cajá (*Spondias lutea*) are collected from the forest floor during the rainy season to prepare a tart and refreshing drink. The juicy mesocarp provides a welcome snack, particularly for hunters. The football-sized fruit of frutão (*Pouteria pariri*) is eaten raw, mixed with sugar to make a dessert, or stirred into water for a drink. Towering frutão drops its fruit in the rainy season. The powerful fragrance of the damaged fruits permeates the forest for dozens of meters around the base of the tree, alerting settlers, particularly hunters, to the presence of the much-appreciated food. A drink is made from the generous pulp of genipapo (*Genipa americana*), a forest tree that may owe its distribution in some cases to Indians, who prepare a black dye from the fruit juice. The oily fruits of the less common uxi (*Endopleura uchi*) and piquí (*Caryocar villosum*) are cooked with manioc flour and sugar to make a gruel. The aromatic pulp of cupuaçu (*Theobroma grandiflorum*) is much sought after in the forest during the wet season to make a tangy drink. The sticky white mesocarp is also blended with grated Brazil nuts and eaten as a dessert. Settlers also prepare a refreshing drink from the fruits of the related but smaller cacau bravo (*Theobroma speciosum*).

Second growth

Early plant colonizers of fields, particularly species of Compositae and Solanaceae, are a major reason why settlers usually abandon cultivated plots within a couple of years. Weeds often become such a problem after two years of rice or maize cultivation on the same site that most colonists prefer to clear a fresh field from the forest. A similar pattern of shifting cultivation in response to weed invasion is reported from other regions of Brazil (Lynn Smith, 1972 : 366), the Peruvian Amazon (Sanchez and Nureña, 1972; Scott, 1974), and the tropical forests of Sri Lanka (Joachim and Kandiah, 1948), Mindanao (Kellman, 1969), and New Guinea (Clarke, 1967 : 251). Soil exhaustion is not usually an important factor in the farmer's decision to abandon a plot after two years of cultivation along the Transamazon (Smith, 1976a : 105).

In 1971 weeds were not a great nuisance in fields. But as the forest edge was pushed back from the roads second-growth communities proliferated. By 1974 farmers were usually forced

Figure 13. Family weeding six-week-old rice near Nova Fronteira in March 1974. The weeds, mostly *Leptochloa virgata* (Gramineae), are placed on tops of stumps and logs to prevent rerooting.

to weed two or three times during the rice-growing season from December to May (Fig. 13). Although the cutting of forest requires more time and energy than slashing weeds, settlers still prefer to clear a new field for annual crops after cultivating the same site for two years. Sometimes a field is planted to a perennial, such as banana or cacao, which effectively shades out competition from weeds.

Weeds do not provide much material for a good burn, and the resultant ash is very thin. Furthermore, weed-choked fields can be extremely unpleasant places to work. In early second growth and in fields, seemingly ubiquitous fire ants (*Solenopsis* sp.) swarm over the feet and legs of workers to deliver painful stings. *Azteca* ants that live in the hollow internodes of embaúba (*Cecropia* spp.) severely punish those that brush against their homes. Solanaceous shrubs with sickle-shaped thorns, such as jurubeba (*Solanum cyananthum*) and *S. toxicaria*, or coarse leaves, such as *S. asperum*, tear and irritate the skin. By clearing a new patch of forest, settlers also temporarily escape the excessive build-up of crop pests and pathogens.

Although weeds are considered a nuisance, they are nevertheless a vital component of agro-ecosystems along the Transamazon, as in other tropical areas (Popenoe, 1957; Greenland and Nye, 1959; Nye and Greenland, 1960; Kellman, 1969). The rapid weed invasion of fields during and after cropping initiates the recuperation of swidden soils (Fig. 14). Second growth restores organic matter and nitrogen, checks soil erosion, and in later stages draws up nutrients leached to lower horizons. Nutrients are also reintroduced to the abandoned site by colonizing animals.

Half of the 100-ha lots are supposed to be left as a biological reserve. If 20 percent of the remaining area is inappropriate for crops, owing to water courses, rocks, or buildings, then each colonist has roughly 40 ha to farm. Colonists plant an average 8 ha (s = 9, n = 97) a year, so the fallow period would be ten years if each field was cultivated for two years. Except in the case of very sandy soils, a ten-year fallow period is probably adequate for the restoration of soils cultivated once.[4] It is not known how many ten-year swidden cycles Transamazon soils can endure without unfavorable and potentially irreversible biochemical and physical changes.

The composition of seral plant communities varies considerably along the Transamazon. A thorough inventory of second-growth associations along the highway is beyond the scope of

4. Estimates on the length of the fallow period required to recuperate tropical soils vary according to climate, soils, vegetation, and cropping history. For example, a four-year fallow is considered adequate for the restoration of limestone-derived soils of the Petén region of Guatemala after one maize crop (Cowgill, 1960). A seven-year fallow is required to restore the chemical and physical properties of the same soil after two years of maize cropping. In southeastern Mindoro Island, a minimum of five to eight years of secondary succession is necessary to recuperate soils (Conklin, 1954), whereas in Mindanao a five-to-ten-year fallow is required (Kellman, 1969). In Sierra Leone, a minimum of seven to nine years of fallow is necessary to restore the fertility of red-brown soils derived from sedimentary rocks (Newton, 1960). Shorter fallows impoverish the soil and lead to the invasion of *Imperata* and *Andropogon* grasses. An eight-to-ten-year fallow is considered necessary to repair cultivated loamy soils in forested regions of Sri Lanka (Joachim and Kandiah, 1948) In Dipterocarp forest of Sarawak, twelve years is apparently the minimum fallow for the restoration of swidden soils (Freeman, 1955), whereas Coene (1956) claims that in the Congo basin, at least fifteen years are needed. Croat (1972) asserts that in Panama twenty-five years of fallow are necessary to restore cultivated soils.

Figure 14. Second growth, mostly *Eupatorium macrophyllum* (Compositae), three months after harvesting rice; *terra roxa* soil near Nŏva Fronteira, October 1973

this study. Nevertheless, a few generalizations are possible, based on field observations and some collecting (Table 5).[5] Members of the sunflower family are particularly conspicuous in second growth, two to three months old, on *terra roxa* and latosols. The white-flowered *Eupatorium macrophyllum* often dominates harvested fields on *terra roxa* within a few months. In the vicinity of Coco Chato, composites are less common; various solanaceous shrubs are especially important members of early second growth on podzolic soils and latosols. After about a year of succession, the sun-loving composites and solanaceous plants are shaded out by small trees, such as *Cecropia* spp., *Cassia* spp., *Didymopanax* sp., and *Trema micranthum*.

Birds are important dispersal agents for many second-growth species (Table 5). *Cecropia*, one of the most common colonizers of waste places along the Transamazon, is dispersed by birds in

5. Plant material was identified by Paulo Cavalcante and is deposited with the herbaria at the Museu Goeldi, Belém, and INPA, Manaus. Information on dispersal mechanisms of the second-growth plants was gathered from field observations, Adams (1972), and personal communications from Herbert Baker, Spencer Barrett, and Jonathan Sauer.

Table 5. Some Plants of Second-Growth Communities up to Sixteen Months Old in Transamazon Fields

Scientific name	Family	Principal dispersal mechanism
Erechtites hieraciifolia	Compositae	Wind
Conyza floribunda	Compositae	Wind
Eupatorium macrophyllum	Compositae	Wind
Eupatorium maximiliani	Compositae	Wind
Porophyllum ruderale	Compositae	Wind
Vernonia sp.	Compositae	Wind
Solanum asperum	Solanaceae	Birds
Solanum toxicaria	Solanaceae	Birds
Solanum americanum	Solanaceae	Birds
Solanum cyananthum	Solanaceae	Birds
Solanum sp.	Solanaceae	Birds
Digitaria sanguinalis	Gramineae	Fringillid birds
Digitaria insularis	Gramineae	Wind, hairy mammals, birds
Cenchrus echinatus	Gramineae	Hairy mammals
Sorghum arundinaceum	Gramineae	Birds
Phytolacca rivinoides	Phytolacaceae	Birds
Amaranthus spinosus	Amaranthaceae	Birds, wind
Cecropia spp.	Moraceae	Birds, wind
Ipomoea sp.	Convolvulaceae	Birds
Christiana sp.	Tiliaceae	
Cassia sp.	Leguminosae	Birds, mammals
Trema micranthum	Ulmaceae	Birds
Gouania pyrifolia	Rhamnaceae	Birds
Didymopanax sp.	Araliaceae	Birds

at least thirteen families, as well as by bats (Vázquez-Yanes et al., 1975).[6] I saw blue-gray tanagers (*Thraupis episcopus*) and silver-beaked tanagers (*Ramphocelus carbo*) eating fruits of *Solanum* spp. and *Trema micranthum*. Both blue-gray tanagers and palm tanagers (*Thraupis palmarum*) feed avidly on ripe papaya (*Carica papaya*) fruits in the vicinity of settlers' homes. Papaya occurs as a weed on relatively fertile soils, such as *terra roxa*, where tan-

6. According to Eisenmann (1961), Olson and Blum (1968), Leck (1972), and Skutch (1980), birds in the following families have been observed feeding on *Cecropia* catkins: parakeets (Psittacidae), woodpeckers (Picidae), thrushes (Turdidae), honeycreepers and bananaquits (Coerebidae), wood-warblers (Parulidae), tanagers (Thraupidae), finches (Fringillidae), pigeons (Columbidae), trogons (Trogonidae), toucans (Ramphastidae), flycatchers (Tyrannidae), thrashers (Mimidae), and oropendolas (Icteridae).

Figure 15. The opening of the Transamazon landscape to second growth and grassland, km 75 of the Altamira–Itaituba stretch, September 1979

agers have defecated. Wind is the primary dispersal agent for weeds of the sunflower family.

Buried seed may be another source of weeds (Guevara and Gómez-Pompa, 1972; Kellman, 1974). Seeds of some species of heliophytes can remain viable in the soil for long periods, waiting for a chance to germinate. The intense heat of swidden fires destroys some of the seeds (Moody, 1974), but others probably survive and sprout.

Ruderal grasses, especially escaped pasture grasses such as colonião (*Panicum maximum*) and jaragua (*Hyparrhenia rufa*), as well as rabo de rapôso (*Andropogon bicornis*), capim amargoso (*Digitaria insularis*), *D. sanguinalis, Paspalum conspersum, P. conjugatum, Eleusine indica, Panicum mertensii,* and the abundant *Leptochloa virgata* (Fig. 13), provide a food base for finches, such as the blue-black grassquit (*Volatinia jacarina*) and yellow-bellied seedeaters (*Sporophila nigricollis*). Neither of the birds is a serious agricultural pest at present, but their numbers are likely to increase as the swath of second growth and grassland expands (Fig. 15).

In 1974 *Sorghum arundinaceum* was a rare escapee, but by 1979 almost pure stands of the tall cereal could be found in patches of up to 0.5 ha in the Nova Fronteira area. Spontaneous sorghum provides shelter for flocks of around fifty red-breasted blackbirds (*Leistes militaris*), a post-1975 arrival in the vicinity of the *agrovila* and at *agrópolis* Miritituba. The blackbirds prefer to feed on the ground in open places and may become agricultural pests.

The uniform canopy level of second growth contrasts noticeably against the forest. Until about the eighth year of succession, second growth is referred to as *capoeira* or *juqueira*. Older second-growth communities are called *capoeirão* until they blend in with the forest after about a century. The game yield from second growth is considerably lower than in forested areas. Of the important game species only brocket deer, nine-banded armadillos (*Dasypus novemcinctus*), and agouti (*Dasyprocta* sp.) thrive in *capoeirão* (Smith, 1976c).

Second growth is depauperate of edible fruits and nuts. Babaçu palm is the only wild plant that provides food for colonists and thrives in the presence of man. Fire liberates the nuts, from one to five, encased in the extremely hard endocarp, and they then germinate readily in the nutrient-rich ash. In the forest the palm has a very scattered distribution, but after swidden agriculture dense stands often form (Smith, 1974). Settlers eat the flavorful nuts raw or pound them in a mortar to extract the oil for use in cooking. Other palms, such as tucumã, najá, and bacaba, are normally left standing when settlers clear their fields, but they are often severely damaged by fire and regenerate poorly in *capoeira*.

Cerrado

A scrub savanna characterizes the extreme eastern portion of the Transamazon between the Tocantins and Araguaia rivers. An enclave of cerrado also occurs on the outskirts of Humaitá in the western portion of the highway. Gnarled and charred specimens of *Curatella americana*, *Byrsonima* sp., and *Tabebuia* sp., the latter providing the cerrado with a brilliant flush of yellow blooms in the dry season, are the main woody species. Grasses, a few herbs, and terrestrial bromeliads occupy spaces between the stunted trees.

The factors responsible for the zones of cerrado along the Transamazon are not fully understood. Frequent summer fires, set to improve forage for free-roaming cattle, keep the landscape open. Climate is not a factor, since the deep taproots of cerrado trees protect them against desiccation (Ferri, 1973). Along the Transamazon, cerrado is associated with heavily textured soils. Hueck (1972 : 298) and Müller (1973 : 190) suggest that patches of cerrado in Amazonia are relicts of a more extensive xeromorphic vegetation that supposedly covered large areas of the region during a postglacial dry period. Scrub savanna islands could also have originated by long-distance dispersal from the central plateau region of Brazil.

In the cerrado zone along the eastern section of the Transamazon, spontaneous settlers cultivate plots cleared from galeria forest along water courses. The fingers of alluvial soils are generally fertile, and the strips of forest provide nutrient-rich ash after the burn. The small quantity of cinders resulting from cerrado fires does not fertilize the soil sufficiently to promote good crop development. The poor game yields from cerrado is a further deterrent to settlement by subsistence farmers.[7]

Grassland

Isolated patches of open grassland (*campo limpo*) are found in the Jacareacanga and Humaitá areas of the Transamazon. The *campo* of Jacareacanga, covering some 100 sq. km, appears to be associated with a groundwater podzol that may be seasonally flooded by the Tapajós River. Scattered *Mauritia* palms attest to the damp condition of the soil. From the air I saw outliers of smaller grasslands along the Jacareacanga–Prainha trajectory of the highway. The 388-sq.-km Humaitá grassland grows on a groundwater lateritic soil (Braun and Ramos, 1959).

Sombroek (1966 : 220) states that open grasslands are found on groundwater laterites, groundwater podzols, and freely drained

7. Armadillos and rabbits (*Sylvilagus* sp.) are the only game animals that occur relatively frequently in cerrado areas of the Transamazon. Larger mammals, such as brocket deer and tapir, occasionally slip out of the forest in the early morning or late afternoon to browse in scrub savanna, but hunters rarely encounter these animals far from the cover of forest or old second growth. The low species diversity of vertebrate fauna in the cerrado areas of Brazil is attributed, in part, to the historically limited distribution of the vegetation type (Vanzolini, 1963).

podzols. Forest also grows on poorly drained lateritic soils (IPEAN, 1974), so soil is a predisposing rather than a determining factor in the formation of grasslands in upland areas of Amazonia. All savannas observed by Heinsdijk (1958) between the Tocantins and Xingu rivers showed evidence of fire. Aubréville (1961) asserts that all *campos* are derived from the burning of low woods (*campina*) that grow on podzols. Man-induced fires are surely responsible for the maintenance and expansion of most *campos* in Amazonia.

The agricultural potential of the Transamazon grasslands is limited by the strongly acid and highly leached soils, poor drainage in many cases, and low plant biomass. Even if *campos* on hydromorphic lateritic soils could be drained, such action could lead to plinthite hardening (Sanchez, 1973 : 9). Expensive fertilizers and lime would be needed to compensate for the lack of combustible material. The grasslands are used for extensive grazing by ranchers in Humaitá and Estreito. A colonist with 100 ha of *campo* would have a hard time trying to eke a living from his lot. Wisely, savannas have not been divided into parcels for small-scale farmers.

Campina

Open, stunted woodlands (*campina*) grow on lenses of well-drained podzols along the Jacareacanga–Humaitá stretch of the Transamazon. Unlike cerrado, the bases of *campina* trees are covered with a mound of litter up to half a meter deep. Stretches of bleached sand separate the tree islands. *Campina* podzols are usually abandoned river bars of Pleistocene age.

Extensive *campinas* grow on sandy soils washed into the upper Rio Negro region from the crystalline basement complex of the Guiana shield. The Rio Negro *campinas* are a source of potential dispersal, by birds and wind, to podzols in other areas of Amazonia. Small *campinas* may be relicts of dry climatic cycles in the region, and are now being enveloped by forest. *Campinas* are usually associated with potsherds, suggesting that they have been cleared by Indians (Prance and Schubart, 1978).

Campinas account for less than 1 percent of the highway transect, which is fortunate from the point of view of agriculture. The unusual accumulation of spongy organic matter around *cam-*

pina trees perishes in fires.[8] The porous soil exacerbates the already acute moisture deficit during the dry season. Pineapples and cashews are the only crops that produce reasonably well on highly leached *campina* podzols.

The ecological impact of the Transamazon

Much has been written about the present or potential ecological impact of the Transamazon.[9] Many of the concerned voices were shrill, in tune with the wave of environmental awakening in the late 1960s and early 1970s. Some saw the controversy over the ecological impact of the highway as a means to attack capitalism and a military regime. The specter of red deserts and scrub savannas loomed in the destructive wake of the highway (Denevan, 1973; Goodland and Irwin, 1975). All the literature, including this section, is highly speculative (Anderson, 1972; Modenar, 1972; Paula, 1972; Lovejoy, 1973; Dasmann, 1975 : 122; Jahoda and O'Hearn, 1975; Bunker, 1980; Norgaard, 1981).

Concern for the ecological effects of development in Amazonia, or any other part of the globe, is warranted. All projects should be designed so that they minimize the disruption of natural ecosystems. But in the case of the Amazon basin and other economically backward areas, hyperbole is likely to damage conservation efforts. The pressures to gain access to the natural resources of the region are immense; in the view of some, conservation is a luxury of the developed nations. It is

8. Singer and Araujo (1979) argue that the accumulation of a thick mat of organic matter in *campina* and the denser *campinarana* is due to the presence of ectotrophic mycorrhiza on the roots of the dominant trees. Direct nutrient cycling, aided by the ectotrophic mycorrhiza, apparently robs saprophytic fungi of an essential part of the available nitrogen and phosphorus compounds. Furthermore, the ectotrophic mycorrhiza exude antibiotics, which probably reduces the population of litter microorganisms. Secondary compounds in *campina* leaves, produced to discourage predation, may also inhibit litter decomposers (Janzen, 1974).

9. In 1970 alone, at least a hundred articles on the Transamazon appeared in fourteen of Brazil's leading newspapers. For examples of the concern for the ecological impact of the highway in the foreign press, see "Taming of the Amazon" (*Newsweek*, 2 November 1970), "Transamazonia: The Last Frontier" (*Time*, 13 September 1971, p. 36), and "Brazil Warned of Amazon Destruction" (*Los Angeles Times*, 2 May 1975, p. 1).

more effective to argue environmental causes in a social context: unless the survival needs of the masses of rural and urban poor are met, more forest will inevitably fall, regardless of the number of elaborate conservation strategies drawn up.

Because of the much lower colonization rate than was anticipated, the Transamazon has not provoked any major ecological disasters so far. The highway and its associated side roads are but a hairline fracture across the vast canopy (Fig. 16). If the entire 200-km zone expropriated along the highway is occupied and developed, as much as 600,000 sq. km of forest could disappear. This, together with deforestation in other areas of the basin, could result in a significant drop in rainfall. Between 50 and 60 percent of the precipitation in the region derives from evapotranspiration from forest (Molion, 1975 : 101; Villa Nova et al., 1976; Salati et al., 1978). A mosaic of crops, pasture, and second growth in developed zones cannot match the moisture contribution of the forest. In cleared areas, much of the rain quickly drains into streams and rivers. The water is thus rapidly removed from the system. The forest, on the other hand, acts much like a sponge.

How much rainfall would diminish if 600,000 sq. km of forest were removed is unknown. But even a slight drying of the climate could upset the complex functioning of the forest ecosystem; the character of biological preserves and parks would change, and many species of plants and animals are likely to disappear. In a computer simulation model, 34 percent of the earth between latitudes 5° north and 5° south is assumed to be covered by forest. If the vegetation is removed, the following sequence of events is projected: the reflectivity (albedo) of the land surface increases, less heat is absorbed at the surface, and so convectional activity diminishes. Rainfall dwindles in the tropics, and global temperatures drop, owing to the increased reflection of energy and because less latent heat is released when water vapor condenses (Potter et al., 1975).

Whereas it is plausible that rainfall might decrease in the tropics with large-scale deforestation, global temperatures are less likely to drop. The extensive burning of forests would release substantial amounts of carbon dioxide into the atmosphere, thereby probably raising temperatures through the

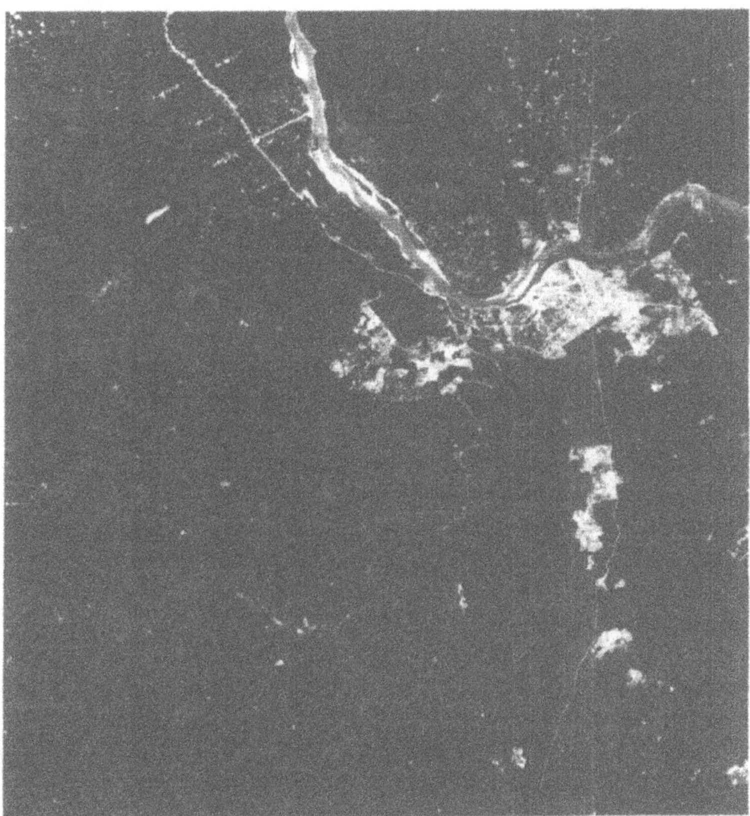

Figure 16. The Transamazon in the vicinity of Marabá (large gray area in the center-left of image). The Transamazon extends northwest from Marabá and roughly parallels the Tocantins River. Note the side roads at intervals along the Transamazon. Landsat satellite image taken in August 1973. The scale is 1:500,000.

greenhouse effect (Goodland and Irwin, 1975:25; Woodwell, 1978). Ice caps would melt. Sea level would rise and flood some cities. How much the oceans will swell is in dispute, but the atmospheric carbon dioxide content is projected to double by the year 2050, thereby raising global temperatures by 2° to 3° C. More ominous still is the likelihood that a stepped-up contribution of CO_2 will disrupt rainfall regimes, resulting in a drier climate for the major temperate cereal-growing areas (Butzer, 1980). A paradoxical situation could develop when more forest is cleared in the tropics to produce food and rainfall decreases in the maize- and wheat-growing belt of North America, thus producing a net loss of food for the world.

Such arguments are unlikely to brake the land rush to Amazonia. First, development planners will argue that the global ecological impact of tropical deforestation is highly speculative. And they are correct. Nevertheless, the projections are based on reasonable assumptions, and if a laissez-faire attitude is adopted, the concrete evidence desired by policy makers may bring tragic consequences. But even if a persuasive case can be made for slowing down the rate of tropical deforestation, such as that which has been put forth by Myers (1980), Brazilians would naturally resent the idea that they should lock up their last frontier to keep cereal farmers happy in North America. In 1972, at the United Nations conference in Stockholm on Man and the Biosphere, the Brazilian delegation rejected the notion that they should preserve their forests to purify the air of pollutants caused by the industrial nations.

Ecological arguments are more likely to be incorporated into planning policy if tangible benefits can be demonstrated. One adverse environmental effect of deforestation along the Transamazon which is immediately obvious to the visitor is the disruption of water courses. During the rainy seasons, the streams and rivers are charged with sediments. The silting of rivers in Amazonia is jeopardizing agriculture. The annual floods of the Amazon River, for example, have been higher of late, thus destroying many crops and reducing the effective growing season on the floodplain (Gentry and Lopez-Parodi, 1980; Smith, 1981). Deforestation in the basin is deemed responsible for the shift in the hydrological cycle. The flooding of towns along the Tocantins and Araguaia during the high-water season has also grown increasingly intense in recent years. Increased run-off and aggradation of river channels is probably largely responsible. Since 1965 large areas of forest have been cleared in the watersheds of the rivers for cattle ranches.

The silting of water courses due to deforestation also diminishes the potential of hydroelectric projects. The useful life of the Tucuruí dam across the Tocantins is expected to be less than twenty-five years. Deforestation along the Transamazon between Marabá and Altamira will disgorge more sediments into the reservoir, further curtailing its long-term capacity to generate electricity. A site for a future dam across the Xingu is being investigated close to Altamira. At the moment, the Xingu is classified as a clear-water river; its waters are a deep green, with few suspended sediments. But as deforestation progresses along the Transamazon, the murky affluents will change the hydrochemistry of the Xingu as well as the Tapajós, another major tributary of the Amazon under consideration for a hydroelectric dam.

The Transamazon has most likely caused the extinction of numerous potentially economic species. Many taxa have restricted ranges. Bulldozers surely crushed some plant and insect species into oblivion. Settlers eliminate more species every year as they puncture holes in the forest rim. A complete inventory of all the plant and animal species living in the forest along the trajectory of the highway before construction began would have been a costly and time-consuming task. Scientists in Amazonia are regularly documenting new species, particularly of insects and plants, but financial and manpower shortages postpone the day when the flora and fauna are well known. In the meantime, thousands of species are likely to become extinct, reducing future options for new agricultural crops and drugs for the pharmaceutical industry.

The new highway system in Amazonia will radically alter the zoogeography of the basin. As the cleared paths widen, blocks of forest will be left, forming isolated gene pools. Many taxa, such as spider monkeys (*Ateles* spp.), are unable to cross broad expanses of modified habitats. Many species of birds that live in the dim interior of the forest are unlikely to venture out into the open. When the Transamazon had been recently built, herds of white-lipped peccaries were observed to emerge from the wall of forest, appear momentarily confused, then cross the road. Although the peccaries swim across broad rivers, such as the Negro, they may avoid a journey of several kilometers across poor cover. Some forest species, such as nine-banded armadillos, agoutis, and titis (*Callicebus moloch*), are not hindered by pasture or second growth.

If the remaining tracts of forest are large, as they are at

present, then speciation may occur in the same manner postulated for the Pleistocene refugia. Species diversity could increase as a result of human activities. A patchwork of different crops, pasture, and second growth at various stages of succession will create opportunities for the influx of new species to the basin.

In the long run, though, the Transamazon and associated PIN highways will inevitably lead to a decline in species diversity. Man-made habitats cannot match the complexity of the forest ecosystem. According to article 44 of law 4.771 (1965), 50 percent of all properties destined for agriculture must remain in forest as a reserve. In practice, the regulation is largely ignored because there is virtually no control. IBDF has far too few personnel to check on the ratio of forest to cleared areas on the thousands of properties scattered throughout the basin. Landsat satellite images can be used to monitor clearing, but many of the large companies involved in ranching projects in Amazonia exert a great deal of economic and political leverage. Along the Transamazon, some lots have been completely cleared with impunity.

The 50 percent rule is seen mostly as an obstacle to development by many officials and settlers along the Transamazon. With such a large expanse of forest left, it is argued, why not clear the 100-ha lots? Some interpret the 50 percent rule to mean that half of their lot must be in forest or perennial crops, or any combination of the two. Artificial pasture is considered a perennial crop, although 50 ha of grassland with exotic cattle hardly constitutes a biological preserve. Besides, it is argued, five forest reserves have been created along the Transamazon to compensate for possible excesses in clearing lots.

INCRA set aside the reserves (Table 6) in a haphazard manner, mainly on the basis of the occurrence of particularly poor soils. No attempt was made to systematically preserve various habitats on other soil types. All the reserves have been invaded by squatters, except the one between km 120 and km 140 of the Altamira–Itaituba stretch of the highway, where fear of attack by the Arara Indians has kept spontaneous settlers at bay. At least sixteen families live within the 10-sq.-km forest reserve located between km 50 and km 60 of the Altamira–Marabá portion of the highway. The lack of boundaries for the reserves encourages their expropriation by speculators and the genuinely needy.

Table 6. Forest Reserves Created by INCRA along the Transamazon

Extension km	Location	Area sq. km
10	Km 50 to km 60 Altamira–Marabá stretch, north margin of highway to Xingu river	10
20	Km 120 to km 140 Altamira–Itaituba stretch of highway, both sides	Undefined
25	Km 350 to km 375 Altamira–Itaituba stretch of highway, both sides	Undefined
7	Km 395 to km 402 Altamira–Itaituba stretch of highway, both sides	Undefined
15	Km 435 to km 450 Altamira–Itaituba stretch of highway, both sides	Undefined

Squatters have even cleared plots along the roadside of the reserves. The authorities have taken no measures to remove the illegal settlers, probably because such moves could provoke violence. Furthermore, squatters would expect reimbursement for "improvements" to the land. Expelled families would only move on to invade another reserve, or someone's property, along the Transamazon or in another part of the basin.

The awesome size of Amazonia is a buffer against imminent ecological demise. The environmental problems are not nearly so serious as in some densely settled regions, such as Haiti or El Salvador. There is still time to set aside a large array of the habitats in the basin for preservation. The federal government is showing signs of taking seriously the responsibility for conserving portions of the Amazon region. The Tapajós park east of Itaituba, a million hectares in size, is an example (Barrett, 1980). But ways will have to be found to accommodate the influx of settlers streaming into Amazonia. The Transamazon scheme was designed as a rational alternative to spontaneous settlement, but it has evidently not proved very successful. The agricultural underpinnings of the project will now be examined.

chapter 4

Agro-Ecosystem Productivity

Disappointing agricultural productivity has been a major factor in the slowdown of the colonization rate. This chapter focuses on the main bottlenecks to increased farm production; no attempt is made to identify all the complex cultural, sociopolitical, and ecological factors that influence agricultural yields. The problems associated with annual and perennial crops are reviewed, and the role of credit is examined. Finally, difficulties encountered with the formation of cooperatives are discussed.

Annual crops

Government planners envisaged upland rice *(Oryza sativa)* as the principal cash and subsistence crop for Transamazon colonists (Fig. 17). Favored by fiscal incentives, rice accounted for 30 percent of the income of 155 settlers

Figure 17. Rice field ready for harvesting near Nova Fronteira in June 1979. Note the large *Ceiba pentandra* tree in the center, a relatively common tree on *terra roxa*.

sampled in 1978. But heavy dependence on one crop for food and subsistence is always a risky policy, and rice cultivators have encountered a series of ecological and economic difficulties with the crop.

Rice yields are generally very low along the highway, averaging only 1,593 kg/ha (s = 679, n = 97).[1] Only one rice crop a year is grown along the Transamazon because of the pronounced dry season. The selling price for harvested rice does not justify the expense of installing irrigation equipment. During the 1979 harvest, for example, a 60-kg sack of rice was worth only $9 (U.S.) to the farmer. The average area planted to the crop each year is 8 ha. Thus the expected income from a 8-ha rice field would be $1,900. Out of the gross earnings from his harvested cereal, the settler must pay the workers who helped him gather the crop, and repay the bank loan.

Most settlers plant IAC 101, a rice developed in the temperate area of Campinas, São Paulo. The variety is unsuited to the climatic conditions of the Transamazon. The long stems easily lodge during storms at harvest time, when the inflorescences are heavy. A flattened crop takes longer to harvest. In the meantime, rats and ground doves (*Columbina talpacoti*) feed avidly on the seeds on or near the ground. INCRA ignored other varieties, better suited to the ecological environment of the Amazon, because they were considered inferior.

Planners opted for a single variety for the entire Transamazon. The dangers of monocultures, especially in the tropics, are well known to ecologists. Apparently, the many cases of single-crop disasters, such as the collapse of the Ford rubber plantation along the Tapajós, escaped the attention of the designers of the Transamazon scheme. In late 1972 and early 1973, INCRA distributed *barbalha*, a rice variety from the northeastern state of Pernambuco, to Transamazon colonists. Yields from the variety were well below expectations, averaging only 445 kg/ha (Smith,

1. The *s* in parenthesis after average yields refers to standard deviation. Colonists were asked how large an area was planted to each crop, the quantity harvested, and income in 1978. The area-weighted average yield for rice was 1,454 kg/ha (Appendix 3). Many settlers are not familiar with the hectare unit. Conversion rates for other means of measuring area are as follows: 3.3 *tarefas* = 1 ha, 3.3 *linhas* = 1 ha, 1 *alqueire* = 5 ha. Two sack sizes are used along the Transamazon: the traditional 60 kg size, and 50 kg, introduced by INCRA.

1978). *Barbalha* was not tested in trial plots along the Transamazon before distribution. The variety proved ecologically unsuited to the highway, and many settlers did not even bother to gather the meager crop.

Rice farmers encounter major difficulties at harvest time. Labor must be contracted to cut the crop. Some settlers help each other at the task, but most are in competition to hire workers, which are usually in short supply. If the ripe crop is left a long time in the field, the yield declines because of predation by birds, especially blue-headed parrots (*Pionus menstruus*) and painted parakeets (*Pyrrhura picta*). Noisy flocks of the forest birds, numbering up to 150 in the case of blue-headed parrots, swoop down on rice fields and devour kernels from the vantage of fallen logs and branches. Scarecrows are not used and would probably be ineffectual, since the parrots and parakeets are alarmed by movement and quickly resume feeding if the observer remains still. Shotgun shells, at twenty-five cents each, are too expensive to spend on a bird that will render at most 100 g of meat.

After a colonist has managed to harvest his rice crop, usually with machetes or sickles (Fig. 18), he must then secure a threshing machine (*trilhadeira*) to separate the kernels from the stalks. During the first two years of settlement, INCRA distributed *trilhadeiras* along the highway for use by colonists. But within a couple of years, the machines fell into disrepair and rusted. Some settlers brought their own threshing machines, but few can afford to purchase one at $4,300 (Fig. 19). Consequently, settlers have to wait until they can rent one of the machines. Colonists along badly eroded side roads are often denied access to *trilhadeiras*. The owners are reluctant to risk having their machines stuck during the height of the rice harvest season.

For subsistence, rice is cut with a knife just below the inflorescence. The seed heads are then carried home, where women pound them in wooden mortars to separate the chaff from the kernels. The dull thud of the pestle quickly attracts chickens, which eagerly wait for rice to spill over the mortar. The rice is then transferred to a large, circular, flat basket and is tossed into the air to remove the husks. The manual method of dehusking provides an adequate supply of the cereal for home consumption, but it is not suitable for large-scale commercial

Figure 18. Settler from Rio Grande do Sul harvesting rice near Nova Fronteira in May 1974

Figure 19. A *trilhadeira* brought to the Transamazon by a family from Rio Grande do Sul, near Nova Fronteira, May 1974

production. Many kernels are broken in the mortar, thereby reducing the sales value. Furthermore, the manual method is very time-consuming.

After separating the kernels from the stalks, farmers must send their sacked rice to a drier before it ferments and moulds. Few storage facilities are available for harvested crops along the Transamazon. Most colonists cover their rice harvest under canvas or plastic sheets. Others store the cereal in a hut or in their homes until transportation can be arranged. During the first two years of colonization, INCRA trucks took the rice to CIBRAZEM warehouses in Marabá, Altamira, *agrópolis* Brasil Novo, and Miritituba, whence it was shipped to Belém for consumption in the internal market. Since 1973 settlers have had to contract privately operated trucks to remove their rice harvest.

The importance of CIBRAZEM as the preeminent marketer of rice along the Transamazon is being eroded. In 1977 trucks at the CIBRAZEM warehouses at *agrópolis* Brasil Novo and *rurópolis* Medicilandia had to wait up to ten days to unload rice. The sacks had to be weighed individually, thereby causing the trucks to back up and the rice to ferment in the hot sun. While the quality of the rice deteriorates, colonists must pay freight charges as the vehicles remain idle (Bunker, 1979). At each of the CIBRAZEM warehouses the rice is classified according to quality. To obtain a favorable rating, it is apparently sometimes necessary to provide a commission. Surprisingly, settlers do not generally express much moral outrage when faced with corruption; most would probably supplement their income in the same manner if they had the chance.

Although CIBRAZEM pays the official minimum price, several discounts are deducted from the total. The settler must wait for payment at the Banco do Brasil. A delay of several weeks, and numerous trips to town, are often necessary before the colonist receives any income from his rice harvest sold to CIBRAZEM.

Private firms in Marabá, Altamira, Miritituba, and Itaituba now purchase the bulk of the rice along the Transamazon. The companies usually have large scales that weigh the vehicles before and after unloading, thus eliminating the need to wait. Buyers often remove the harvest from the lot and pay the colonist cash. Settlers along some of the transverse arteries often lose much of their rice crop because trucks are unable to reach their lots after the rainy season has dissected the roads. Some access roads were never built; colonists must extract their harvests by mule.

Manioc (*Manihot esculenta*), the basic staple of Amazonia, could have provided a much more reliable source of cash and subsistence, particularly during the first few years of colonization. In spite of its widespread use in the basin, the starchy cultivar is perceived as a low-status crop, with little nutritional value (Smith, 1978). Although *mandioca* has less than 1 percent protein, settlers generally obtain adequate quantities of amino acids from beans, game, and domestic animals.

Yields from manioc vary, but are always much higher than rice. Along the Transamazon, manioc yields attain 60 tons/ha within a year when planted as a first crop on fertile *terra roxa*. Manioc is traditionally planted as the last crop in the sequence in many areas of the tropics, therefore yields are reduced because of weed invasion and the loss of soil nutrients through leaching and run-off. No serious pests or diseases attack manioc along the Transamazon. Yields average 20 tons of tubers per hectare on plots recently cleared from forest.

Figure 20. Box-type manioc press weighted with logs. Note manioc in the background and the oven for making flour to the left. Km 400 of the Altamira–Itaituba stretch, 1973.

Most of the manioc harvested along the highway is converted to flour. The tubers are peeled and grated on a board or by machine; then the dough is placed in a press, of which there are several varieties in use along the Transamazon. In one model, used mostly by settlers from the south, a viselike device squeezes the dough stuffed into sacks. A defect with this method is that the sacks sometimes split under the pressure, releasing the dough onto the dirty floor. Northerners and Nordestinos place grated manioc in a box lined with leaves. Weight is then applied by rocks or wood (Fig. 20). The traditional, sleeve-like *tipití* (Fig. 21), of Indian design, is also employed to squeeze water out of the dough. The compacted mass is then pushed through a sieve to remove large pieces of fiber. Finally, the dough is agitated with a paddle on an iron griddle over an oven for a couple of hours until it is dry. The granular flour can be stored for months without spoiling.

Both sweet (*macaxeira*) and bitter (*mandioca brava*) varieties of manioc are used to make flour. The poisonous prussic acid of *mandioca brava* is driven off when the dough is heated. To pre-

Figure 21. *Tipití* manioc press near Nova Fronteira, 1974

pare *farinha puba,* a flour with a distinctive yellow color which is higher in protein and vitamin A, the tubers are soaked in water for several days so that they become pulpy. The grating step is thus bypassed. An average 3.3 kg (s = 0.4, n = 4) of peeled roots are required to make 1 kg of flour.[2] Allowing for a 30 percent reduction in yield because of rotted portions, attached earth, and peelings, a 1-ha field of one-year-old manioc containing 20 tons of tubers would produce 4,242 kg.

Manioc provides far more carbohydrates per unit area than rice. The calorific value of milled rice is about 360 Kcal/100g, compared with some 330 Kcal/100g for manioc flour (Chatfield, 1954; Leung and Flores, 1961; Platt, 1962). The yield of dried and dehusked rice along the Transamazon averages approximately 1,300 Kg/ha, or 4.6 million calories. An equivalent area of manioc can produce 14 million calories in the form of flour, and is thus three times as productive as rice.[3]

Manioc can also generate more income than rice. A 60-kg sack of manioc flour was worth $15 in 1979. A family of six can comfortably harvest 3 ha of the root crop and produce 12,726 kg of flour within a year, thereby earning $3,000. A rice farmer would make an average of $1,900 from 8 ha of the cereal. The profit advantage of manioc varies according to soil and market conditions, but the crop can usually provide more calories and income for settlers.

Manioc is well suited to the cultural and ecological conditions of a pioneer rainforest environment. Harvesting can be staggered from eight months to three years after the stems are planted, although the fiber content of the tubers increases after eighteen months. In this manner, a sick family can wait until they recover without ruining the crop. Manioc cultivation fosters cooperation and social cohesion, instead of the competition for labor and machines characteristic of rice farming. Families assist each other in processing flour during the protracted harvest. The flour-making hut (*casa da farinha*) forges reciprocal working re-

2. If unwashed and unpeeled tubers are considered, the ratio is 4.3:1. Other reported ratios range from 2.5:1 (LeCointe, 1922), to 3.2:1 (BNB, 1971:17) and 3.6:1 (Normanha and Pereira, 1950).

3. In eastern Nigeria, manioc, with a yield of 12,654 kg/ha, produces twice as many calories as rice, which averages 1,362 kg/ha (Miracle, 1973).

lationships and provides an opportunity for settlers to exchange information, especially gossip.

The technology required for making manioc flour is simple and easy to acquire. A circular iron griddle is the only item usually bought to make top quality flour. A griddle two meters in diameter can be readily purchased in a Transamazon town for $80. Colonists fashion cruder oven pans from kerosene cans or oil drums, but the flour is usually inferior because the heat is not distributed evenly. Ceramic griddles, employed by some Indian tribes, are not used by highway settlers. Some colonists have bought 7-h.p. gasoline-fueled graters for $240, though manually operated ones are also used successfully. Other materials needed to equip a *casa da farinha*, such as bricks for the oven walls and wood for fuel and the press, can be prepared from clay and trees on the lot.

Neither pests nor diseases significantly affect manioc yields along the highway, or in other parts of Amazonia. Leaf-cutter ants (*Atta sexdens*) and brocket deer crop sprouting manioc in a few isolated cases, but their overall effect is negligible. Rodents, especially spiny rats (*Proechimys* sp.) and introduced brown rats,[4] gnaw small portions of sweet manioc tubers at or close to the surface. Fungi and bacteria invade the damaged roots and cause more appreciable losses through rotting.

Bitter manioc is supposed to be toxic to mammals, yet white-lipped peccaries, white-collared peccaries (*Tayassu tajacu*), agoutis, and pacas (*Agouti paca*) occasionally raid *mandioca brava* fields. Humans become violently ill if they eat bitter manioc (Clark, 1936). McGaughey (1951) found a high mortality rate among captive nutrias (*Myocastor coypus*) fed bitter manioc. In Africa the roots of sweet manioc are raided by wild pigs and baboons, but the poisonous variety can be left unguarded (De Schlippe, 1956). The latter is sometimes planted around the perimeter of sweet-manioc fields to discourage predation (Jennings, 1970).

In the upper-Xingu region of the Brazilian Amazon, peccaries also eat bitter manioc in fields planted by the Camayurá and

4. The two species were caught in rat traps baited with sweet manioc in plantations of the root crop. The rats were identified with the aid of Pine (1973).

Kuikuru (Oberg, 1953; Carneiro, 1961). Carneiro argues that peccaries are able to root out and consume manioc in fields because interred tubers contain no prussic acid, only manihotoxine, a cyanogenetic glucoside. The roots apparently become toxic after they are exposed to the air and enzymes have converted cyanogenetic glucoside to prussic acid.

Although the delayed enzyme reaction in bitter manioc roots may be partly responsible for the ability of wild animals in Amazonia to raid the tubers in fields, other factors may be involved. It seems likely that peccaries and some other animals have acquired the ability to detoxify prussic acid, as other fauna have done with a variety of chemical compounds produced by plants for defense (Freeland and Janzen, 1974). Peccaries have been interacting with manioc fields much longer in the New World than wild pigs have in Africa, where the crop was introduced in colonial times.

Cattle and pigs can also eat bitter manioc with impunity, provided that the tubers are covered with earth; the colloidal clay apparently absorbs prussic acid (BNB, 1967:240). Along the Transamazon I have watched chickens drinking the juice squeezed from bitter manioc with no apparent ill effects. Different clones of bitter manioc contain varying amounts of prussic acid, and this may partly account for the observed differences in the physiological effects. Bitter manioc may have conferred better protection in the past, but its advantages over sweet manioc appear to be declining in Amazonia. Still, losses due to mammalian predation are insignificant when compared with the high tuber yields.

A biased system of fiscal incentives is the main reason why manioc has not assumed a more important role as a commercial crop along the Transamazon. Bank financing is not available for the root crop. Many settlers depend on Banco do Brasil loans, arranged by EMATER, to hire labor to clear forest, as well as to plant and harvest their crops. Furthermore, CIBRAZEM will not buy manioc roots or flour. Consequently, manioc provided only 1 percent of the income of surveyed settlers in 1978. Only 7 percent of the 155 colonists interviewed sold manioc tubers or flour in that year.

Manioc is not a panacea for the agricultural problems of the

Transamazon. But it would provide a sounder basis than cereals to launch settlement projects in Amazonia. Manioc flour finds a ready market in Transamazon towns such as Marabá, Altamira, and Itaituba, and could become a significant trade item to larger towns such as Belém, Santarém, and Manaus if more incentives were provided.

Maize (*Zea mays*), as in the case of rice, is an unreliable source of income. Yields are modest, averaging only 1,320 kg/ha (s = 646, n = 13). The price a Transamazon settler receives for a 60-kg sack of maize varies according to locality and time of year, but averages only $5.80, well below that of rice. Few settlers grow the crop on a commercial scale; only 16 of the 155 colonists interviewed sold maize in 1978, representing a meager 1 percent of the settlers' income. *Milho,* as the crop is known in Brazil, is grown mainly to feed pigs and chickens.

One reason for the depressed yields is that colonists save kernels produced by hybrid corn for planting the following year. The F2 generation is much more variable in quality and quantity of seeds produced. Rats and chickens reduce yields by uncovering and eating recently planted seed. In some areas, leafcutter ants denude maize fields up to 0.5 ha in size. As the crop ripens, rats gnaw the kernels. Cobs on collapsed stalks are eaten by diurnal agoutis and nocturnal pacas.

Maize cobs infested with aphids (*Rhopalosiphum maidis*), hidden under the husks, show no damage by predators. Ground-nesting fire ants (*Solenopsis sp.*) milk the aphids and indirectly protect the maize plants.[5] Any attempt to molest the maize elicits an immediate stinging response from the ants. Although fire ants are commonly regarded as a nuisance, they serve a useful function in Transamazon maize fields. Ants are known to protect wild plants from mammals, as in the associations between *Pseudomyrmex* ants and *Acacia* trees and between *Azteca* ants and *Cecropia* (Janzen, 1969; Berg, 1978), but the mutually beneficial relationship is unusual among cultivars. Settlers harvest most of

5. I sent the ants and aphids to the Systematic Entomology Laboratory, U.S.D.A., Beltsville, Maryland, for identification. L. M. Russel kindly determined the aphids, and D. R. Smith identified the ants. It was not possible to determine the fire ants as to species because I did not include soldiers in my sample.

the crop with impunity, since they collect the cobs after they have dried on the stalks and the aphids have left.

The greatest damage to maize occurs when it is stored. Cosmopolitan snout beetles (*Sitophilus zeamais*) quickly bore into the kernels and render the crop commercially worthless within four months. The cobs are generally piled close to the ground. There the harvest moulds and is invaded by beetles that feed on fungi and whose larvae tunnel into the kernels. Maize provides a striking illustration of the diversity of agricultural pests in the tropics. From one pile of the cereal in a lot near Coco Chato, I collected seven beetle species in four families (Nitidulidae: *Carpophilus pilosellus, C. dimidiatus, C. freemani, C. mutilatus;* Cryptophagidae: *Hapalips* sp.; Cucujidae: *Ahasverus advens;* Curculionidae: *Sitophilus zeamais*).[6] The Arara Indians, who formerly inhabited the area around Nova Fronteira, suspend their three varieties of maize from the ceiling of their communal house. The harvest thus remains dry, and smoke from household fires helps discourage predation.

Kidney beans (*Phaseolus vulgaris*), planted after the rice harvest by some settlers for domestic consumption, do not provide a significant cash income for Transamazon settlers (Fig. 22). Few colonists have been able to take advantage of the favorable market for *P. vulgaris*. Brazil used to be largely self-sufficient in kidney beans. Then in response to the doubling of the price of soybeans (*Glycine max*) on world markets in 1973, large areas of fertile *terra roxa* in southern Brazil were planted to the crop (L. Brown, 1978 : 154). Brazil exports soybeans to Japan and western Europe and is now the world's second largest producer, after the United States. Whereas soybean exports have generated much-needed foreign exchange, the production of foodstuffs for the domestic market has slackened. Brazil is forced to purchase kidney beans from Argentina and Mexico to satisfy home demand. A 60-kg sack of *P. vulgaris* sells for an average of $27 along the Transamazon, three times the price of a sack of rice.

During the first year of settlement, beans produced well in

6. The nitidulid beetles were determined by W. A. Connel, the Cryptophagidae by J. M. Kingsolver, the Cucujidae by T. J. Spilman, and the Curculionidae by R. W. Warner, care of the Systematic Entomology Laboratory, U.S.D.A., Beltsville, Maryland.

Figure 22. Colonist weeding kidney beans near Leonardo da Vinci in June 1979. Note the stakes ready for the planting of pepper.

areas recently cleared from forest. By 1973 various species of fungi, particularly *Thanatephorus cucumeris*, were seriously damaging the crop. Bean sprouts are frequently cropped by rabbits (*Sylvilagus brasiliensis*), which have colonized the avenues of disturbed habitats along the highway. The average yield on thirty-one lots in 1978 was only 506 kg/ha (s = 322, n = 31).

Yields are further reduced after the harvest by at least two species of beetles, *Callosobruchus maculatus* and *Zabrotes subfasciatus*.[7] The bruchids bore into most of the stored pulses within four months, a problem noted in other parts of Amazonia and in Africa (Sefer, 1959; Jurion and Henry, 1969 : 247). Seed for planting is preserved with insecticide in bottles or steel drums. The bruchid pests were probably introduced along the highway with beans destined for planting. Another source of the beetles may have been beans purchased for food; in 1973 I saw packages infested with bruchids for sale in stores in Altamira.

Perennial crops

Perennial crops are often cited as one of the most rational means of farming the uplands of Amazonia, since they provide better soil cover than annuals (Alvim, 1977a, 1978). Through Banco do Brasil credit, colonists are encouraged to plant perennials as a long-term source of cash. Sugarcane (*Saccharum officinarum*), cacao (*Theobroma cacao*), coffee (*Coffea arabica*), pepper (*Piper nigrum*), bananas (*Musa* spp.), and guinea grass (*Panicum maximum*) have been especially promoted by INCRA and EMATER as sources of revenue for colonists.

Sugarcane was envisaged as one of the most promising perennial-crop candidates for *terra roxa* along the highway. INCRA built a mill with an annual production capacity of 500,000 sacks of sugar at km 92 of the Altamira–Itaituba stretch, in the largest *terra roxa* patch along the Transamazon. The mill was assembled with domestic and imported machinery. Some parts were flown to Altamira, others were trucked from São Paulo. To justify the expense of building a $6 million mill, INCRA strongly

7. The bruchid beetles were determined by J. M. Kingsolver, care of the Systematic Entomology Laboratory, U.S.D.A., Beltsville, Maryland.

encouraged colonists to plant cane within a 20-km radius of the mill.

The INCRA-operated mill was inaugurated in 1974, even though there was not nearly enough cane in the area to keep it operating. As of August 1974 only 300 ha of the crop had been established in the vicinity of the mill. To hasten the planting schedule, credit was liberated so that colonists could purchase tractors to pull up stumps from the land as well as plough and load cane onto trucks. INCRA even bulldozed forest on some lots to accelerate planting. By July 1977, the area planted to cane had increased to slightly under 1,000 ha. The modest production of semirefined sugar, well under capacity, was distributed through COBAL stores. In 1976 the mill produced 1.4 million liters of alcohol to fuel government vehicles as an experiment.

Sugarcane produces well on *terra roxa,* averaging 81 tons/ha (s = 17) in a sample of fifteen lots in 1978. Some colonists reap up to 107 tons/ha on the first cutting. Settlers report that yields are lower in bulldozed areas; the D-8 Caterpillars scrape away the more fertile topsoil and compact the earth (Smith, 1978). Yields may slip in the future unless ash from the bagasse is returned to the fields. In November 1978 I collected *Atta sexdens* that were removing leaf blades from sugarcane 12 km east of the mill.[8] The ants could proliferate, as they have in other tropical areas of South America (Weber, 1947; Gonçalves, 1957, 1967; Butt, 1970), and seriously damage cane and other crops along the highway.

A favorable political climate awaits further expansion of sugarcane plantations along the Transamazon as well as in other parts of Brazil. Through the *pro-álcool* program, the country is attempting to drastically reduce oil imports by fueling the national fleet of some 12 million vehicles with ethanol. The Brazilian automobile industry produced approximately 200,000 alcohol-powered cars in 1980 and has set a target of 900,000 ethanol-fueled cars by 1982 (Anon., 1980a). In addition, 270,000 vehicles with gasoline engines are to be converted to burn alcohol. Cars with alcohol motors can be purchased over three years, whereas credit for gasoline-powered automobiles is available for only

8. The leaf-cutter ants, known as *saúva* in Brazil, were identified by C. R. Gonçalves, Instituto de Biologia, Universidade Federal Rural do Rio de Janeiro.

twelve months. Finally, alcohol sells for at least 35 percent less than gasoline and can be purchased at the pump over the weekend when the latter fuel cannot be legally sold.

Transamazon settlers are unlikely to reap any immediate benefit from the improving market for sugar and alcohol. During the 1978 harvest, the mill was able to crush only a small fraction of the mature cane because of broken machinery and administrative difficulties. In 1979 much of the cane crop was condemned as useless. The saccharose content was too low because a lot of the cane was more than two years old. Some settlers set fire to their cane fields in preparation for cutting, then lost the crop because trucks were unable to negotiate the slippery and rutted side roads. Once cane has been burned, it must be processed within seventy-two hours. A longer delay ruins the crop because of fermentation.

The official buying price of $18 per ton of cane was an incentive to colonists. When those colonists who managed to dispatch their crop to the mill appeared to collect payment, they received an unpleasant surprise. Taxes, fees, freight charges, and commissions shrank the average payment in 1978 to only $8 per ton. Many of the colonists who made a commitment to growing cane felt they had been let down. In 1979 the mill was leased to a co-op from the south of Brazil. The latter organization wants to operate the mill on a money-making basis, so sugarcane may yet prove to be a financially viable crop for a limited number of settlers along the highway.

Cacao, at a selling price of $2 per kg, is one of the most promising perennial crops along the Transamazon. As of 1979 some 6,000 ha of cacao had been planted along the Altamira–Itaituba stretch of the highway. Brazil exported 310,000 tons of cacao beans in 1979, becoming the world's second largest producer after the Ivory Coast. CEPLAC (Comissão Executiva do Plano de Lavoura Cacaueira) has announced an ambitious plan to expand the area planted to cacao and thereby propel Brazil into the forefront of world producers of the commodity. At present, Amazonia has only 45,000 ha of cacao plantations (Alvim, pers. comm.), representing 1 percent of the national production. But by 1985 some 160,000 ha of cacao groves are to be planted in the region, 40,000 ha along the Transamazon alone

(Alvares-Afonso, 1979). In 1978 cacao already accounted for 5 percent of the income of the surveyed settlers.

Colonists receive cacao seeds from CEPLAC if their project is approved and they have been granted credit by the Banco do Brasil. To qualify for CEPLAC seeds, a colonist must own a lot with good soil, preferably *terra roxa*. The seeds are germinated in small plastic bags in nurseries with palm-thatch covers on the settlers' lots. After the seedlings have reached approximately 50 cms in height, they are transplanted under the shade of manioc or banana trees. No long-term shading is provided for cacao along the Transamazon.

On *terra roxa*, cacao plantations have already formed dense stands and are healthy. Yields vary, but are as high as 1,000 kg of beans per ha in four-year-old groves. In podzolic soils, such as in the vicinity of Coco Chato, cacao trees are generally stunted and produce poorly. Along the Transamazon, cacao plantations produce all year round. The harvested beans are dried on large canvas sheets; thus far, no sheds with sliding drawers have been built to help protect the seeds from showers. A few colonists roast some of their crop to make a rich, fatty, chocolate drink for home consumption. The tart, pulpy seeds are relished as a snack.

At least three factors may limit the potential for cacao along the Transamazon. First, the area of suitable soil, *terra roxa*, is very restricted. The red clays account for only 3 percent of the highway transect. Second, fertilization is recommended in unshaded plantations (Alvim, 1977b). The economic viability of such treatments is questionable. There is no fertilizer plant in Amazonia; the product has to be imported from the Northeast and southern Brazil. Fertilizer prices have been climbing steeply in recent years, partly as a result of the rise in oil prices. In Amazonia they are especially high because of the additional transportation costs. One kg of superphosphate costs forty-one cents in Altamira (Smith, 1978). Third, cacao is native to the Amazon region, and several wild species of *Theobroma* occur in the forest along the highway. Consequently, disease reservoirs exist in close proximity to Transamazon cacao plantations. If witches' broom (*Crinipellis perniciosa*) or black pod (*Phytophthora palmivora*) invade cacao groves along the highway, settlers will suffer severe financial reverses. Fungicides are expensive and largely ineffective, since they must be applied during the rainy season when the spores are being released. The rain rapidly washes away the applied chemicals.

Coffee, Brazil's most popular hot beverage and the leading agricultural export, was initially thought to offer great promise as a cash crop along the Transamazon. The output of coffee plantations in Brazil has been slipping for about a decade owing to frosts and the introduction of coffee rust (*Hemileia vastatrix*). The disease reached Bahia, probably by plane from Africa, in 1970 and soon spread to other states (Purseglove, 1974: 476). Unusually severe frosts in 1973, 1975, 1976, and 1979 further devastated plantations in São Paulo and Paraná (Margolis, 1979; Marshall, 1980). To compensate for the demise of many of the coffee groves, the government has encouraged planting of new disease-resistant varieties of the crop in warmer climates.

EMBRAPA (Empresa Brasileira de Pesquisa Agropecuária), a research organ of the Ministry of Agriculture, introduced *Mundo Novo* to the Transamazon in 1972. The variety, developed in southern Brazil and reportedly resistant to coffee-rust disease, was planted at the EMBRAPA experimental station at km 23 Altamira–Itaituba and distributed to several settlers on a trial basis. Weekly applications of insecticides were soon required in some cases to control leaf miners (*Perileucoptera cofeella*, Lepidoptera). Whereas the well-tended experimental plot at km 23 remained green and impressive to visiting dignitaries, none of the colonists could afford to spray their coffee groves.

Other varieties introduced to the highway have also met with limited success. *Bourbon* sheds its leaves excessively and fruits poorly. *Canelão* produces a flush of berries in the dry season, but yields are modest. The low productivity of coffee along the highway, even when relatively free of diseases and pests, is probably due to the high mean annual temperature of 26° C (Appendixes 1 and 2). Average yearly temperatures in excess of 24° C inhibit coffee growth (Maestri and Barros, 1977). For this reason, the crop is not usually planted on a large scale in equatorial lowlands. Although coffee has limited potential as a commercial crop along the highway, some settlers keep several bushes in their backyards for domestic consumption. Ground coffee costs $3/kg in Transamazon stores, relatively cheap by North American or European standards, but expensive for settlers.

The Transamazon was seen as an opportunity to create new pepper plantations and thereby escape the buildup of diseases and pests in the traditional growing areas. The crop was first cultivated on a commercial scale in the Brazilian Amazon in the mid 1940s by Japanese immigrants who established a colony at Tomé-Açu, Pará, in 1929. Pepper commands a high price on the international market, and the crop soon became Pará's leading agricultural export. But in the 1960s the extensive plantations around Tomé-Açu became infested with a fungus disease, *Fusarium solani piperi,* and production fell. Root nematodes (*Meloidogyne* sp.) also attack the vines, further reducing yields and the profit margin. Farmers at Tomé-Açu plant marigolds around the base of pepper plants to combat the worms, but no effective fungicide has been developed against *Fusarium s. piperi.* The useful life of a pepper grove has been reduced from fifteen to seven years in diseased areas. Shriveled pepper plantations are being replaced by cacao at Tomé-Açu.

INCRA and EMATER promoted pepper as one of the most viable perennial crops for Transamazon settlers (Fig. 23). At a selling price of $1.20/kg, the high cost of fertilization is rewarded. Banco do Brasil credit was extended for settlers to buy the 2.5-meter-high wooden stakes (Fig. 22), a thousand of which are required per hectare, and to purchase cuttings.

Although pepper is currently one of the most important perennial crops along the Transamazon, accounting for 8 percent of the 1978 income of the colonists surveyed, its future is uncertain. By 1975 *Fusarium s. piperi* had appeared in plantations along the highway (Fearnside, 1978:366, 1980), possibly introduced with infected cuttings or stakes. The disease is dispersed by wind-borne spores to new plantings along the Transamazon within a couple of years. Yellow leaves, withered stems, and stark, sun-bleached stakes bear witness to the efficiency of the pathogen.

Bananas, of which there at least six varieties planted along the highway, produced abundantly during the first few years of colonization.[9] Much of the production during the early years

9. Banana cultivars observed growing along the Transamazon include *comprida* (plantain), *congo*, *inajá*, *nanica*, *ouro*, and *roxo*. Though *inajá* and *ouro* yield less than other varieties, they are relished for their creamy texture and sweet taste.

Figure 23. Japanese-born colonist drying pepper on plastic sheets near Nova Fronteira, September 1979

rotted on the ground because the small local markets were saturated. None of the highway towns had more than 25,000 inhabitants in 1973.

Two factors converged after 1974 to improve the prospects for banana growers along the Transamazon. After the Belém–Brasília was asphalted in 1974, trucks from the south could reach colonists along the BR-230 more cheaply and quickly. Furthermore, as in the case of coffee, severe frosts destroyed many banana groves in the south. A large market in central and southern Brazil was thus opened to Transamazon banana growers.

Truck drivers, operating independently, pay colonists about thirty cents a stalk. A driver is only interested in dealing with growers who can quickly fill his vehicle, usually a diesel-powered Mercedes or Ford. The cargo area is lined with banana leaves, and up to 2,000 stalks of the green fruit are loaded tightly and covered with tarpaulin. When the truck reaches Minas Gerais or São Paulo, after some five to seven days, the bananas are beginning to ripen. A major breakdown on the journey to market results in considerable financial loss, since the cargo spoils rapidly.[10]

As the market conditions improved for Transamazon banana growers disease struck. Several fungi, especially *Fusarium oxysporum cubense*, now severely damage banana plantations, often before the colonist can cut a crop. Banana groves on poor soils are particularly vulnerable to disease, and even on relatively fertile *terra roxa*, plantations do not survive more than three years. Whereas in the first few years of colonization banana groves were mostly green, now a large number of the plants have brown and yellow leaves. The cores are often rotten.

Some settlers sow guinea grass with rice so that pasture may form after the cereal is harvested. Colonists regard the substitution of unproductive second growth with pasture as a potential solution to their cash-crop problem along the Transamazon. Settlers are attracted to the idea of cattle-raising because of the prestige associated with ranching in Luso-Brazilian culture. Many settlers dream of a day when, from the comfort of a hammock on a shaded and breezy veranda, they will gaze upon a herd of cattle grazing contentedly on lush pasture. Life on a *fazenda* is considered far more leisurely and civilized than crop-farming in the hot sun. Because of the widespread enthusiasm for cattle-ranching, and generous bank credit, beef production accounted for 14 percent of the income of interviewed settlers in 1978.

Few colonists are able to make money from ranching on their 100-ha lots. Only 10 percent of the 155 settlers surveyed sold cattle in 1978. Cattle-raising is concentrated in the hands of a small group of the wealthier colonists. Tossing grass seed into rice fields is a relatively easy task, but keeping pastures open from weed invasion and stump sprouting is onerous and costly. Fencing is expensive and time-consuming. Many settlers sowed more pasture than they could keep clear with cattle-grazing and machetes. Consequently, much of the pasture along the Transamazon is choked with second growth (Fig. 24).

10. Bananas produced on large-scale plantations in Central America are cut when much greener than along the Transamazon. The boxed fruit is transported in chilled holds for the journey of one to two weeks by ship to the United States or Europe. At the port of destination, the bananas are gassed with ethylene to promote uniform ripening (Purseglove, 1975:368).

Figure 24. Weed-infested pasture at km 17 of the Altamira–Marabá stretch of the Transamazon in 1979. Note the fire-damaged Brazil-nut tree in the center.

Some settlers purchased more cattle than their pastures could support. The herds soon became weak and diseased; the cattle then died or were sold off. The settlers inherited badly eroded grassland and a Banco do Brasil loan to pay off. To liquidate their financial obligations, some have sold their lots. Entrepreneurs typically consolidate several adjacent lots, place a few cowhands on their recently acquired properties, then reside in Marabá, Altamira, or Itaituba.

Even if a colonist is able to convert up to 80 percent of his 50-ha cropping area to good pasture, beef production on such a small area is a marginal enterprise at best. The year-round carrying capacity of new artificial pastures in upland Amazonia averages only one head per hectare.[11] Cattle in The Brazilian Amazon usually require four years to reach a slaughter weight of 350 kg (IDESP, 1970; FAO, 1973); thus the productivity of such pastures is only 44 kg/ha/yr, allowing for calves and reproducers. Under optimal conditions, a colonist might be able to produce 1,760 kg of undressed beef a year on 40 ha, thereby earning $739 (based on a live-weight price of forty-two cents per kilogram). Manioc-farming is clearly more profitable than cattle-ranching; flour from a 3-ha plot of the tubers can earn a settler $3,000. Furthermore, manioc cultivation is far less destructive of the environment.

A limited area of grassland for dairy cattle, local beef demand, and draft animals is warranted, but converting most of the cropping area to pasture for meat export is risky. Productivity is likely to decline as the pasture is impoverished owing to soil

11. Based on interviews at ranches in upland areas with artificial pasture as follows: Fazenda Sossêgo, gleba 23, lote 9, km 79 Altamira–Itaituba, *Panicum maximum* of 15 ha, 0.8 head/ha/year; Fazenda California, Paragominas, Belém–Brasília, 1,500 ha of *P. maximum* and jaragua (*Hyparrhenia rufa*), 0.6 head/ha/year; Fazenda Santa Lucia, Marabá, 5,000 ha of *P. maximum* and *H. rufa*, 1.5 head/ha/yr (supplemental feeding with chopped elephant grass *Pennisetum purpureum*); Fazenda Boa Esperança, Itupiranga, 400 ha of *H. rufa* and *P. maximum*, 0.5 head/ha/yr. Fearnside (1979) suggests that the average carrying capacity of artificial pastures up to three years old in Amazonia is only 0.3 head/ha. The latter figure has little relevance to the Amazon region, since it is based on productivity data from experiments with *Brachiaria decumbens* and models of African cattle-raising systems. *B. decumbens* has never been an important pasture grass in the Brazilian Amazon, partly because it is highly susceptible to pest damage by cigarrinha (*Deois* spp., Cercopidae).

compaction and nutrient loss through fires, leaching, and removal of cattle. It will be extremely difficult to recuperate pasture soils for crop-farming without massive additions of fertilizers and possibly ploughing. Many of the Transamazon farmers opting for a monoculture of pasture are thus entering an ecological and economic cul-de-sac.

The credit system

The credit system along the Transamazon is complicated, especially for the majority of settlers who have never dealt before with banks and can hardly read. Colonists often owe on as many as four loans, both short and long term. Short-term Banco do Brasil loans are arranged by EMATER to cover the costs of cultivating rice. Payment is due at harvest. The unpaid balance is charged interest at 10 percent per annum. Long-term loans are also available to purchase livestock, power saws, pumps, barbed wire, and asbestos roofing and to plant cacao and pepper. The latter loans come with a three-year grace period at 7 percent annual interest, then capital payments beginning in the fourth year with 10 percent due, 15 percent in the fifth year, 20 percent in the sixth year, 25 percent in the seventh year, and the balance in the eighth year. Some settlers are indebted to INCRA for their homes and the six-month welfare loans. All colonists owe INCRA for their lots. Because of the generally depressed agricultural yields, the majority of colonists are in arrears with the Banco do Brasil and INCRA.

While credit has undoubtedly enabled some settlers to expand their cropland and increase production, the system sometimes works against the interests of colonists. Even when paper work flows smoothly, colonists need to make frequent, and financially onerous, trips to town to receive their loans, which are liberated in parcels. Sometimes, because of a bureaucratic delay, part of the loan is released too late. A colonist near Altamira received the first portion of a loan to prepare one hectare of his land for pepper. He hired labor, put in the stakes, and lined up a source of cuttings. With the onset of the rains, he returned to the bank to receive the second loan parcel to buy the cuttings; however, the money arrived several months late. The colonist finally managed to plant his pepper, but most of it died. The dry season had begun.

A major blow to the financial solvency of colonists came in 1973 with the disastrous *barbalha* rice crop. Although the responsibility for the poor crop does not rest with colonists, only in 1979 were some of them compensated for their losses. Many settlers still have an unfavorable credit rating with Banco do Brasil because they were unable to repay the short-term loans in 1973. Inadequate and inefficient administration by some government agencies has been highlighted as a principal factor in the demise of the Transamazon scheme (Wood and Schmink, 1978).

Cooperatives

Cooperatives are often seen as a panacea for agriculturally underdeveloped regions. The idea that farmers should control the harvesting and marketing of their crops and thus obtain better prices by eliminating middlemen is attractive. Government policy encourages the formation of such organizations along the Transamazon; INCRA is phasing out its activities, and there is concern that private enterprise will fill the vacuum and exploit colonists.

The history of co-op movements along the Transamazon is dismal, as is the case throughout most of the Brazilian Amazon. Two co-ops functioned briefly in the Altamira and Marabá areas shortly before the arrival of the highway. The Cooperativa Mista Agropecuária do Vale do Xingu was founded in 1965 with 304 members. Within two years it had collapsed with an outstanding debt of close to $100,000 at BASA (INCRA, 1972b). In the Marabá region, 60 percent of the colonists now living in *agrovila* Coco Chato were deceived as members of the COPEMBA co-op in the late 1960s when, after a few years of operation, the president absconded with the funds.[12] The sad performance of these co-ops hardly created a favorable climate for the establishment of new ones along the Transamazon.

Colonists generally recognize the intrinsic value of co-ops, but few trust each other enough, or can invest sufficient capital, to

12. COPEMBA maintained an office in Marabá opposite the old electricity-generating plant. The co-op was known locally as Valmir, after the first name of its president.

join and maintain one. Three co-ops were launched along the highway in 1973, but two of them soon foundered owing to inadequate financial and popular support. CAMNOF (Cooperativa Agropecuária Mista Nova Fronteira), registered in Altamira with INCRA (no. 513/15.6.73), was based at *agrovila* Nova Fronteira. It never functioned. Not enough colonists paid the $285 joining fee. The more prosperous settlers were suspicious of CAMNOF, since the most vociferous supporters of the movement were the least successful, or most heavily indebted, colonists. The Nova Paraná co-op was formed in 1973 at *agrópolis* Brasil Novo, but quickly disintegrated when the funds were mismanaged (Moran, pers. comm.).

The longest-lasting co-op along the Transamazon, COMACI (Cooperativa Mista Agropecuária Colonial de Itaituba), started in October 1973 at *rurópolis* Medicilandia. The co-op, with 293 members, has only two small warehouses and no vehicles. Although 28 percent of the colonists in the region of the *rurópolis* are nominally members of COMACI, most sell their rice to private dealers or CIBRAZEM. COMACI is operated essentially by INCRA.

In spite of the disappointing results, INCRA continued to promote co-ops. Cooperativa Umberto de Alencar Castelo Branco was created in December 1977 at *agrovila* Coco Chato when the INCRA-backed candidate was elected by colonists. Some of the settlers, wary because of the COPEMBA fiasco, finally agreed to pay the $300 membership fee. Within a year the president allegedly fled with the funds, reportedly about $10,000, a considerable sum for an impoverished community. The co-op promptly dissolved.

CAMNOF was resurrected in 1977 with funds from the POLAMAZÔNIA program.[13] It was renamed COOPERFRON (Cooperativa Nova Fronteira). Although the president is a colonist, the administrative staff are from EMATER. As of September 1979, 300 members had paid, or were making installments on,

13. POLAMAZÔNIA (Pólos Agropecuários e Agrominerais da Amazônia) was created in 1974 (Decree 74.607) to support the integrated development of agricultural and mineral resources in fifteen key areas of the Brazilian Amazon. POLAMAZÔNIA was provided with a fund of $211 million, 26 percent of which was to be spent on agricultural projects (Brazil, 1976).

the $424 membership fee. COOPERFRON is the best-equipped co-op along the Transamazon. It is based in Altamira, where it offers the use of a medium-sized warehouse. A larger one with a 500,000-sack capacity is operating at km 180 Altamira–Itaituba, and a small storage facility is under construction at Nova Fronteira. COOPERFRON also runs five trucks, several of them borrowed from INCRA. In spite of the relatively well endowed infrastructure, only 8 percent of the colonists in the Altamira area are members of the co-op.

CIRA (Cooperativa Integral de Reforma Agrária) was established by INCRA to organize cane growers and to operate the mill at km 92 Altamira–Itaituba. In order to sell cane to the mill, colonists were required to join CIRA. New members were billed $1,700, payable in six annual installments. As of 1978, 200 settlers had applied for membership, but the co-op soon ran into serious difficulties. The mill fell into disrepair and operated well below capacity in 1978. Checks with no supporting funds were issued to some settlers in payment for their cane. By 1979 CIRA was extinct.

In an effort to inject dynamism into the co-op movement along the Transamazon, INCRA ceded a 400,000-ha *gleba* to a large and powerful organization from the south, COTRIJUI (Cooperativa Regional Tritícola Serrana). The co-op acquired the land, located near the sugarcane mill (Fig. 5), for $3.60/ha, payable over twenty years with a three-year grace period and 6 percent annual interest. COTRIJUI hopes to relieve the overcrowded agricultural land of northwestern Rio Grande do Sul by bringing 2,000 families to the *gleba* by 1987 (Silva Lima et al., 1978). It is not clear how Transamazon colonists will benefit from COTRIJUI, since no plans have been announced to extend membership to highway settlers.

The future of COTRIJUI along the Transamazon is uncertain. The forest sold to the co-op contains the remnants of the Arara Indians, now reduced to between 100 and 200 individuals. The Carib group has had sporadic and sometimes violent contact with Brazilian society for close to a century. They remain hostile to foreign intrusion into their land. In May 1976 three workers on a government-sponsored geological survey were killed by the Arara inside the area now belonging to COTRIJUI. A year later a Transamazon settler was killed by the same group when he strayed into their territory.[14] In June 1979 the Arara badly wounded two FUNAI employees as the latter were trying to make peaceful contact with the tribe. The FUNAI workers were evacuated by helicopter to Altamira with several arrows protruding from their bodies.

According to the Brazilian constitution, it is illegal to occupy aboriginal lands. Some settlers do not believe that the Arara exist. Terrorists in the service of multinational corporations are masquerading as natives while an inventory of the natural resources of the area is being completed. According to the perception of others, the Indians are being paid by land speculators who wish to create confusion so that they can become established within the *gleba*. FUNAI has prohibited entry into the COTRIJUI parcel by unauthorized personnel until the situation is resolved. In the meantime, the co-op is operating the sugar mill and two sawmills, one at Brasil Novo and the other at km 180 of the Altamira–Itaituba stretch of the highway.

Several major problems retard co-op movements along the Transamazon. First, settlers do not share a common cultural heritage, since they come from different regional backgrounds. Southerners do not generally regard northeasterners or northerners very favorably; they are considered backward. Colonists belong to a great diversity of religious sects, ranging from the Catholic church to Adventists, Lutherans, Methodists, Presbyterians, Baptists, Jehovah's Witnesses, Evangelical Christians, and the fast-growing Assembly of God.[15] Azevedo (1979) emphasizes the important role of the chapel as a unifying element among Italian immigrants, all Catholic, who settled in rural areas of Rio Grande do Sul in the latter part of the nineteenth century.

Each Transamazon *agrovila* is supposed to have an ecumenical church. In practice, the various sects worship separately in pri-

14. Source: *O Estado de São Paulo* (20 July 1977, p. 12).

15. Among the 155 colonists sampled, 64% professed to be Catholics, whereas 10% claimed they were atheists or agnostics. The remainder are accounted for by Seventh-Day Adventists, the Assembly of God, and the Batista da Congregação Brasileira (4% each), Presbyterians, Lutherans, Spiritualists, and the Pentecostal church (2% each), Congregação Cristã, Methodists, Adventista da Promessa, Buddhism, Jehovah's Witnesses, and the Batista Independente church (1% each).

vate homes or small chapels. The pioneer rainforest environment has not nurtured religious harmony. Catholics are frowned upon by some Protestants because the former drink alcoholic beverages and dance at social gatherings. Even bingo or raffles, promoted by Catholics to raise money for community projects, are considered harbingers of moral decay by the more fundamental Protestant (Crente) sects. Even within the Crente order, there is little spiritual cohesion. Seventh-Day Adventists, for example, harbor doctrinal disagreements with members of the Adventista da Promessa. Assembly of God members feel that Presbyterians and Methodists are too quiet in church and somewhat permissive in behavior and dress. The safe destiny of the latter's souls is by no means assured.

A second obstacle to the smooth functioning of co-ops is the absence of a tradition of working together. Colonists did not build their communities, erect bridges, or organize themselves politically. It is arguable that a frontier society, with little government control, breeds an independent spirit that would not be necessarily beneficial to the development of cooperatives. Such a society flourished during the opening up of the American West (Turner, 1928). On the other hand, a paternalistic attitude by government agencies can stifle initiative, as happened along the Transamazon.

In an effort to overcome the lack of spontaneous organization of co-ops along the highway, INCRA assumed the task of setting them up. The co-ops were administered from above; members had no real voice in policy or management. Consequently, the movements withered, in part because there was little effective grass-roots support. Finally, a co-op is usually doomed at conception because few colonists have sufficient capital or managerial ability to maintain one.

chapter

5

Settlement and Disease

An examination of health problems faced by colonists is essential to an assessment of the current and future prospects for settlement along the highway. Disease significantly affects the productivity of Transamazon agro-ecosystems. The first section of this chapter looks at forest zoonoses that can be transmitted to settlers. The second part investigates the impact of diseases introduced with, or exacerbated by, settlement.

Forest zoonoses

A large number of wild animal parasites circulate in forest ecosystems in Amazonia. Complex transmission cycles have evolved between infected hosts, usually mammals, birds, or reptiles, and arthropod vectors. Occasionally, man inadvertently becomes involved in a zoonosis cycle, such as when he comes within biting range of a vector. No attempt is made here to inventory all the animal parasites in the forest along the highway transect which can adversely affect the health of settlers. Attention is focused on the most serious pathogens that infect transamazon colonists.

Sylvan yellow fever, a zoonosis among monkeys, is endemic to the Amazon region (Causey and Maroja, 1959). The disease is potentially fatal to man, but rarely affects inhabitants of Amazonia because transmission occurs mainly in the canopy zone. Humans occasionally become infected when they clear forest and bring the vectors—which include *Haemagogus spegazzini, H. capricornii, Aedes leucocelaenus* and *Sabethes chloropterus* (Kumm, 1949; Lacaz et al., 1972 : 204)—down to ground level. In 1959, for example, two minor outbreaks of sylvan yellow fever were reported in the vicinity of Belém. Ten workers involved in clearing forest for a rubber plantation became infected, and in the second outbreak, thirty-six people became ill with yellow fever in another forested area. A large population of squirrel monkeys in the latter area may have served as a reservoir of the disease (Causey and Maroja, 1959). Five deaths due to yellow fever occurred in the vicinity of Belterra, 120 km north of *rurópolis* Medicilandia, in 1978. All the fatalities were males between fourteen and fifty-seven years old; they probably contracted the disease in forest (F. Pinheiro, A. and J. Travassos da Rosa, et al., 1978).

Two cases of yellow fever have been confirmed along the Transamazon, one of them fatal. The latter was a woodcutter working near km 100 of the Altamira–Itaituba stretch of the highway. He died at the Altamira FSESP (Fundação Serviços de Saúde Pública) hospital in June 1977, a week after the onset of symptoms (Anon., 1977). The second patient, who became ill the same year, was a carpenter working at km 92, close to the preceding case. Other cases may have occurred undetected; yellow fever may be diagnosed as hepatitis in some instances.

The incidence of sylvan yellow fever is determined by a variety of factors, including the size and movements of reservoir and vector populations. Mosquito populations responsible for transmission of the disease increase during the rainy season when breeding places, such as rain water trapped in epiphytes and tree holes, are more abundant (Kumm, 1950). The greater humidity of the wet season also favors the survival of the mosquitos. Settlers clear forest during the drier months when vector populations are likely to be at their lowest. The chances of being bitten by an infected mosquito are thus minimized. The low incidence of sylvan yellow fever among inhabitants of Amazonia is probably due largely to the timing of clearing, which does not coincide with the main transmission peak of the zoonosis.

At least sixty different arboviruses occur in the Brazilian Amazon, sixteen of which have been isolated from humans (Woodall, 1967). Surveys of the blood and viscera of wild animals along the Transamazon have revealed six arboviruses, one of which, St. Louis encephalitis, can seriously affect the health of man (F. Pinheiro, Bensabath, Andrade, et al., 1974). Colonists are being exposed to Mayaro, Guaroa, Itaporanga, and Oropouche viruses, all of which provoke fever and muscular aches, but are not usually fatal (F. Pinheiro et al., 1977). In a 100 percent sample of cases from the Transamazon admitted to the FSESP hospitals in Altamira and Marabá, I found nine diagnosed as fever of unknown etiology. It is possible that some of the latter cases were due to arboviruses.

Leishmaniasis (*Leishmania braziliensis* complex) is another zoonosis endemic to the Amazon region which is pathogenic to humans. The parasites can cause disfiguring skin lesions, particularly of the nasopharyngeal area. The open sores are also vulnerable to secondary infection by bacteria and fungi. Human infections of *Leishmania mexicana amazonensis* are rare and are therefore not considered here. In the Brazilian Amazon, rodents are the known natural hosts of *L. braziliensis,* and several species of phlebotomine sandflies act as vectors for the parasites (Lainson, Shaw, Ward, et al., 1979). Because of its strongly anthropophilic habit, *Psychodopygus wellcomei* is the main vector for *Leishmania b. braziliensis* among humans in the Serra dos Carajás area in Pará and possibly other areas of the basin (Lainson et al., 1973). For the same reason, the tiny *Lutzomyia umbratilis* is principally responsible for transmission of "pian-bois" (*Leishmania b. guyanensis*) to man in the region (Lainson et al., 1976; Ward and Fraiha, 1977; Lainson and Shaw, 1978). The diurnal behavior and understorey abode of the vectors increases the chances that people might be bitten while they are on hunting-and-gathering excursions in the forest. Although the disease is an important public health problem in some areas of the region, few cases have yet been diagnosed among Transamazon settlers (F. Pinheiro, Bensabath, Andrade, et al., 1974).

Chagas's disease is another zoonosis that has been detected in forest animals along the Transamazon and which can adversely affect the health of settlers. The etiological agent, a flagellated protozoan (*Trypanosoma cruzi*), is maintained in a sylvan cycle by reduviid bugs acting as vectors and by marsupials (Didelphidae), porcupines (*Coendu* spp.), nine-banded armadillos, coatimundis (*Nasua nasua*), anteaters (*Tamandua tetradactyla*), various rodents, tayras (*Tayra barbara*), squirrel monkeys (*Saimiri sciureus*), and several species of bats serving as hosts (Lainson, Shaw, Fraiha, et al., 1979). Because of the strongly zoophilic feeding preference of the vectors, man is rarely infected with *T. cruzi* in Amazonia. No human cases have so far been reported from the Transamazon.

A popular image of the forest as a dangerous and unhealthy environment has not proved to be the case along the Transamazon. Zoonoses are not currently important diseases among the highway settlers. Nevertheless, habitat modification and the influx of different vectors and infected people, discussed in chapter 6, may create new epidemiological links involving the zoonoses and man. The major public health problems along the Transamazon have been introduced by settlers.

Major public health problems

In an effort to assess the relative importance of diseases along the highway, I sampled all patients from the Transamazon, excluding preexisting towns, admitted to the FSESP hospitals in Marabá and Altamira in 1978. All causes for internment, except for cases related to gestation, were recorded and ranked according to the number of admissions (Table 7). The highway population served by the two hospitals in that year is estimated at 53,300.[1] Data from a similar sample of admissions to the same

1. Based on a total of 6,630 families settled by INCRA in the Altamira and Marabá regions (Table 2). The number of families is increased by 20 percent, to

Table 7. Patients from the Transamazon Admitted to the FSESP Hospitals in Altamira and Marabá in 1978

Disease	Cases Altamira	Cases Marabá	Total cases	Deaths
Malaria	349	315	664	11
Injury	138	27	165	5
Respiratory	101	42	143	12
Gastrointestinal	88	44	132	19
Miscellaneous	76	7	83	3
Genital	38	14	52	0
Cardiovascular	18	11	29	4
Infectious hepatitis	21	7	28	2
Anemia	27	0	27	1
Poisoning	17	2	19	0
Hemorrhagic synd. Altamira	17	0	17	1
Scorpion sting	15	0	15	0
Snakebite	13	2	15	1
Toxic hepatitis	11	3	14	0
Malnutrition	11	1	12	1
Appendicitis	10	1	11	1
Kidney	8	3	11	2
Nervous disorders	9	1	10	0
Helminthiasis	8	2	10	1
Fever (cause unknown)	7	2	9	0
Liver cirrhosis	6	2	8	0
Arthritis	5	1	6	0
Tetanus	3	0	3	1
Hernia	0	3	3	0
Measles	1	1	2	0
Rheumatic fever	2	0	2	0
Diabetes	1	0	1	0
Polio	1	0	1	0
Leprosy	1	0	1	0
Meningitis	1	0	1	0
Totals	1,003	491	1,494	65

hospitals in 1973, when the highway population served by the hospitals was approximately 31,300, provides an opportunity to assess changes in the public health picture (Table 8). In 1973 the Marabá hospital contained 50 beds, whereas the one in Altamira had 45 beds. In 1978 the Marabá hospital still had only 50 beds, but the Altamira one had expanded to 75 beds.

account for squatters, and multiplied by 6.7, the average household size encountered on my survey of 155 families.

Table 8. Patients from the Transamazon Admittted to the FSESP Hospitals in Altamira and Marabá in 1973

Disease	Cases Altamira	Cases Marabá	Total cases	Deaths
Malaria	501	784	1,285	26
Gastrointestinal	132	86	218	32
Injury	139	61	200	8
Respiratory	103	96	199	13
Miscellaneous	75	60	135	6
Helminthiasis	84	3	87	0
Genital	42	15	57	0
Liver	45	10	55	6
Hemorrhagic synd. Altamira	52	0	52	2
Malnutrition	31	0	31	0
Measles	10	19	29	1
Hernia	17	10	27	0
Snakebite	21	0	21	0
Kidney	18	1	19	1
Cardiovascular	8	9	17	3
Scorpion sting	6	0	6	0
Totals	1,284	1,154	2,438	98

The hospital records do not indicate disease rates among settlers, nor the total number of workdays lost. Only the tip of an iceberg is portrayed. Extrapolation from hospital admissions statistics to the population as a whole is risky, since a number of variables are involved, such as the admissions policy of the doctor on duty and the number of available beds. In spite of the limitations, the records reveal some of the critical public health problems along the highway and provide a useful point of departure for discussion.

Health problems are examined in order of importance according to the number of cases admitted. The four most significant causes of hospitalization—malaria, injuries, and respiratory and gastrointestinal diseases—are discussed first. Then the impact of other diseases, such as helminthiasis and the hemorrhagic syndrome of Altamira, are also analyzed in spite of their poor representation in the hospital data, since they significantly affect the health of settlers.

To provide a framework for examining each disease, the morbidity and mortality rates are considered to assess the proportion of the highway population affected. The age/sex spread of the hospital cases is used to gauge the impact of the disease on the working capacity of colonists. Whenever possible, the spatial distribution of cases is included in the discussion so that the average does not obscure the gravity of the illness in certain critical areas. Particular attention is paid to the temporal variation of diseases to see whether morbidity peaks coincide with important phases of the agricultural calendar.

Malaria

Malaria is a chronic and serious public health problem along the Transamazon, where it is caused by three species of protozoan parasites (*Plasmodium falciparum, P. vivax,* and rarely *P. malariae*). The disease was responsible for 53 percent of hospital admissions in 1973 and 44 percent in 1978 (Tables 7 and 8). Malaria also accounted for 23 percent of hospital deaths in 1973 and 1978.

It is difficult to gauge what percentage of the highway population is affected by the disease. Many settlers suffering with malaria go directly to drugstores for treatment and thus bypass statistics gathered by the hospitals and SUCAM (Superintendência de Campanhas de Saúde Pública), an agency of the Ministry of Health responsible for malaria control. SUCAM sends teams along the highway to draw blood samples from people with fever, or from anyone who has been febrile within the preceding thirty days. Other suspected cases make their way to the SUCAM posts in Altamira, Marabá, and Itaituba to be screened for the parasites.

A major problem with SUCAM data is that there are gaps for certain stretches of the highway for some months, owing to a lack of equipment or logistical support. Another drawback is that malaria cases detected in hospitals and private clinics are not reported to SUCAM. In June 1977 the Ministry of Health ordered the suspension of reporting malaria data by stretch along the Transamazon, allegedly because the information was unreliable. Malaria cases from the highway were to be included in reports of morbidity by municipality, thereby making it virtually impossible to assess the epidemiological importance of the disease along the Transamazon.

Table 9. Malaria Cases Registered by SUCAM along the Araguaia–Jacareacanga Stretch of the Transamazon, 1975 to June 1977

Year/Month	Slides examined	Slides positive malaria	% Positive malaria
1975 Jan.	1,570	214	14
Feb.	1,558	220	14
Mar.	1,805	146	8
Apr.	3,498	285	8
May	2,621	118	4
June	3,577	187	5
July	3,490	121	3
Aug.	2,893	143	5
Sept.	2,634	153	6
Oct.	2,040	131	6
Nov.	2,105	175	8
Dec.	1,487	133	9
1975 Totals	29,278	2,026	7
1976 Jan.	574	90	16
Feb.	1,090	152	14
Mar.	1,715	163	10
Apr.	1,555	91	6
May	1,592	60	4
June	1,517	87	6
July	1,473	117	8
Aug.	931	81	9
Sept.	1,258	82	7
Oct.	1,306	145	11
Nov.	815	130	16
Dec.	1,448	218	15
1976 Totals	15,274	1,416	9
1977 Jan.	1,427	219	15
Feb.	1,086	208	19
Mar.	1,576	203	13
Apr.	3,197	354	11
May	2,598	152	6
June	1,601	99	6

Source: SUCAM, Belém.

In spite of the deficiencies of the SUCAM data, it is possible to gain some idea of the proportion of the highway population contracting the disease and the annual fluctuations in transmission. During 1975 and 1976 at least 7 percent of the 50,000 people living along the highway became ill with malaria along the Araguaia–Jacareacanga stretch of the highway (Table 9). The

SUCAM statistics reveal little variation in incidence between the two years. In 1973 at least 11 percent of the highway population within a 250-km radius of Altamira contracted the disease, while some 12 percent of the highway settlers were affected in the Marabá region (Smith, 1976a: 210). Approximately 4 percent of the Transamazon population in the Marabá and Altamira areas required hospital treatment for malaria in 1973, whereas in 1978 only 1 percent were admitted to the FSESP hospitals because of the disease. Between 5 and 25 percent of the Transamazon residents contract malaria every year.

Malaria afflicts both sexes and all age groups approximately equally (compare Figs. 25 and 26).[2] The anomalous bulge of hospital cases among males between the ages of twenty-five and twenty-nine is most likely due to the population of migrant workers, which is not included in my household survey. Malaria transmission must occur mostly at night inside homes, or in their immediate vicinity, because very young children become infected. Malaria is also acquired in the forest, since topographers and woodcutters were frequent victims of the disease during the surveying and construction phase of the highway. So far, no reservoirs of human malaria have been found in wild animals in Amazonia; infected people introduce the parasites to forest areas where suitable vectors live.

Malaria incidence varies considerably along different portions of the Transamazon. For example, 80 percent of the malaria cases admitted to the Altamira hospital in 1978 came from the first 280 km of the road in the direction of Marabá. Of the 349 malaria cases interned that year, 36 percent came from the vicinity of Anapu at km 160 of the Altamira–Marabá stretch, and 30 percent originated in the immediate area of Pacajá, at km 280 of the same stretch. Thus, approximately 150 km of the highway, about a third of the area served by the Altamira hospital, accounted for two-thirds of the malaria cases admitted for treatment in 1978. There is no obvious ecological reason why the Pacajá and Anapu areas have such a high incidence of malaria. Both areas are traversed by small rivers, but so are many other places along the Transamazon.

Highway settlers are infected with malaria all year round, but

2. Only people living at home, including relatives and adopted children, are considered in Figure 25. Offspring who have moved away are not included.

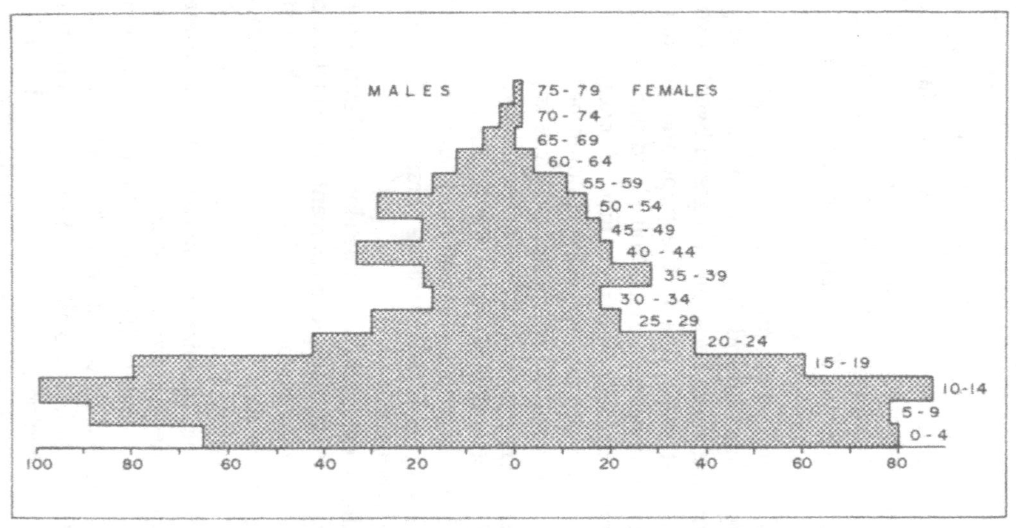

Figure 25. Age/sex distribution of 155 households along the Transamazon, 1978

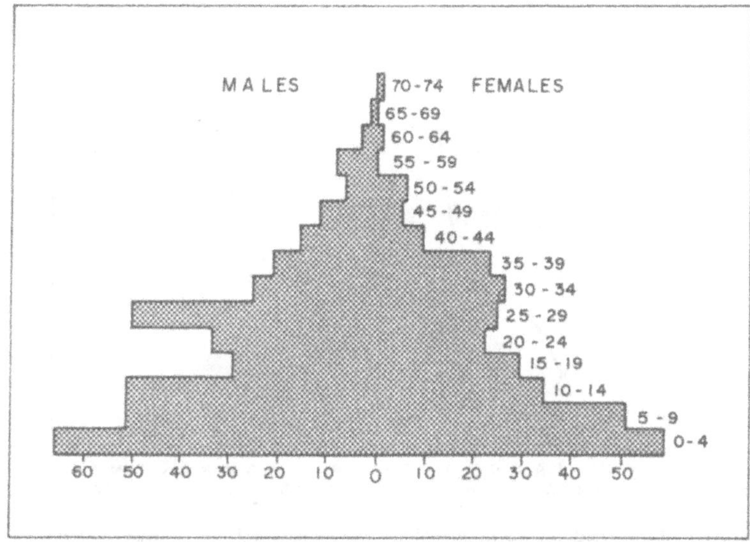

Figure 26. Age/sex distribution of 664 malaria cases from the Transamazon admitted to the FSESP hospitals in Altamira and Marabá during 1978

two main peaks of transmission coincide with important agricultural activities. The major transmission peak usually occurs at the beginning of the rainy season in December or January (Figs. 27 and 28) when farmers are planting their fields. The effect of malaria at such a time can be particularly serious, as an entire family can be incapacitated for several weeks with fever. If planting is postponed for more than a month, crop yields are reduced.

The peak of malaria transmission with the onset of the rainy season is probably due to a buildup of vector populations during the drier months. Along the pioneer Manaus–Boa Vista highway, opened to traffic in 1976, the number of malaria cases increases markedly toward the end of the dry season (Hayes and Charlwood, 1979). The surge in morbidity is attributed mostly to population dynamics of the main vector, *Anopheles darlingi.*

Instead of an increase in the incidence of malaria with the arrival of the rains, the opposite occurs. The drop in malaria morbidity during the wet period is probably a result of the swollen streams that flush away anopheline eggs and larvae. Only after the rains slacken does malaria increase again, producing a minor peak at the beginning of the dry season (Figs. 27 and 28).

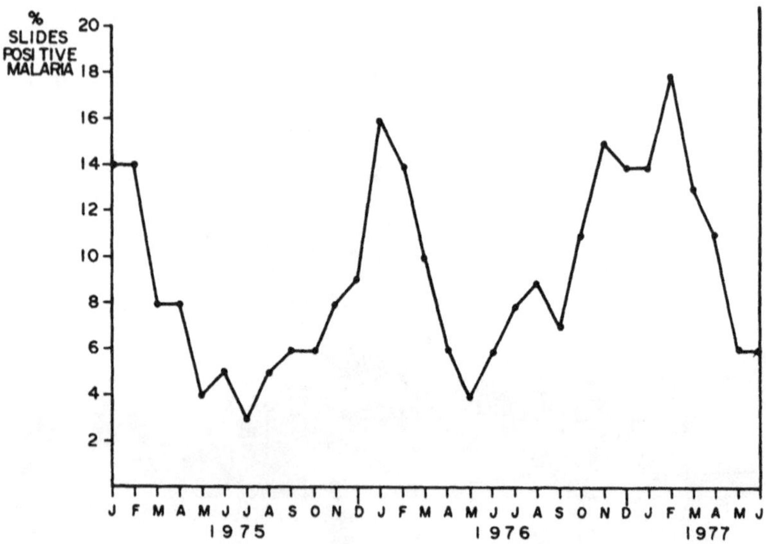

Figure 27. Malaria incidence by month along the Araguaia–Jacareacanga stretch of the Transamazon, 1975 to June 1977 (Table 9)

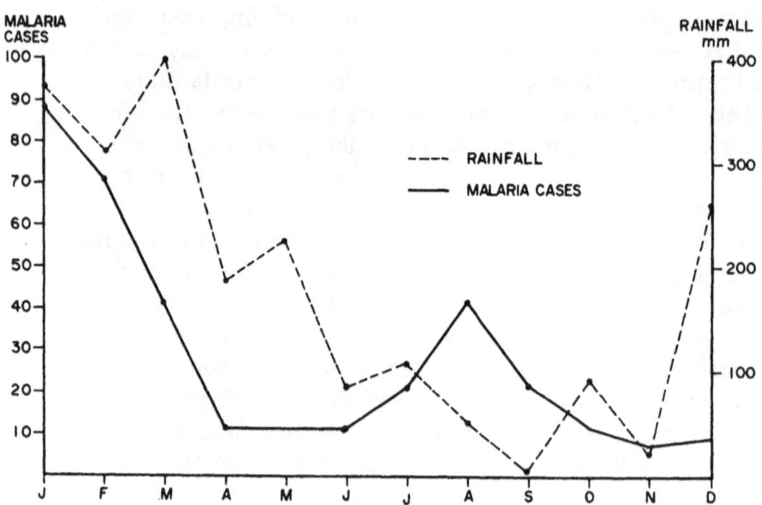

Figure 28. Monthly admissions of malaria cases from the Transamazon at the Altamira FSESP hospital, 1978

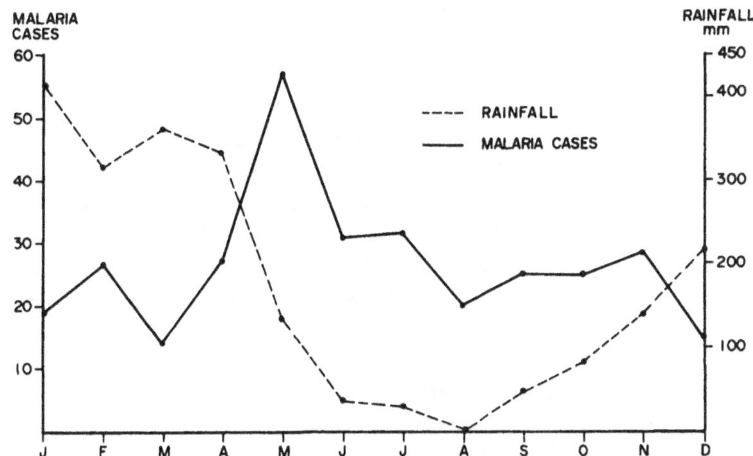

Figure 29. Monthly admissions of malaria cases from the Transamazon at the Marabá FSESP hospital, 1978

In the Marabá region the main peak of transmission occurred immediately after the rains in 1978 (Fig. 29). The second morbidity peak occurs during the rice harvest season and when new fields are being cleared. A delay in the reaping of the cereal substantially reduces yields through lodging and predation. If a family is forced to put off the task of cutting forest or second growth, the slash may not have sufficient time to dry for a thorough burn. A similar problem with malaria has been noted in parts of Paraguay, where the disease markedly restricts the area that can be cleared and planted to crops (Conly, 1975).

The dry-season peak of malaria cases is probably due to two factors. First, the velocity of streams slows, thereby providing more tranquil waters for mosquito breeding. Second, a large flow of workers arrives on the Transamazon after the rains to help with harvesting and the clearing of new fields. Many of the laborers come from malarious zones, such as western Maranhão, and some undoubtedly bring the blood parasites with them. In Nigeria, for example, migrant workers return to Sokoto province with malaria and thereby help to maintain a reservoir of the disease in their home region (Prothero, 1965: 106).

It is difficult to place a quantitative value on the impact of malaria on agricultural productivity because of the paucity of data and the great temporal and spatial variation of the disease. If 10 percent of the Transamazon population is infected during a year, and if each victim is ill for an average of 38 days,[3] then some 234,000 days are lost because of malaria. For some families malaria has seriously affected their livelihood; for others the disease is insignificant.

The hidden costs of malaria must also be taken into account. Considerable sums are spent by families on trips to town to consult with doctors and purchase remedies. Sometimes it is necessary to lodge overnight to wait for the results of blood smears. The psychological burden of the disease adversely affects morale. Aspirations for a better life in a new frontier are sometimes dashed by the high cost of effective treatment. Malaria also weakens the body's resistance to other illnesses.

Malaria control is difficult because the epidemiology of the disease along the Transamazon and throughout most of Amazonia is poorly understood. One of the major obstacles to an effective control program is that the vector along the Transamazon has not been established with certainty. Since *Anopheles darlingi* is the main vector for the disease in the region away from the coast,[4] I shall assume that the mosquito is primarily responsible for transmission along the highway. The species prefers partially shaded, neutral, unpolluted, and relatively still water for breeding (Giglioli, 1938; Deane et al., 1946, 1948, 1949; Vargas and Sá, 1949; Pinotti, 1951a; Bustamante, 1957). These conditions are only occasionally encountered in *terra firme,* such as by the margin of small rivers. Forest streams are usually heavily shaded and strongly acid (Fittkau, 1967).

Whereas *A. darlingi* lives in forested areas, human modification of the landscape increases the number of favorable breeding sites. In eastern Colombia, for example, the species breeds in partially shaded ditches in areas cleared from forest (Renjifo and De Zulueta, 1952). In forest zones of Guyana, Giglioli (1968) found the same species in dammed streams and

3. Hayes and Ferraroni (1978) estimate that males older than ten years lost an average of thirty-eight days of work per malaria infection along the Manaus–Boa Vista highway.

4. Along the coast of Amazonia, *Anopheles aquasalis* is the principal vector for malaria, since the vector is capable of breeding in brackish water.

gravel pits around mining camps. Forest disturbance also favors *Anopheles maculatus,* an important vector for malaria in Malaysia (Meade, 1976).

Along the Transamazon, stream ponds are relatively common, since water culverts were often installed above stream gradients. In some cases, no outlet was provided when the smaller swales were filled along the highway transect. Consequently, the streams often back up and kill the forest. The artificial ponds range from 0.5 to 10 ha and are frequently covered with floating vegetation such as algae pads, lilies, and *Salvinia* sp. I collected eight species of anopheline larvae from vegetation on the perimeter of stream ponds along the Transamazon. Four of the species—*A. brasiliensis, A. noroestensis, A. rangeli,* and *A. triannulatus*[5]—have been incriminated as vectors of human malaria in various parts of South America. One or several of the species collected may be involved in the transmission of malaria to settlers along the highway. Although I did not find *A. darlingi,* the species probably breeds in the more shaded portions of some of the ponds.

Malaria vectors are thus probably breeding close to settlers' houses along the Transamazon. Anopheline mosquitos are likely to feed on males as they bathe in ponds and streams at sunset; women usually bathe during the day after they have washed clothes, when vectors are likely to be resting. The whole family is susceptible to infection in the evening when they are assembled at home. Mosquito nets deter malaria vectors, but few settlers use them. Of the 155 households surveyed only 2 use mosquito nets. One family employs several hammock nets to escape from diurnal black flies during the rainy season. The mosquito net belonging to the second family is used exclusively to protect the baby.

There are three main reasons why colonists do not generally use mosquito nets. First, probably less than half of the Transamazon settlers believe that malaria is transmitted by mosquitos. Of the 155 families surveyed only 42 percent understand the

5. Anopheline larvae were captured with a white dip pan and were preserved in a solution of water containing 70 percent alcohol. The larvae specimens were identified by M. Cotrim and E. Galeti of the Faculdade de Saúde Pública, Universidade de São Paulo.

basic epidemiology of the disease.[6] Nearly as many of the settlers interviewed feel that one acquires malaria by drinking, smelling, or bathing in water, especially stagnant water with a lot of decomposing leaves. The notion that malaria is associated with sluggish water can be traced to Hippocratic medicine. Malaria means literally "bad air"; 4 percent of the colonists sampled suggest that one can become infected with the disease by inhaling smoke or unwholesome odors from privies.

The high cost of mosquito nets is another reason why they are infrequently used along the Transamazon. A net for a hammock costs around $14 (U.S.) along the highway, and a larger circular one for a bed sells for $18. It would cost $80 to protect a family of six sleeping in hammocks with the cocoon-shaped shrouds. Third, the veils are considered impractical and hot; they are in constant need of repair, and the small-mesh size substantially reduces any breeze. Screens for windows and doors are rarely employed along the Transamazon, for the same reasons that *mosquiteiros* are not normally used.

In an effort to control malaria vectors, SUCAM teams spray the interior of Transamazon buildings with DDT every six months. The efficacy of the expensive spraying program is questionable, since the disease remains a serious public health problem after ten years of DDT treatments. The inside walls of houses and huts are sprayed under the assumption that malaria vectors rest on the insecticide-coated surfaces for at least twelve hours after taking a blood meal, the minimum period for *Anopheles* to absorb a lethal dose of DDT (Elliott, 1972). A program of residual spraying with DDT successfully reduced *A. darlingi* populations in coastal Guyana, Minas Gerais, and Bahia (Pinotti, 1951b; Giglioli, 1952), but it is having limited, if any, effect on malaria vectors in the Brazilian Amazon.

The main reason for the ineffectiveness of the DDT control program is that some populations of *Anopheles darlingi* have

6. The heads of households were asked how they think a person gets malaria. Settlers are familiar with the symptoms of the disease, such as alternating fever and chills, often accompanied by headache and muscular pains. Along the Transamazon, malaria is known locally as *malária*, *malára*, *paludismo*, and *cezão*. In a survey of 163 homes along the Manaus–Boa Vista road, Hayes and Ferraroni (1978) found that only 45 percent of the settlers believe that mosquitos transmit malaria.

evolved a behavioral resistance to the insecticide. Along the Manaus–Boa Vista highway, for example, the species feeds inside houses but rests outside on vegetation if the home has been treated with DDT (Hayes and Charlwood, 1977). In DDT-free buildings, *A. darlingi* rests on interior walls. The mosquito is irritated by the insecticide and therefore avoids surfaces coated with the chemical (Charlwood and Paraluppi, 1978).

In 1947 *A. darlingi* was strongly endophilic in the Brazilian Amazon (Deane, 1947), but by 1959 the species frequently fed and rested outside (Bustamante, 1959). A similar behavior change in response to DDT spraying has been observed with *Anopheles nuneztovari,* an important malaria vector in Venezuela (Gabaldon, 1972). Populations of *A. darlingi* in forested zones of Guyana and the Brazilian Amazon are now considered more exophilic than in other regions (Bustamante, 1959; Giglioli, 1963; Bruce-Chwatt, 1970). The malaria vector, or vectors, along the Transamazon may have acquired physiological resistance to DDT, allowing them to alight on the insecticide with impunity, as has occurred with at least nineteen species of *Anopheles* in various countries (Wright et al., 1972).

The DDT-spraying program thus appears to be of little benefit. *Culex quinquefasciatus,* a mosquito commonly found inside Transamazon homes and a potential vector for Bancroft's disease, is unaffected by the insecticide (Scaff and Gueiros, 1967; Charlwood and Paraluppi, 1978). Cockroaches die in large numbers after houses are sprayed with the chemical, but populations of the cosmopolitan pest soon rebound. Chickens feed avidly on dying arthropods after the houses have been sprayed; settlers may gradually acquire toxic doses of DDT by eating poultry and their eggs.

The mobility of the Transamazon population and house materials may also account for the failure of the malaria vector control program. Migrant workers often lash together a makeshift shelter after SUCAM teams have sprayed buildings in the area, as has been noted in other parts of the region (Schmidt, 1965). Many settlers, particularly from the North and Northeast, assemble wattle-and-daub houses on their lots. The potency of DDT declines on earth surfaces because of absorption and catalytic decomposition, especially if the soil is rich in iron oxides

(Bordas et al., 1953). Red soils, owing to the presence of ferrous oxide, are common along the Transamazon.

Destruction of anopheline breeding grounds would reduce the incidence of malaria along the Transamazon, but before such measures can be taken, the vector or vectors must be identified and their ecology better understood. Stream ponds are incriminated as important breeding grounds for the disease vectors along the highway. Even if the ponds are drained, malaria transmission is likely to continue. *Anopheles darlingi* may reproduce along the margins of partially shaded streams and rivers flowing through deforested areas. Small lakes, shaped like swimming pools, were left by earth-scrapers along the highway and may also provide suitable breeding grounds for malaria vectors. The deep lagoons would have to be filled to eliminate them. If the margins of water courses remained in forest, as is required by law, the opportunities for anopheline mosquitos to breed could well diminish.

Chemical prophylaxis is not a viable means of controlling malaria along the Transamazon. Chloroquine, the most commonly prescribed drug for protection against the disease, is seldom effective. *Plasmodium falciparum,* which accounted for 33 percent of the malaria infections recorded along the Araguaia–Jacareacanga stretch of the highway between 1975 and 1977, and for 64 percent of the cases interned in the Altamira and Marabá FSESP hospitals in 1978, has evolved a resistance to the synthetic chemical in Amazonia since at least 1948 (Mein and Rosado, 1948). Chloroquine-resistant strains of the parasite now thrive throughout the basin (Rodrigues, 1961; Silva et al., 1961; Box et al., 1963; Giglioli, 1968; García-Martin, 1972; Ferraroni and Hayes, 1979).[7] Even as much as 1,000 mg of chloroquine per week is insufficient to provide adequate protection against *P. falciparum.* Doses in excess of one gram a week are likely to damage the liver and retinas if continued indefinitely. Whereas people may become more resistant to malaria after repeated infections, there is no immunity.

7. Chloroquine-resistant strains of *Plasmodium falciparum* have also appeared in Guyana, Surinam, Venezuela, and Panama (Nájera-Morrondo, 1979), Colombia (Moore and Lanier, 1961; Young and Moore, 1961; Comer et al., 1968), Thailand (Young et al., 1963), East Africa (Fogh et al., 1978), Bangladesh and Malaysia (McKelvey et al., 1971; Rosenberg and Maheswary, 1977).

Treatment of malaria along the Transamazon is also largely ineffective, and this ineffectiveness helps to maintain a pool of infected people. In the case of *P. falciparum* infections, SUCAM distributes chloroquine tablets free of charge. Unfortunately, after a day or two of treatment, a settler may feel better and stop taking the pills. The symptoms often return some time later, but detection of the parasites in blood slides becomes extremely difficult because of the repressive action of the drug. According to FSESP doctors, colonists sometimes swallow too many pills in their haste to free themselves from the fever and pain of malaria. By so doing, they damage their livers. Hospital cases registered as toxic hepatitis are sometimes a result of overdoses of chloroquine.

Chloroquine, usually administered by drip bottle, is the standard medication used to combat malaria infections in the FSESP hospitals. In resistant cases, quinine is used. But, as with many other drugs, quinine is often lacking, or in short supply. After spending an average of four days in hospital ($s = 2.7$, $n = 664$), many malaria patients are thus released, clinically improved but not cured. Relapses of the disease are common.

Sulphur-based drugs, such as Fansidar,[8] are lethal to chloroquine-resistant populations of *P. falciparum* (Ferraroni et al., 1978), but they are very expensive and hard to find in the interior. Public health officials are reluctant to promote the widespread use of Fansidar, for they wish to reduce the chances of creating *P. falciparum* strains resistant to the drug. Fansidar is a weapon of last resort (if the patient can afford to buy it). Antibiotics, such as minocycline, have been used effectively to treat chloroquine-resistant strains of *P. falciparum* (Colwell et al., 1972; Ferraroni and Dourado, 1977). In the Brazilian Amazon, antibiotic treatment of malaria has been attempted on an experimental basis only. Two problems may prevent its widespread use. First, minocycline is expensive. Second, the drug takes longer than other treatments to suppress malaria symptoms.

Treatment of *Plasmodium vivax* infections along the Transamazon is also largely ineffective. Primaquine is the only drug capable of eliminating the parasite. The drug is imported from

8. Fansidar, produced by Roche, is a combination of pyrimethamine and sulfadoxine. It has been marketed in the Brazilian Amazon since about 1970.

the United States and is available only at SUCAM. A confirmed case of vivax malaria is instructed to remain close to the post in Marabá, Altamira, or Itaituba to receive one pill a day for two weeks. The entire dosage is not given to the patient at once lest he take an overdose, take too few pills, or sell the tablets. Few colonists can afford to stay in lodgings for two weeks; they thus often return promptly to their homes. Primaquine is not used in the hospitals; consequently, a large reservoir of the disease is maintained along the highway. Along the Araguaia–Jacareacanga stretch, for example, 67 percent of the malaria infections between 1975 and 1977 were attributed to *P. vivax*.

In view of the complexity of ecological, biological, and cultural factors influencing the incidence of malaria along the highway, the disease is likely to persist as a major public health problem. The lack of progress in malaria control has also been noted in other areas of tropical America (Nájera-Morrondo, 1979). After some initial widespread successes in reducing malaria morbidity, evolution of the parasites and vectors, as well as administrative and financial difficulties, have combined to weaken control efforts. Research into new antimalarial drugs may provide temporary gains. A vaccine would provide the best protection, but no such breakthrough is imminent.

Injury

Injuries, such as burns, cuts, and broken bones, are the second most important cause of hospitalization among the Transamazon population. Trauma accounted for 8 percent and 11 percent of the cases admitted to the FSESP hospitals in Altamira and Marabá during 1973 and 1978 respectively (Tables 7 and 8). Although only 0.3 percent of the highway inhabitants in the regions of the two towns were interned for treatment of injuries in 1978, the work loss was greater than the hospital data suggest.

Males aged from twenty to fifty years are particularly prone to serious injury (Fig. 30). Adult males perform most of the agricultural tasks, so injuries depress farm yields. A major peak of injury cases resulting in hospitalization occurs in September, and is probably related to accidents incurred while clearing forest and second growth (Fig. 31). Hospital records rarely include the cause of injuries, but according to doctors, road accidents are

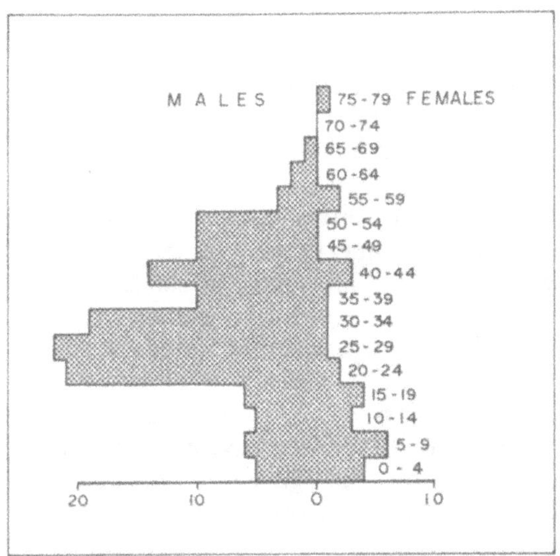

Figure 30. Age/sex distribution of 165 injury cases from the Transamazon admitted to the FSESP hospitals in Altamira and Marabá during 1978

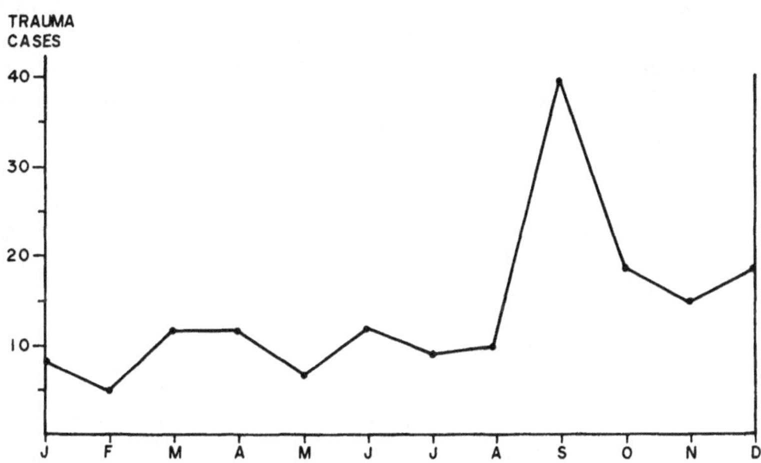

Figure 31. Monthly admissions of injury cases from the Transamazon at the FSESP hospitals in Altamira and Marabá during 1978

also a significant source of trauma cases admitted for treatment. Dust clouds, whipped up in the wake of vehicles in the dry season, sometimes fatally obscure the vision of drivers. During the rainy months the slippery road surface also causes serious traffic accidents.

Of the four leading causes of hospitalization, injury cases usually take the most time to recuperate. A traumatized patient stays in a hospital bed an average of six days (s = 9.2, n = 165). After release, most patients cannot immediately resume arduous labor, and this is particularly burdensome in the dry season when fields must be prepared. If the highway were asphalted, some accidents due to blinding dust and the slick surface would be avoided, but no such plans have been announced. Trauma is thus likely to continue to figure prominently in hospital admissions along the Transamazon.

Respiratory diseases

Pneumonia, bronchitis, asthma, and influenza were the third and fourth most important causes of hospitalization along the Transamazon in 1973 and 1978 respectively (Tables 7 and 8). Respiratory infections produce particularly severe symptoms in the young (Fig. 32). Diseases of the respiratory tract are a leading cause of deaths in the Marabá and Altamira hospitals, accounting for 18 percent of all the mortalities in 1978. Of the twelve hospital deaths attributed to respiratory complaints in that year, 67 percent were children under ten years old. The high birthrate of settlers more than offsets infant mortality due to pneumonia and bronchitis. Tuberculosis is not common along the highway, and since adults usually suffer only mild colds, diseases of the respiratory tract do not seriously affect agricultural productivity along the highway.

Gastrointestinal diseases

Illness due to pathogenic enterobacteria, protozoa, and viruses was the second and fourth most important cause of hospitalization along the Transamazon in 1973 and 1978 respectively (Tables 7 and 8). In both years, gastrointestinal disorders were responsible for 9 percent of the hospital admissions. Although less than 1 percent of the highway settlers require hospital treat-

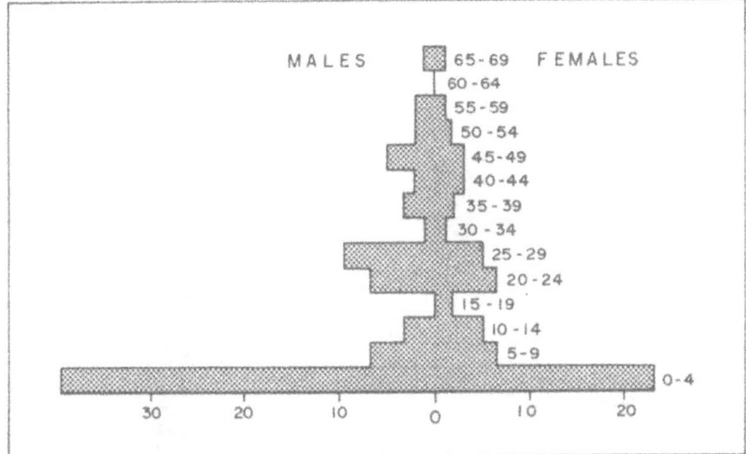

Figure 32. Age/sex distribution of 143 respiratory-disease cases from the Transamazon admitted to the FSESP hospitals in Altamira and Marabá during 1978

ment for intestinal problems in any given year, it is a safe assumption that the entire population suffers from a gastrointestinal infection during the course of a year.

Gastrointestinal infections produce particularly severe symptoms in the very young (Fig. 33). Of the 132 cases admitted to the Altamira and Marabá FSESP hospitals in 1978, 64 percent were babies under a year old. Juveniles are more prone to a serious loss of body fluids and salts as a result of diarrhea and vomiting. Gastroenteritis with its associated dehydration is the principal cause of infant mortality along the Transamazon, as in many other lesser-developed regions (Ascoli et al., 1967). Diarrheal diseases were responsible for 48 percent and 51 percent of the hospital deaths in children up to five years old in 1973 and 1978 respectively.

The high incidence of gastrointestinal infections among inhabitants of the Transamazon is linked to the prevailing low standards of hygiene. If a pacifier falls to the ground, it is often put straight back into the child's mouth. Contaminated bottles and artificial teats are another source of infection among babies. Breast-feeding is considered a social stigma among many moth-

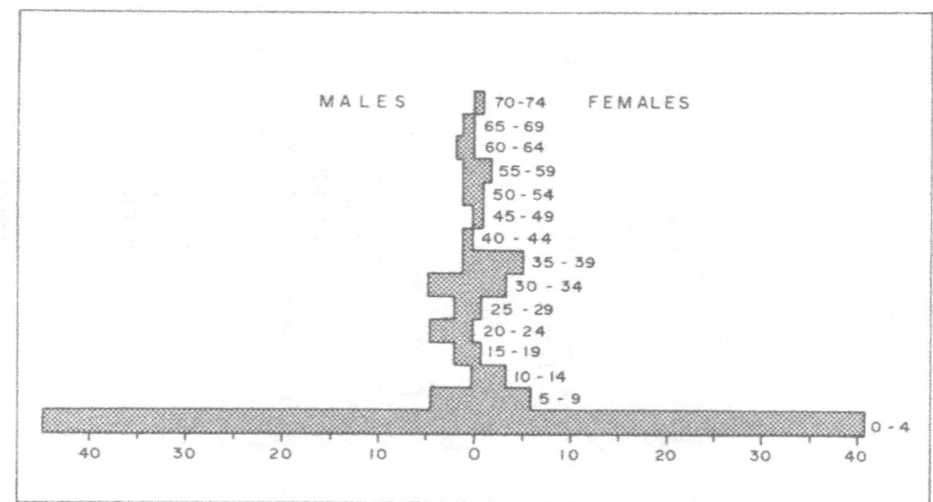

Figure 33. Age/sex distribution of 132 cases of gastrointestinal disease from the Transamazon admitted to the FSESP hospitals in Altamira and Marabá during 1978

ers, even in the rustic, frontier environment of the Transamazon. Since bottles and teats are rarely sterilized in boiling water, the culture of pathogenic bacteria is certain. Infants protected by breast-feeding during their first few months of life become vulnerable to gastroenteritis when they are given solid food and untreated water.[9]

Contaminated drinking water is a major source of gastrointestinal disease among all age groups along the Transamazon. As of September 1974 only four of the twenty-six *agrovilas* had a piped-water system. By December 1978 FSESP had extended the service to nineteen of the twenty-seven communities.[10] The water system in all the *agrovilas* functions precariously. The concrete-lined wells quickly run dry, especially after the rainy season, since they are only five to fourteen meters deep. The water table appears to be dropping, probably because of increased forest clearing. In the wet season, when there is sufficient water in the wells, the pumps can operate for no more than two hours a day because of the strict quota of diesel fuel for each community. Although each of the *agrovilas* has a large storage tank, it usually remains empty. When the water arrives, settlers leave their taps on, to fill as many receptacles as possible; within twenty minutes the liquid often ceases to flow. Leaks are common because the pipes are made of plastic and are installed near the surface.

Breakdowns in the pumping equipment are relatively common. When I visited Coco Chato in September 1979, the water pump had not been working for nine months because of mechanical failure. *Agrovila* dwellers thus frequently resort to

9. Breast milk provides antibodies against enterobacteria. Gram-positive anaerobic bacilli of the genus *Bifidobacterium* dominate the intestinal flora of breast-fed children. *Bifidobacterium* metabolizes sugars, thereby producing acetic and lactic acid, which inhibit the development of pathogenic bacteria and protozoa. The intestinal ecosystem of bottle-fed infants is composed mostly of species of gram-negative *Bacteroides* in an alkaline environment, which favor the proliferation of pathogenic enterobacteria (Béhar, 1975).

10. The following *agrovilas* have a piped-water system installed: Leonardo da Vinci, Vale Piauiense, km 40 Altamira–Itaituba, Grande Esperança, Jorge Bueno da Silva, Nova Fronteira, Abraham Lincoln, km 100 Altamira–Itaituba, Princesa do Xingu, União, Novo Paraíso, Getulio Vargas, Café Filho, Areia Branca, Presidente Kennedy, Princesa Isabel, Duque de Caxias, Verde Floresta, and Coco Chato.

streams and ponds for their drinking water. Colonists who live on their lots usually build a shallow, open well close to their homes. Such water sources are frequently polluted with human and livestock feces.

Fecal contamination of water used for drinking and food preparation is a well-known source of gastrointestinal disease (Gordon et al., 1964; Barker, 1975). Cysts of pathogenic amoebas and flagellates, such as *Entamoeba histolytica* and *Giardia lamblia,* are easily washed from feces into streams, ponds, and wells. A sizable portion of the Transamazon population is infected with intestinal protozoa, as was detected by SUCAM during routine screening for health cards (Table 10). The particularly high rate of infection in 1971 is probably due to the crowded and unsanitary conditions of the temporary camps erected by INCRA for incoming settlers. Fecal pollution of the water supply by pathogenic bacteria, such as *Shigella dysenteriae* and *Salmonella,* is also implicated in the epidemiology of intestinal infections along the highway.

Only ten of the *agrovilas* are equipped with latrines. None of the side-road communities or any of the lots have INCRA-installed toilets. Few of the colonists who live on their lots have built privies. Even *agrovila* toilets are underused. Children usually defecate in the yard; they are scared of falling down the murky hole of the privy, or of encountering spiders in the wooden outhouse. The avoidance of latrines by infants has also been noted in settlement projects in Malaysia (Meade, 1976). Potent odors emanating from the generally untreated toilets also discourage their use. Several settlers regard privies as undesirable because they think mosquitos breed therein, especially malaria vectors. Most settlers prefer to take care of their physiological necessities in a banana or maize patch close to home.

Boiling and filtering water is an effective method of reducing the incidence of gastrointestinal disease. Of the 155 families surveyed only 2 percent boil water for drinking, and then only for infants. When asked why water is not boiled regularly for the whole family, settlers replied that it would entail too much work. Furthermore, boiling allegedly makes water "heavy," thus adversely affecting its flavor. Only half of the families surveyed had filters in their home. Clay filters are effective barriers against

Table 10. Transamazon Population with Gastrointestinal Infections Caused by Pathogenic Protozoa, 1971–1977.

Region	Year	People examined	% With Entamoeba histolytica	% With Giardia lamblia
Altamira	1971	1,050	23.4	22.6
	1972	6,601	8.1	15.3
	1973	8,067	3.0	7.1
	1974	5,120	5.7	13.2
	1975	7,018	2.4	7.1
	1976	6,496	4.2	5.3
	1977	5,420	4.5	9.6
Marabá	1971	362	43.6	23.3
	1972	4,750	5.1	24.8
	1973	5,161	12.4	27.9
	1974	4,779	11.6	23.8
	1975	5,985	5.8	27.4
	1976	5,093	6.1	14.7
	1977	5,654	4.4	23.5

Source: SUCAM, Belém.

amoebas, but not against viruses or bacteria. The presence of a filter in the home does not guarantee adequate protection against amoebic dysentery or giardiasis. Many filters are too small for a large family; consequently, members frequently dip a cup into the top portion of the pot before the water has had an opportunity to filter to the bottom. Settlers frequently drink water from ponds and streams when working in their fields.

A medium-to-large-size filter sells for $13 to $17 along the Transamazon. Although a filter is a modest investment for improved health, it is often not perceived as necessary. Of the 155 colonists interviewed 32 percent said that they do not know what causes diarrhea or dysentery. Twenty-three percent attributed the symptoms to water, but only 6 percent to potentially unpotable stagnant or stream water. Half of the colonists who feel that the liquid is involved in the epidemiology of gastroenteritis consider warm water sufficient to provoke diarrhea. For the most part, settlers filter water to improve its color, not to eliminate pathogens.

Unhygienic methods of garbage disposal and food storage are also responsible for the high incidence of gastrointestinal disease along the Transamazon. The rubbish dump at *rurópolis* Medicilandia is only 250 meters from the FSESP hospital. No garbage collection service has been organized in any of the *agrovilas*. Chickens, pigs, dogs, and cats eat much of the waste food, but some is discarded in backyards, where it provides breeding grounds for flies. Various species of flies feed on feces and contaminate unprotected food with pathogenic bacteria and amoebic cysts (Greenberg, 1965; G. Hunter et al., 1966:289). Cockroaches, potential vectors for at least forty-four species of pathogenic bacteria and amoebic dysentery (James and Harwood, 1970), are abundant in settlers' homes. Ubiquitous rats (*Rattus rattus*) are also implicated in the transmission of gastroenteritis, since they feed and defecate on food in the houses of colonists. Few settlers can afford kerosene-fueled refrigerators at $500 each.

Helminthiasis

Although helminthic diseases do not figure prominently among hospital admissions, they are nevertheless a widespread and important public health concern along the Transamazon. Approximately 65 percent of the highway population is infected with at least one parasitic worm species (Table 11). A high incidence of helminthiasis is not peculiar to the Transamazon; the disease is hyperendemic wherever standards of hygiene are poor and where there is unsanitary disposal of sewage.[11] Man has introduced the nematode and flatworm parasites to the Transamazon.

Roundworms (*Ascaris lumbricoides*) feed in the intestines of at least 60 percent of the highway population. *Lombriga*, as the nematode is known in Brazil, interferes with the digestion and absorption of dietary proteins and fat and thus exacerbates the poor health of undernourished children (Venkatachalam and Patwardhan, 1953; G. Hunter et al., 1966:433; Tripathy et al.,

11. In the Brazilian Amazon, helminth infection rates of 65 percent or more are common among urban residents of poorer districts (Causey et al., 1947; O. Costa et al., 1955; M. Azevedo and Maroja, 1956; Lowenstein, 1963; Franco, 1967; M. Pinheiro et al., 1977; Montoril Filho et al., 1978). High rates of infestation with intestinal nematodes are also found in other regions with low hygiene standards, such as in Costa Rica and Puerto Rico (Scrimshaw et al., 1953; Guardiola-Rotger et al., 1964).

Table 11. Helminthiasis among Transamazon Population, 1971–1977

Region	Year	People examined	% With Ascaris lumbricoides	% With Necator americanus	% With Trichuris trichiura	% With Strongyloides stercoralis	% With Enterobius vermicularis	% With Schistosoma mansoni
Altamira	1971	1,050	84.6	42.4	49.2	9.1	0.4	0.8
	1972	6,601	81.1	40.2	37.9	7.5	0.2	1.0
	1973	8,067	69.2	47.3	42.2	7.5	0.2	1.7
	1974	5,120	61.9	46.8	42.6	7.8	0.3	1.3
	1975	7,018	71.5	42.5	37.8	6.4	0.3	0.8
	1976	6,496	63.6	37.7	35.0	4.9	0.2	0.5
	1977	5,420	62.4	35.4	31.6	5.8	0.1	0.9
Marabá	1971	362	62.3	23.4	50.3	6.8	0.2	0.0
	1972	4,750	64.3	35.8	47.8	0.2	0.7	0.2
	1973	5,161	64.0	36.3	43.0	1.8	0.7	0.2
	1974	4,779	57.1	30.2	36.4	1.4	0.6	0.2
	1975	5,985	59.3	31.6	39.9	0.4	0.7	0.4
	1976	5,093	58.2	24.5	41.4	4.7	0.5	0.4
	1977	5,654	58.8	41.6	42.8	6.9	0.2	0.6

Source: SUCAM, Belém

1971). Intestinal parasites were most likely partly responsible for the internment of forty-three cases of malnutrition in the Altamira and Marabá FSESP hospitals in 1978.

Roundworm eggs are passed in feces and remain viable in the soil for months, since they are resistant to desiccation. Backyards of Transamazon homes are well stocked with *Ascaris* eggs; the daily output of *A. lumbricoides* ova from a child can range from 4.8 to 22.5 million (Tripathy et al., 1971). A single gram of feces from an adult with a moderate roundworm infection can contain as many as 20,000 eggs of the parasite (Dunn, 1972). Children acquire roundworms by ingesting embryonated ova while playing in backyard soil. Improperly washed vegetables, house flies, and polluted drinking water are also implicated in the transmission of the disease along the highway.

Whipworm (*Trichuris trichiura*) is another common intestinal nematode along the Transamazon, occurring in about 40 percent of the population (Table 11). The epidemiology of the disease is similar to that caused by roundworms. Whereas a light burden is unlikely to provoke any significant pathological effects, a large concentration of the parasites can cause chronic diarrhea, dehydration, and anemia, especially in children.

Hookworm (*Necator americanus*) is another intestinal parasite of major importance along the Transamazon. The helminths infest some 40 percent of the settlers (Table 11). Large burdens of *N. americanus* can produce anemia, depending on the host's general state of health and diet. The nematode ingests blood from the small intestine and leaves small wounds which bleed. In Brazil the disease is aptly called *amarelão:* big yellow, the pallid, waxy, skin tone characteristic of victims with heavy hookworm infections. The twenty-seven cases of anemia admitted to the FSESP hospital in Altamira during 1978 were probably due partly to intestinal parasites, especially hookworms.

Numerous eggs of *N. americanus* are passed onto the ground in human feces around Transamazon homes. The highway's warm and moist climate is ideal for the development of the ova. Settlers are constantly reinfected with hookworms when they walk barefoot around the yard and visit their customary site for defecating. The parasitic larvae penetrate their hosts through the skin. Very few children regularly wear shoes. Footwear for infants is saved for Sundays, particularly for church.

Hookworm infections are likely to remain high along the Transamazon. Only half of the colonists surveyed believe that they can acquire helminth infections by walking with barefeet. Nearly a quarter profess to have no idea about how one acquires worm infestations. Posters are displayed on various government buildings along the highway explaining the epidemiology of hookworm infections. But many colonists cannot read. Fewer still can afford to buy shoes regularly for the whole family.

Hemorrhagic Syndrome of Altamira

Cases of local as well as disseminated cutaneous hemorrhaging, sometimes associated with apparently spontaneous nose-bleeding, first came to the attention of public health personnel in Altamira during 1971.[12] No etiological agent for the disease, named the hemorrhagic syndrome of Altamira (HSA), has been found (F. Pinheiro, Bensabath, Costa, et al., 1974). One case required hospitalization in Altamira in 1971. The following year the number had increased to twenty-five, and by 1973 fifty-two people were interned for treatment of HSA. In 1978 seventeen cases were admitted to the FSESP hospital because of the disease (Table 7). Although the symptoms are alarming, the death rate is low. Two of the HSA cases died in 1973, and one in 1978. Children are particularly prone to the disease (Fig. 34).

The hemorrhagic syndrome is provoked by black-fly bites. The symptoms are attributed to a hypersensitive reaction to toxin injected when the simuliids take a blood meal. Why the disease occurs only in the Altamira area remains a mystery. Large black-fly populations also thrive in other areas of Amazonia, such as around Marabá and along the Tapajós and Aripuanã rivers. The disease probably occurred with a low incidence in the Altamira region prior to the Transamazon. After the highway was opened for traffic, HSA became a public health problem because of the large influx of people unaccustomed to black-fly bites.

The disease strikes mostly in the rainy season when simuliids are abundant (Fig. 35). Black-fly biting becomes so intense during the rainy months, with as many as 250 bites per man-hour (F. Pinheiro, Bensabath, Costa, et al., 1974), that some families tem-

12. F. Pinheiro et al. (1977) state that the hemorrhagic syndrome was first recorded in the Altamira region in 1972; however, a case of the disease was admitted to the FSESP hospital in Altamira in March 1971.

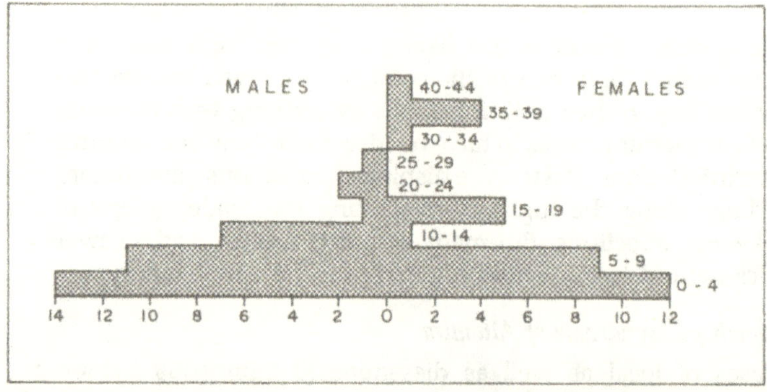

Figure 34. Age/sex distribution of 69 cases of hemorrhagic syndrome of Altamira admitted to the FSESP hospital in Altamira during 1973 and 1978

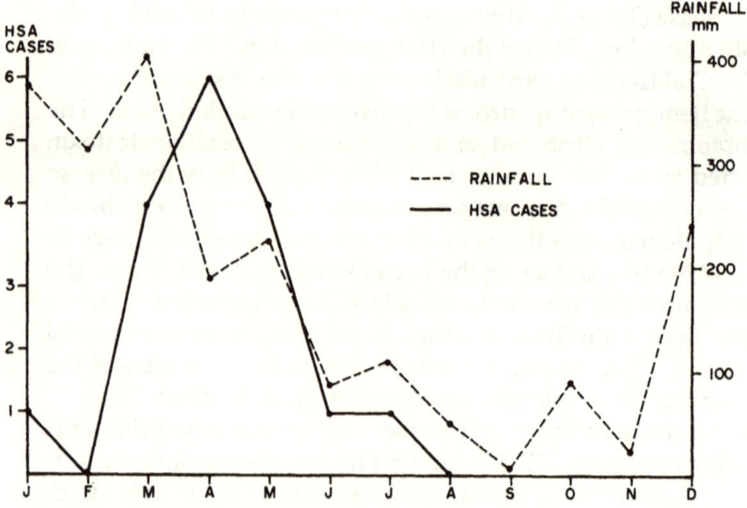

Figure 35. Monthly admissions of hemorrhagic syndrome of Altamira cases admitted to the FSESP hospital in Altamira during 1978

porarily abandon their lots to seek some respite in the *agrovilas* or in Altamira. One family built a small wooden tower in an unsuccessful attempt to flee from black flies (F. Pinheiro et al., 1977). Agricultural yields may be reduced in some cases because weeding is neglected. In some years, the flies are particularly bothersome. In 1974, for example, some colonists along the Altamira–Belo Monte stretch of the highway encountered difficulty in contracting labor to help with the rice harvest. Few workers were willing to endure the seemingly incessant attacks of *pium,* as the simuliids are known locally.

The population density of black flies varies considerably along the Transamazon. Simuliids are particularly common near rapids, such as the Xingu between Altamira and Vitoria. For this reason, the Altamira–Belo Monte stretch of the highway, which accompanies the river relatively closely, is notorious for *pium* attacks. Simuliids along the highway concentrate where they are likely to find a blood meal. They shun the interior of forest where they are less likely to encounter a human. The airport on the outskirts of Altamira is a favorite feeding ground for the flies, especially when flights are delayed. Traffic bottlenecks due to quagmires, slippery hills, or washed-out bridges are also major feeding zones. When the vehicle stops, simuliids immediately swarm onto the hapless passengers. If a car breaks down on a good stretch of the highway, several minutes usually pass before black flies appear.

At least three simuliid species (*Simulium amazonicum, S. incrustatum,* and *S. pintoi*) feed on man in the Altamira region of the Transamazon (Moraes, 1974). The numerous streams along the highway, especially in undulating terrain, as well as the Xingu rapids, provide ideal breeding grounds for *pium* during the rainy season. Black-fly larvae filter food from swift-flowing water while attached to rocks or immersed branches. The increased humidity of the wetter months also favors the development of simuliid populations.

Black-fly populations are difficult to control. Eliminating the breeding grounds would not be feasible. Poisoning the water courses to kill the larvae would have potentially serious ecological repercussions: fish populations would most likely be adversely affected and the water would become unpotable. Some colonists have tried plastering their exposed skin with axle grease. Although the flies become trapped and inoffensive in the sticky coating, the greasy film clogs pores, thereby reducing the cooling effect of sweat evaporation. Settlers cover as much of their skin as possible with clothes during the *pium* season (Figs. 13, 17, 18). Long-sleeved shirts, T-shirts, socks, scarves, and hoods reduce the number of bites, but the diurnal black flies invariably find and exploit even the smallest gap. Colonists face an unenviable decision: tuck their clothes in tightly and become hotter, or surrender to the full brunt of *pium* attacks.

The public health importance of HSA seems to be declining (Tables 7 and 8). The flow of settlers to the Transamazon has slowed. Residents of the highway are becoming used to black flies. During the first season of exposure to *pium,* painfall swelling and itching from the bites are common, but in succeeding years the symptoms generally abate. The continued opening of the Transamazon landscape is also likely to lead to a reduction in HSA cases. Black flies are particularly abundant close to the forest edge, such as along side roads. In large cleared areas, such as downtown Altamira, the population of simuliids is smaller. The flies may rest in the humid microclimate of the forest edge while waiting for a potential blood meal to pass nearby.

The impact of diseases on the Transamazon scheme

Diseases are not as important as are defects in agricultural planning and the credit system in depressing the productivity of Transamazon farms. Nevertheless, the synergistic effect of multiple illnesses, such as polyparasitism and gastroenteritis, does reduce the overall health and working capacity of the highway population. In industrial societies, the impact of diseases on working capacity can be calculated by the number of workers reporting sick and the number of days lost. The economic loss can then be calculated by multiplying the amount of time away from the job by daily wages. Such analyses are not possible along the Transamazon, where much of the labor is unpaid because it is performed by family members.

The major public health problems along the highway, as reflected in hospital admissions, differ from those of major metropolitan areas in developed countries. In industrial cities, cancer and cardiovascular disease are important causes of hospital internment. The hazards of air pollution and a sedentary lifestyle are not shared by Transamazon settlers. The main health risks for the highway colonists do not come from "exotic" tropical diseases. Vivax malaria, for example, was a serious problem in many temperate zones until drainage and better housing reduced its importance. Man is responsible, through his cultural habits and modification of habitats, for the introduction and maintenance of most of the illnesses along the Transamazon.

The public health picture has not changed much since 1973. The top four causes of hospital admissions in 1973 and 1978 were the same. No improvement in the health of settlers is likely until the general standard of living is raised. Radio programs, posters, and lectures by public health officials appear to have little effect on the incidence of diseases such as gastroenteritis and helminthiasis. A patient takes the prescribed medication to eliminate the parasites and soon becomes reinfected.

It has been argued that a population must be healthy before it can improve its standard of living. But remedial treatment without ameliorating the underlying causes is not a long-term solution. The benefits of improved sanitation in reducing the incidence and intensity of intestinal parasites are well known. But medical posts, latrines, and piped-water systems are not enough to ensure low rates of disease among a pioneer population. Economically and ecologically viable farms are a prerequisite to a healthier environment along the Transamazon. The difficult problems of crop choice, rotation systems, marketing, and credit will have to be tackled and at least partly solved in order to improve the general health conditions along the highway. In the meantime, the public health situation may deteriorate in view of the possible spread of hitherto unimportant diseases.

chapter

6

Potential Public Health Problems

The purpose of this chapter is to illustrate the dynamic nature of the public health picture along the Transamazon by focusing on the dangers of epidemics of new, or currently rare, diseases. Man-induced environmental disturbance and the introduction of vectors and parasites may create favorable conditions for outbreaks of onchocerciasis, Bancroft's filariasis, schistosomiasis, Chagas's disease, and yellow fever. If just one of the above diseases becomes established among the Transamazon population, then agricultural productivity and the livelihood of settlers is likely to suffer.

Onchocerciasis

Onchocerciasis, an Old World disease caused by the filarial worm (*Onchocerca volvulus*), was unknown in Brazil until recently. In 1973, autochthonous cases were first documented in the country among the Waica Indians of northwest Amazonas near the Venezuelan border (Moraes et al., 1973). At least one of the vectors for the disease in the state of Amazonas, *Simulium amazonicum*, is also present in the Altamira region of the Transamazon (Moraes, 1974; Rassi et al., 1975). Workers and peasants from the Northern Perimeter highway could contract the disease in the isolated endemic area and bring the infection to other areas of Amazonia, such as the Transamazon (Rassi et al., 1976).

Control of the vectors, as in the case of the hemorrhagic syndrome of Altamira, would be difficult. In Africa, aerial spraying of DDT in water courses has effectively reduced black-fly populations (G. Hunter et al., 1966:479), but such a course of action would not be advisable along the Transamazon. If the disease spread to the highway, it would severely limit the prospects for improving living standards, since the microfilariae of *O. volvulus* can cause blindness. In the Red Volta region of northern Ghana, for example, formerly intensively cultivated land has been abandoned largely because of the disease (J. Hunter, 1966).

Bancroft's disease

Bancroft's filariasis, caused by another tissue-inhabiting nematode, *Wuchereria bancrofti*, also of Old World origin, may become a public health problem along the Transamazon. The pathological effects of the parasite depend on a number of factors, such as the frequency of infected bites and the number of microfilariae inoculated each time. The host generally experiences discomfort and restricted mobility. In advanced cases, known as elephantiasis, the disease is disfiguring and debilitating.

The principal vector for Bancroft's filariasis in Brazil, *Culex quinquefasciatus* (Causey et al., 1945; Lacaz et al., 1972:338), thrives along the Transamazon. I collected larvae of the mosquito in man-made pools along the highway created by tire ruts, drinking troughs for chickens, wallow holes for pigs, storage tanks, discarded tin cans, and empty seed pods (*ouriços*) of Brazil nuts.[1] The highway created an avenue for dispersal of *C. quinquefasciatus* from preexisting towns. The species feeds avidly on settlers at night during the rainy and dry seasons and rests in dark spots in homes, such as behind furniture, or outside in sheds.

In the Brazilian Amazon, the disease is confined mostly to large towns, such as Belém. In the capital of Pará state, the infection rate among the population was reduced from 12.3 percent to 1.7 percent between 1955 and 1965 by employing a large-scale chemotherapy program (Scaff and Gueiros, 1967). Although Bancroft's disease is no longer an important public health problem in Amazonia, an epidemic may still occur wherever there are large populations of the vector (Charlwood, 1979). The onset of severe symptoms takes several years, so the disease could spread along the Transamazon for some time before coming to the attention of public health officials.

Schistosomiasis

Schistosomiasis, caused by several species of blood flukes (*Schistosoma mansoni, S. haematobium, S. japonicum*), is a major public health problem in the tropics. The blood flukes infest some 200 million people in the Old and the New World. In Brazil schistosomiasis is mainly a result of *S. mansoni,* which infects about 8 million inhabitants of the Northeast, Central-West, and the Southeast (Lacaz et al., 1972 : 305).

Schistosomiasis is not yet an important public health problem in Amazonia. Only three isolated foci of the disease have so far been reported from the basin, all in Brazil. The first isolated pocket of the disease was documented at Fordlandia on the right bank of the Tapajós (Machado and Martins, 1951; Maroja, 1953; Sioli, 1953); the others are found in Belém and in the vicinity of Quatipuru in the Bragantina zone (Galvão, 1968; Moraes, 1972).

1. Larvae were identified by M. Cotrim and E. Galeti of the Faculdade de Saúde Pública, Universidade de São Paulo.

Concern has been expressed that schistosomiasis may disseminate to other areas of Amazonia, particularly along pioneer highways (Freitas, 1972; Moraes, 1972; Cooper et al., 1974; Paulini, 1974; Pimentel, 1974; Getz et al., 1975; Goodland and Irwin, 1975:51; Fraiha, 1977).

In spite of control programs, schistosomiasis is spreading in many tropical regions, mostly as a result of human modification of ecosystems. In Africa hydroelectric and irrigation schemes have been primarily responsible for creating favorable conditions for planorbid snails, intermediate hosts for the disease (Wright, 1970; Hughes and Hunter, 1972; Schalie, 1972; Shiff, 1972). The disease is also encroaching on new areas in Brazil. Infected workers on the Rio–São Paulo highway brought schistosomiasis to the Paraíba valley between 1928 and 1930 (Piza et al., 1959). Within the last two decades, thousands of Nordestinos have migrated to northwestern Paraná in search of land to plant subsistence crops, cotton, and coffee. Forest clearing and the construction of numerous small reservoirs furnished favorable environments for the proliferation of *Biomphalaria straminea*, an important intermediate host of the disease. The snails became infected as a result of the unhygienic methods of sanitary-waste disposal by settlers carrying the helminths (Lacaz et al., 1972:163).

To assess the potential for the dispersal of schistosomiasis along the Transamazon, the epidemiology of the disease will be briefly reviewed. To transmit *S. mansoni*, a carrier must defecate schistosome eggs in or near warm, slow-moving, neutral water so that they can develop. The hatched miracidia seek a planorbid snail in which to undergo further development for about a month; then thousands of cercariae escape from the snail, and now in the infective stage, seek out the definitive host, man. Cercariae penetrate humans while the latter bathe, swim, or drink water. Once through the skin or mucous membrane, the larvae enter the bloodstream and eventually lodge in the mesenteric veins of the abdomen. The laterally spined eggs are passed in feces after they have torn though the intestinal wall.

The intermediate host for *S. mansoni* in the Brazilian Amazon, *B. straminea*, requires abundant aquatic vegetation and relatively neutral water with a high calcium content for optimum growth

(Sioli, 1953). Such conditions are rarely found in upland forest streams. Forest removal allows sunlight to penetrate streams, while ash and exposed topsoil nutrients enter the water courses through percolation and in run-off. Aquatic plants thus proliferate and may provide a favorable environment for planorbid snails. In one sampled stream along the Transamazon, pH, nitrogen, and calcium rose markedly when the water course flowed from forest into a recently burned field.[2]

At Fordlandia, Sioli (1953) found large numbers of *B. straminea* in streams flowing through cleared areas of the former Ford rubber plantation. The snails glean detritus from aquatic vegetation, which flourishes in the exposed streams. The limestone substrate in the area supplies calcium, which reduces acidity and furnishes a raw material crucial for shell development. The numerous impounded streams along the Transamazon are likely to provide suitable conditions for *B. straminea,* particularly in *terra roxa* patches where quantities of exchangeable calcium are generally much higher than in other soil types encountered along the highway.

The planorbid snails have been found in polluted streams draining the disturbed environs of Altamira (Moraes, 1972; F. Pinheiro, Bensabath, Andrade, et al., 1974). The town may serve as a dispersal source for the intermediate host of the disease along the Transamazon. Wattled jacanas (*Jacana jacana*), striated herons (*Butorides striatus*), anhingas (*Anhinga anhinga*), least grebes (*Podiceps dominicus*), sungrebes (*Heliornis fulica*), rufescent tiger-herons (*Tigrisoma lineatum*), and capped herons (*Pilherodius pileatus*) feed in streams and ponds in the vicinity of Altamira and along the Transamazon. The waders could serve as dispersal agents for the snails. Eggs of *B. straminea* attach easily to the legs of aquatic birds and can be carried from one body of water to another.

At least 533 people infected with *S. mansoni* have arrived on

2. The pH of the stream rose from 4.7 to 5.5, while the calcium increased from 2,314 to 5,340 mg/liter. Nitrogen rose from 172 to 216 mg/liter. I collected three one-liter samples from both the forest and the field sections of the stream. One bottle was normal, the second was treated with 5 ml of $CHCl_3$, and the third with 5 ml of sulphuric acid (4N). The samples were sent to INPA, Manaus, for analysis. The sampled stream flows in the vicinity of *agrovila* Coco Chato, an area dominated by red-yellow podzolic soils.

Table 12. Origin by State of Last Residence of Schistosomiasis Cases among Transamazon Settlers Screened by SUCAM in the Altamira and Marabá Areas of the Transamazon, 1971–1978

State	1971	1972	1973	1974	1975	1976	1977	1978	Totals
Minas Gerais	1	20	68	27	32	24	35	26	233
Bahia		4	12	13	18	4	21	11	83
Pernambuco	1	12	15	9	11	9	8		65
Alagoas	2	10	11	7	9	5	10	3	57
R. G. Norte		2	9	4	6	1	5		27
Espirito Santo			2	5	2	4	3	2	18
Paraíba	1	9		1	1		1	1	14
Ceará			3		2	1	2		8
Maranhão		1	3	1		2		1	8
Sergipe			4	1	1	1			7
Pará	1	1			1	1		2	6
Piauí					1		1	1	3
Rio de Janeiro		1		1					2
São Paulo				1					1
Goias							1		1
Totals	6	60	127	70	84	52	87	47	533

Source: SUCAM, Belém, and Altamira

the Transamazon (Table 12). Northeasterners accounted for 51 percent of the cases screened by SUCAM as of the end of 1978. Minas Gerais, a southeastern state, supplied 44 percent of the detected cases. Until 1975 confirmed carriers of *S. mansoni* were given an intramuscular injection of Entrenol, reputed to be 80 percent effective on the first dose. Few follow-up checks were performed, since the colonists had usually dispersed to their lots. In 1975 treatment was switched to a single dose of Mansel pills, administered at a dose of one capsule per 20 kg of body weight.

Many settlers with schistosomiasis have probably slipped through the SUCAM screen. On the day of the stool test, a *S. mansoni* carrier may not have been passing eggs. Treated cases may not have been cured. Squatters and migrant workers are not checked for the parasites. Consequently, hundreds and possibly thousands of people infected with schistosomiasis live along the Transamazon. Other hosts for the disease, albeit less important, such as wild rodents,[3] may also serve as a reservoir of the helminths.

In 1978 two suspected autochthonous cases of schistosomiasis were discovered in the Transamazon town of Altamira (SUCAM, pers. comm.). Both of the *S. mansoni* carriers are residents of the town. One, a woman of thirty years, has spent most of her life in Altamira. She once spent a month in Santarém, a town at the confluence of the Tapajós and Amazon rivers. There is no known enclave of the disease in the vicinity of the latter urban center. The other case, a twelve-year-old girl, has apparently never left the municipality of Altamira.

In the event that schistosomiasis spreads along the Transamazon, the working capacity of settlers is likely to be seriously impaired. In advanced stages, the disease causes irreversible damage to the liver and the lungs. The eggs of the parasite circulate in the host's blood and become trapped in some organs, where they inflict wounds with the spines. The resulting fibrosis impedes the proper functioning of the liver and can lead to death, as occurred with a fifty-nine-year-old woman from the Transamazon in the Altamira hospital in 1978. Serious complications usually take many years to appear, depending on the worm load, so the woman probably acquired the infection in another state. Adults are particularly affected by the pathological impact of the disease (Fig. 36). In a sugarcane estate in Tanzania, workers infected with schistosomiasis made significantly more visits to doctors and took longer to recuperate from illness than those free of the disease (Foster, 1967).

If schistosomiasis becomes established along the highway, it will be difficult to eradicate. Control measures against intermediate hosts of the disease are costly and of limited effect. Molluscicides temporarily eliminate populations of the snails, but the chemicals used are broad-spectrum biocides that adversely affect other aquatic life (Ansari, 1973). Ampullarid snails predate on the eggs and young of planorbids and have successfully reduced schistosomiasis transmission in Puerto Rico

3. In Pernambuco, rats (*Rattus rattus*) have been found passing viable eggs of *S. mansoni* in their feces (F. Barbosa et al., 1953; F. Barbosa, 1972). Wild rodents have also been found naturally infected with *S. mansoni* in the state of São Paulo (Dias et al., 1978).

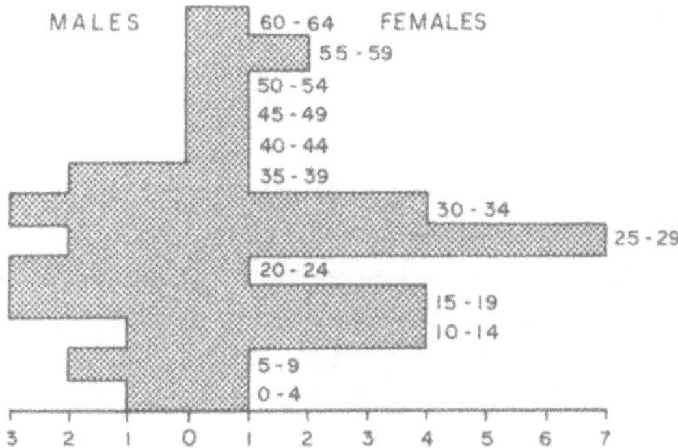

Figure 36. Age/sex distribution of 46 apparently allochthonous cases of schistosomiasis from the transamazon admitted to the FSESP hospital in Altamira during 1973 and 1978

(Oliver-González and Ferguson, 1959; Radke et al., 1961). The effectiveness of ampullarid snails is hampered by abundant aquatic vegetation (Jobin et al., 1973); the biological control method has thus had little effect on the incidence of the disease in other areas. The red and black ocellated carauaçú (*Astronotus ocellatus*) feeds on *B. straminea* (Lacaz et al., 1972: 227), but this popular game fish does not occur along the Transamazon, since it is a lake and river species.

Screening and adequate treatment of all arrivals along the Transamazon would be a difficult task. Buses, trucks, cars, boats, and aircraft daily release passengers at numerous points along the highway. Some of the travelers are transitory, yet they may defecate near a stream and infect intermediate hosts with schistosomiasis. It is unrealistic to expect people to avoid contact with streams and ponds. Long-term, effective control of the disease is again linked to improved standards of living. If all settlers used well-situated, deep latrines, then *S. mansoni* eggs would not reach water.

Chagas's disease

Although Chagas's disease rarely infects man in Amazonia, because the forest vectors feed mostly on wild animals, pioneer highways are likely to facilitate the spread of vectors from other regions of Brazil where they are zoophilic, but also ingest blood from man in and around houses. The intrusion of roads into the forest provides an extensive threshold for forest vectors to adapt to the presence of man.

Only recently have highways been cut through large areas of interfluvial forest in the basin, thereby greatly increasing the ecotone between forest and man-made habitats. At least two forest vectors for *Trypanosoma cruzi* have invaded houses in the region. In the outskirts of Manaus and Belém, *Panstrongylus geniculatus* infected with *T. cruzi* have been found in buildings (Almeida and Machado, 1971; Lainson, Shaw, Fraiha, et al., 1979). In suburban Belém, another forest reduviid infested with the parasites, *Rhodnius pictipes*, has been collected in homes (Lainson, Shaw, Fraiha, et al., 1979). Although no sylvatic vectors have apparently established thriving colonies in houses so far, they may do so in the future.

The importation of vectors already adapted to domestic environments is another manner in which the disease may spread to the Transamazon. Colonists, migrant workers, and cargo trucks from the Northeast may inadvertently introduce eggs, nymphs, or adults of *Panstrongylus megistus* with their baggage. Similarly, southerners may transport *Triatoma sordida* or *T. infestans* with their luggage. The reduviid bugs may also spread on their own or be dispersed by birds. In São Paulo state, for example, house sparrows (*Passer domesticus*) have been found carrying nymphs of *T. sordida* in their feathers (Forattini et al., 1971). The exotic birds have recently become established in Amazonia and are rapidly expanding their range (Smith, 1973; 1980b). In Bahia *T. infestans* has colonized inhabited areas of the São Francisco valley since 1955 and is responsible for outbreaks of Chagas's disease in zones formerly free of the disease (Barrett et al., 1979).

Along the Belém–Brasília, trucks from Goias and São Paulo are apparently transporting vectors of *T. cruzi* in their cargoes (M. Scaff, pers. comm.). Upon arrival in Belém, the bugs evidently die before establishing viable colonies. A local reduviid, *Triatoma rubrofasciata*, not known to transmit Chagas's disease, may be excluding other species from buildings. Other ecological factors, such as the hot, humid climate, may be responsible for the demise of imported reduviids in Belém. Nevertheless, the various domestic vectors for the disease may gradually become adapted to the climate of the North by colonizing the environmental gradient of the major highways, in the same manner as house sparrows.

If vectors for *T. cruzi* became established along the Transamazon, house type would play an important role in determining the incidence of the illness among different families. *Agrovila* homes, with their asbestos roofs and plank walls, would offer fewer diurnal hiding places for the reduviids than other houses along the highway. Homes fashioned from wattle and daub, typical of those built by northeasterners and *caboclos*, would provide numerous resting places for *barbeiros*, as the vectors are known in Brazil. Palm-thatch houses, used mostly by northerners, would also provide an ideal habitat for *barbeiros*.

Fourteen autochthonous cases of Chagas's disease have so far been recorded in the Brazilian Amazon. Four cases, confined to a family in Belém in 1968, were attributed to ingestion of contaminated food (Shaw et al., 1969). Two more cases were found in Belém in 1972 and 1977 (Fraiha, 1977). Another person infected with *T. cruzi* was discovered in Abaetetuba near Belém in 1976. A single autochthonous case has recently been reported from the Territory of Amapá, and six serologically positive cases were found in the region of Barcelos, Rio Negro, in 1977 (Almeida and Mello, 1978). Although the majority of cases are probably a result of chance encounters with forest vectors, transmission by domestic triatomines cannot be ruled out.

Chagas's disease would significantly affect the working capacity of colonists if it became established along the Transamazon. Children suffer most from the acute febrile stage, whereas adults may suffer from megaesophagus, megacolon, and myocardial insufficiency in the latter stages of the illness. The disease can be fatal. Once the acute phase of the disease has passed, there is no cure.

Domestic vectors of *T. cruzi* are resistant to DDT. The elimination of natural predators of the triatomines by spraying homes with the insecticide in the malaria-control program may have aided the spread of *Triatoma infestans* in Brazil (Barrett et al., 1979). Other, more expensive chemicals are effective against the bugs, but frequent treatments are needed to prevent reinfestation. Mosquito nets would discourage the nocturnal feeding visits of the vectors, but few colonists use them, for reasons explored in the discussion of malaria.

Settlers infected with Chagas's disease from endemic areas of Brazil are undoubtedly living on the Transamazon. Potential reservoirs of *T. cruzi,* such as domestic cats, dogs, and rats (*Rattus rattus*),[4] are well established in the colonization zone. Suitable habitats for the disease vectors have been erected. The stage is set for the spread of a new public health problem into Amazonia.

Yellow fever

Yellow fever is another forest zoonosis along the Transamazon that could become a significant public health problem. Although settlers are rarely bitten by infected sylvan vectors, a strongly anthropophilic vector for the virus, well adapted to living in close proximity to man, could easily become established along the highway.

The Old World mosquito, *Aedes aegypti,* responsible for major epidemics of the disease among humans, has been temporarily eradicated from Brazil (Britto and Cardoso, 1973). In spite of surveillance in urban areas by SUCAM, reinfestation of the mosquito occurs periodically from foci in other areas of Latin America. In 1967, for example, boats from the Guianas were deemed responsible for the reintroduction of the vector to Belém. The craft apparently transported *A. aegypti* larvae in water tanks. The species quickly dispersed to São Miguel on the Belém–Brasília highway before it was brought under control (Fraiha, 1968).

Because *A. aegypti* breeds readily in water containers in and around houses, as well as in discarded tin cans and tires, conditions are favorable for the establishment of the vector along the Transamazon. Yellow fever vaccine is reliable and effective for ten years, but only a small segment of the highway population

4. Rats apparently become infected with *T. cruzi* when they eat the vectors (Edgcomb and Johnson, 1970). Humans acquire the parasites in a different manner. After taking a blood meal, the gorged reduviid usually deposits feces close to the puncture wound. The victim scratches the inflamed bite and rubs the *T. cruzi*–infested feces into the lesion, thereby permitting the flagellates to enter the host's body.

has been thus protected. From 1970 to March 1974, 6 percent of the settlers, 2,391 people, were vaccinated against the disease. Spurred by an outbreak of sylvan yellow fever in central Brazil in 1973 that infected at least 71 persons and killed 44 (F. Pinheiro et al., 1978b), SUCAM accelerated the vaccination program along the Transamazon. In the Altamira area, for example, 13,139 people were vaccinated in 1977, and 9,485 in 1978. By the close of 1978 a total of 25,015 had received the vaccine, including residents of Altamira. Less than half of the settlers have been protected against yellow fever. The recent outbreaks of polio in southeastern Brazil, and a case registered from the Transamazon in 1978 (Table 7), attest to the dangers of allowing vaccination campaigns to lag behind population growth or to compensate for migration.

If *A. aegypti* gained a foothold along the Transamazon a serious epidemic of yellow fever could ensue. A man could become infected with the virus while clearing forest, return home to be bitten by *A. aegypti,* and thus initiate a new epidemiological cycle. Increased vigilance for the latter mosquito and a large-scale yellow fever vaccination campaign are needed to ensure that the disease does not become a major public health problem along the highway.

chapter

Public Health Services and Alternative Medicine

When a settler is sick he has three options for treatment. He can visit a medical post, a clinic, or a hospital operated at no cost to the patient by government agencies such as FSESP, FUNRURAL (Fundo de Assistência e Previdência do Trabalhador Rural), SUCAM, INCRA, the army, or Projeto Rondon. He may decide to consult a medical facility operated privately. Finally, he has recourse to spiritual healers and medicinal plants. Some colonists use all three services at different times, depending on need and finances. This chapter describes the three systems of health treatment and analyzes why a need persists for alternative medical services in a pioneer zone.

The public health system

FSESP is the backbone of the public health system along the Transamazon. The government Foundation runs four hospitals with outpatient service in Marabá, Altamira, *rurópolis* Medicilandia, and Itaituba. The Marabá hospital has fifty beds and five doctors, the Altamira one contains seventy-five beds with a staff of four doctors, whereas the Medicilandia hospital has one doctor and eight beds. The Itaituba facility is equipped with sixteen beds and two doctors. In addition, FSESP operates ten medical posts along the Marabá-Itaituba stretch of the Transamazon.[1] A doctor is scheduled to visit the posts, located in *agrovilas* along the main axis of the highway, for four hours each week.

In spite of the extensive infrastructure and the dedication of FSESP employees, the system does not fulfill the needs of settlers. During the rainy season it is sometimes impossible for doctors to visit medical posts, because of the poor road conditions. A restricted gasoline quota and poor vehicle maintenance also contribute to the irregular pattern of visits. Furthermore, the likelihood is slim that on the day a settler becomes ill, a doctor will be on duty at a nearby medical post.

The FSESP hospitals are generally clean and well-disciplined and serve nutritious meals. The care a settler receives therein is usually far better than he has been exposed to before. But FSESP is not able to meet the demand for its services. Only 149 beds are available for 62,000 Transamazon settlers, 85,000 urban residents, and some 80,000 peasants scattered along other roads and rivers. One hospital bed per 1,500 people may be adequate in a region with high standards of living and hygiene, but it is insufficient in an area where the incidence of malaria and gastrointestinal diseases remain high. FSESP doctors are handicapped by a lack of equipment and supplies. The Itaituba hospital has no X-ray machine; patients must be sent to Santarém for this service. Hospital patients are routinely requested to have someone buy medication for them, since stocks are limited.

1. The FSESP medical posts are located as follows: km 42 Marabá–Altamira, km 18 Altamira–Marabá, and at km 23, 40, 46, 60, 70, 80, 90, and 100 of the Altamira–Itaituba stretch of the highway.

The FSESP outpatient service is chaotic. A Transamazon colonist in the Marabá region, for example, must first pass by the INCRA offices in town to obtain a pass certifying that he is a bona fide settler before he can obtain free treatment at FSESP. In order to be included on the list of people for outpatient service that day, the settler must report to the FSESP hospital by 7 A.M. But the INCRA offices do not open until 8 A.M. Consequently, a colonist must remain in town overnight if he wishes to have access to the outpatient service of FSESP. At all the FSESP clinics along the Transamazon, a patient must be in line by 6 A.M. if he hopes to be seen by a doctor. In the morning, only twenty-five consultation slips are distributed, with priority given to children. In the afternoon, only expectant mothers are normally attended.

If a settler manages to draw a consultation number, he may have to wait five hours before he is able to explain his health problem to a doctor. A close relationship rarely develops between a patient and a public health official; settlers are referred to the first available doctor. The impersonal nature of a mass public health system can be an alienating experience. Colonists complain that doctors keep their eyes on the patient's records while the symptoms are explained. Some irritated settlers note that the doctor often starts writing even before the patient speaks. Colonists want individual attention and expect modern medicine to subject them to a battery of tests. Fully aware of the backlog of people to be attended, the doctor usually issues the patient a prescription and quickly ushers him or her to the door.

Other public health services operated by government agencies offer only localized or sporadic help to settlers. A bus operated by FUNRURAL makes irregular trips between km 115 and km 260 of the Marabá–Altamira stretch of the highway.[2] Because of shortages of diesel fuel, the bus now stays mostly at its base at km 115, known as Bacuri. INCRA provides a small medical post and a doctor for the use of colonists at Marabá and Medicilandia, but consultation hours are irregular. A replacement is not provided when an INCRA doctor is absent on vacation or for other reasons. The eighth battalion of the Brazilian army, which built

2. From 1972 until 1975, FUNRURAL operated a twelve-bed hospital on the outskirts of Marabá. The building now serves as a SUCAM post.

the Cuiabá–Santarém highway, runs a medical post at km 112 of the Itaituba–Altamira stretch of the Transamazon as a public service. Projeto Rondon fields several medical students at Marabá, Altamira, and Itaituba, who provide a consulting service for a limited number of patients.[3]

A more useful service to settlers could be provided if the various government agencies involved in the public health system along the Transamazon were consolidated into one organization. In this manner, services could be better coordinated. A much larger injection of funds is needed to expand and improve services. Instead of relying on doctors to treat outpatients along the highway, live-in paramedics could be trained to treat less serious cases within *agrovilas,* similar to the grass-roots medical system in China.

The private sector

The deficiencies of the public health system along the Transamazon create a large market for private health care. Only one organization provides charitable treatment. The Sisters at Itupiranga on the Tocantins River manage the Bom Samaritano clinic free of charge to settlers in the vicinity of Coco Chato. The nuns can care for only a small flock; the majority of colonists who are unwilling, or unable, to use public facilities must pay for treatment.

The only private hospital along the Transamazon, Santo Agostinho in Altamira, caters to a substantial number of highway patients. Inaugurated in 1971, the hospital provides prompt service with four doctors, thirty-two beds, a laboratory, and an X-ray machine. Many settlers prefer to pay the $11 (U.S.) consul-

3. Projeto Rondon, so named in honor of marshall Cândido Rondon, an explorer and defender of Indian causes during the first part of this century, is similar to a short-term VISTA or Peace Corps operation. Students from some Brazilian universities may elect to spend a month in the interior of their country in order to help deprived communities. In Marabá, Projeto Rondon students from the University of São Paulo are flown in by the air force and are lodged at their own base in town. The medical students mostly attend the population of the PA-332 (formerly PA-70) road to the Belém–Brasília. The Projeto Rondon group at Altamira come from the University of Viçosa in Minas Gerais and provide medical consultation in an INCRA building, formerly the topography and map office, in Altamira.

tation fee at the private hospital than to lodge overnight in town and wait in line for FSESP early the next morning. The daily charge for a bed at Santo Agostinho is $12, relatively expensive for many settlers. Nevertheless, a lot of colonists prefer to go to the private hospital, since the FSESP facility, although larger, may be full and is always reluctant to admit patients unless they are covered by a government health plan, such as INPS (Instituto Nacional de Previdência Social) or FUNRURAL. Only the original INCRA colonists are covered by INPS; the majority of highway settlers do not subscribe to any health plan. No needy person is turned down by FSESP, but priority is given to patients armed with the necessary documents. A few settlers make monthly payments to the Association of Rural Workers (Sindicato Rural), since the organization offers the services of a doctor in Altamira. But no hospital care is provided.

If the illness is not very serious, a settler sometimes opts for a private clinic where the rates are more modest than at Santo Agostinho. In Itaituba, for example, Clinica Santana has three beds and the same number of doctors. The consultation fee is only $5 and the daily rate for a bed is the same. A third of the 155 Transamazon settlers interviewed paid for private medical care in 1978 and spent an average of $111 ($s = 179$) per family. Private medical care is not just a luxury of the wealthier colonists; half of the settlers who paid for private medical attention in 1978 earned under $3,350 in that year.

In Marabá, Altamira, and Itaituba, a relatively large selection of doctors work from private offices. Fees for a visit range from under $1 to $18. In Brazil, an M.D. is granted after successful completion of four to five years of undergraduate study. The licensing procedures for medical practitioners in the interior is lax. Transamazon *medicos* at the lower end of the fee scale possess dubious credentials. Some of the less-qualified doctors nevertheless still provide a valuable service, since they are experienced and easily accessible to the poor.[4]

4. In Brazil, anyone with a bachelor's degree expects to be called doctor (*doutor*). The term *doutor* is often used as a signal of respect; people from the lower echelons of the socioeconomic hierarchy in Brazil often refer to a person with a higher social position as *doutor*. Instead of inquiring into the educational background of a person, to be safe, he is often addressed as doctor if he is well dressed and appears to come from a middle-class background.

The majority of Transamazon settlers go straight to a pharmacy when they are feeling ill. The pharmacist is interested in making a sale; he listens sympathetically to the health complaints of a potential customer. A third of the drugstores along the highway invoke the name of a saint, sound business policy in a predominantly Catholic country. Prescriptions for even the most potent drugs are not necessary. Thus, settlers feel that they save time and money when they deal directly with a drugstore.

The impressive number of pharmacies in Transamazon towns attests to the strong demand for their services. Marabá, Altamira, and Itaituba each have from fifteen to seventeen drugstores, although none of the towns has more than 40,000 inhabitants. From five to seven pharmacies compete for customers within a few blocks along the main commercial street of each town. As of 1979, fifty-three drugstores were in business along the Marabá–Itaituba stretch of the highway. The 155 families surveyed spent an average of $216 (s = 314) on drugs in 1978. Transamazon settlers thus spend some $2 million yearly on medication. The drugstores also do a brisk business with urban residents, gold and diamond miners, riverine folk, and settlers along other roads, such as PA-332, which connects Marabá to the Belém–Brasília.

Although pharmacies fill a vital need, they are a mixed blessing. The easy manner in which powerful medicines are dispensed can lead to adverse reactions. The pharmacist is unlikely to be fully aware of the medical history of his customer, and he does not normally explain the situations in which taking the drug is ill-advised. Antibiotics, often perceived as a cure-all by the populace, are regularly sold for treating colds, against which they are useless. The indiscriminate use of a broad range of antibiotics is complicating the treatment of gastrointestinal infections. Pathogenic enterobacteria are becoming increasingly resistant to standard chemotherapy.

All the Transamazon drugstores give injections, usually in the privacy of a booth. Brazilians associate hypodermic syringes with strong and effective medicine. Instead of oral medication, injections are given to treat colds or to administer vitamins. The highway pharmacies do not normally use disposable syringes. Sterilization procedures are inadequate or lacking in most cases. Customers sometimes buy hypodermic syringes and drip bottles for treatment at home, where hygiene standards are also usually precarious. Consequently, infectious hepatitis is a relatively common health complaint along the Transamazon; the disease figures prominently in hospital admissions (Table 7).

Folk medicine

Transamazon settlers often resort to folk remedies when they feel ill, because of the expense and inconvenience of conventional medicine. The use of pharmaceutical plants is not encouraged by public health officials. Some colonists suggest that domestic concoctions are not nearly as effective as modern, synthetic drugs. Folk cures have a low status value along the highway; at times, settlers seem embarrassed to admit that they use medicinal plants. In spite of the low prestige accorded the use of plants for domestic treatment of sickness, 82 percent of the sampled settlers described how they employ parts of herbs, vines, and trees in folk remedies.

A minimum of 127 species of plants in 48 families are used for medicinal purposes along the Transamazon (Appendix 4).[5] I sampled only a small fraction of the colonists, so the total number of plants used for treating health complaints along the highway is undoubtedly much larger. Furthermore, many women were probably reticent to discuss remedies for genital problems. My sample of 155 families nevertheless reveals some of the more common pharmaceutical plants in use. Composites with thirteen species, legumes and mints with nine and eight respectively, euphorbs and Moraceae with six species each, are particularly prominent families among plants used for medicinal purposes along the Transamazon.

Cultivars account for 67 percent of the plants used in folk remedies. At first glance, some Transamazon house-yard gardens appear to be full of ornamentals. On closer inspection, however, many of the herbs and shrubs are grown for their imagined or real pharmaceutical value. Medicinal plants are

5. Whenever possible, I collected specimens of medicinal plants, which were subsequently identified by W. Rodrigues of INPA, Manaus, and M. Pires and M. Van den Berg of the Museu Goeldi, Belém. Some of the material was sterile, so it was not always possible to determine the genus or species of the plants.

mostly the domain of women. Housewives share cuttings and seeds with each other and generally prepare the concoctions. Women tend the plants; some are grown on platforms above ground to escape the depredations of poultry and pigs. Smaller herbs are usually kept in cans containing soil enriched with charcoal and ashes (Fig. 37). Some of the cultivars serve dual purposes. Bom dia (*Vinca rosea* var. *alba*), for example, is grown for its sweet-smelling, attractive white flowers and because a bitter tea is made from its pungent leaves to control excessive menstrual bleeding. Other plants, such as bananas, pineapple (*Ananas comosus*), cashew (*Anacardium occidentale*), guava (*Psidium guajava*), orange (*Citrus sinensis*), papaya (*Carica papaya*), passion fruit (*Passiflora edulis*), mango (*Mangifera indica*), tomato (*Lycopersicon esculentum*), and manioc are cultivated for food as well as for medicinal purposes.

Northerners grow several pharmaceutical plants unknown to settlers from outside of the region. Southerners and Nordestinos were generally unfamiliar with elixir paregórigo (*Piper cavalcantei*), oriza (*Pogostemum patchuli*), vinagreira (*Hibiscus sabdariffa*), rumã (*Cuphea* sp.), crajiru (*Arrabidea chica*), mucuracáa (*Petiveria alliacea*), capim da saúde (*Andropogon* sp.), sete dor, bordo (*Coleus barbatus*), trevo (*Alternanthera bettzikiona*), amor crescido (*Portulaca pilosa*), and chá preto (*Borreria verticillata*) when they arrived on the Transamazon.

Northeasterners encountered some familiar medicinal plants along the Transamazon. Both Nordestinos and northerners attribute pharmaceutical properties to cocinho (*Eleutherina plicata*), pião roxo (*Jatropha gossypifolia*), and pião branco (*J. curcas*). Settlers from the Northeast have introduced several plants of medicinal value, such as erva babosa (*Aloë* sp.), of Old World origin, and pau ferro (*Caesalpinia ferrea* var. *cearensis*) from the dry, thorn scrub woodland (*caatinga*) of the region. Colonists from Goias and Minas Gerais have brought seeds and cuttings of the orange-flowered cordão de frade (*Leonotis nepetaefolia*) and anica (*Pilea microphylla*) to plant around their new homes.

Southerners are responsible for bringing several medicinal plants from temperate and subtropical areas to the Transamazon. Several species of *Eucalyptus* thrive around the homes of settlers; a grove of one species of the exotic has grown eight

Figure 37. Housewife in backyard of her home in *agrovila* Nova Fronteira, 1979. Beside her in the tall can is the large-leafed malva do reino and the smaller hortelão, both used in the treatment of colds and coughs. The tall grass in the foreground is capim santo, which is boiled to make a tea for treating dysentery or upset stomach.

meters high in front of *agrópolis* Brasil Novo within five years. Southerners also cultivate the purple-flowered macaié (*Leonurus sibiricus*), an Asian herb, the white-flowered serraião (*Eupatorium* sp.), the fresh-smelling, pale-flowered macela (*Egletes viscosa*), and the fleshy tuna cactus (*Opuntia tuna*) (Fig. 38). Several cultivated medicinal plants along the Transamazon, such as mastruz (*Chenopodium ambrosioides*), cidreira (*Lantana canescens*), hortelão (*Mentha* sp.), bom dia,[6] melão São Caetano (*Momordica charantia*), and the Old World sabugueira (*Sambucus japonica*), are widely distributed in Latin America and other continents.

Of the medicinal plants used by the sampled families, a third are wild. Forest trees and vines account for 18 percent of the pharmaceutical plants. They are used mainly by northerners who know where to find the plants and how to use them, from long experience and close contact with the *mata*. Women rarely venture into the jungle, so men are mainly responsible for collecting forest plants and for preparing the remedies. One species used in folk cures, babaçu palm, grows in forest and second growth.

Second-growth species account for 15 percent of the medicinal plants used by the sampled colonists. Weeds generally have a wider distribution than forest species. Consequently, some of the pharmaceutical plants from *capoeira,* such as pega pinto (*Boerhaavia paniculata*),[7] picão (*Bidens bipinnata, B. pilosus*), fedegoso (*Cassia occidentalis*), gervão verde (*Stachytarpheta cayennensis*), and capeba (*Potomorphe peltata*) were familiar to settlers from other regions when they arrived on the Transamazon.

Although southerners do not immediately adopt medicinal plants cultivated by northerners, colonists generally share their knowledge of pharmaceutical species. Typically, a *gaúcho* asks a neighbor from Pará to prepare a remedy for some illness for which he has no plants. If the remedy works, the wife might request seeds for her garden. Southerners and Nordestinos are learning to identify forest trees and lianas of medicinal value

6. The first time a medicinal plant is mentioned in the text both the common and scientific names are given. Thereafter, only the common name is used. For scientific names and families, see Appendix 4.

7. The species is known as *pega pinto* (hold chicks) because the abundant, sticky dark seeds sometimes momentarily trap very young chicks in the sprawling plant.

Figure 38. A couple from Rio Grande do Sul with a tuna cactus in their front yard; near Nova Fronteira, 1979

Table 13. Illnesses Treated with Plant Remedies along the Transamazon

Illness	Plant species used
Dysentery, diarrhea	39
Intestinal worms	27
Upset stomach	27
Malaria	26
Liver	23
Colds	23
Fever	13
Headache	9
Lesions	7
Kidneys	6
Coughs	6
Bruises	5
Earache	4
Nervous disorders	3
Edema	3
Heart	3
Constipation	3
Snakebite	3
Measles	2
Sore throat	2
Pain	2
Excessive menstrual bleeding	2
Skin rash	2
Embedded thorns	2
Asthma, pneumonia	2
Eye-ache	2
Urinary tract infection	1
Nausea	1
Hemorrhoids	1
Stiff neck	1
Rheumatism	1
Mouth sores	1
Insomnia	1

when on hunts with northerners. A gradual process of exchange of pharmaceutical plants and methods of their preparation is thus under way along the highway.

Settlers use an impressive array of herbs, bushes, vines, and trees to treat a large assortment of health problems (Table 13). The numerous plants used in preparing remedies for gastro-intestinal disorders, intestinal worms, malaria, liver diseases, and fever suggest that the latter are common health problems along the highway. The ranking of illnesses according to the number of plant species used in their treatment follows reasonably closely the most important causes of internment in the FSESP hospitals (Table 7). A significant difference is that coughs and colds have numerous folk remedies employing plants, but are rarely responsible for hospital admissions.

Intestinal disorders, involving diarrhea or dysentery, are a frequent health complaint among Transamazon families. Instead of seeking out a pharmacy, which can entail a costly trip as far as 150 km from home, colonists commonly resort to remedies prepared from a selection of thirty-nine plants. Almost three-quarters of the plants used to alleviate the distressing symptoms of enteritis are cultivars and thus close at hand. Most of the concoctions are prepared from foliage. A few leaves are plucked, rubbed, or crushed, then boiled. When the liquid cools, some sugar may be stirred in before it is drunk. Sprouting guava leaves are the most common ingredient in cool teas (*chá*) served to abate diarrhea or dysentery, a remedy employed in Brazil since at least the seventeenth century (Marcgrave, 1942 : 105). A *chá* made from the coarse leaves of cidreira is also a popular treatment for intestinal disorders along the highway. Less frequently, remedies using the foliage of arruda (*Ruta graveolens*), an exotic (Cruz, 1965 : 122), pineapple, capeba, cashew, avocado (*Persea americana*), elixir paregórigo, orange, and passion-fruit vine are prepared in similar fashion. An infusion made from a mixture of guava leaves and erva doce (*Pimpinella anisum*) is taken warm or cold.[8] A hot tea is prepared from the pubescent leaves of hortelão, which is sweetened with semirefined sugar, or preferably honey. The hot, bitter drink made from the pounded leaflets of quebra pedra (*Phyllanthus stipulatus, P. niruri*) is not sweetened.

Teas prepared with the small, green leaves of gervão verde, or crushed, yellow foliage of papaya, are taken with salt. Salty brews of chambá (*Lantana* sp.) or sete dor soon provoke vomiting. Presumably, if food is responsible for the gastrointestinal

8. In ancient Greece, *Pimpinella anisum* was used to prepare a mild expectorant (Wheelwright, 1974:48).

distress, the emetic promptly evacuates the source of discomfort.

Infusions of the composites serraião and ficatilha or the mint macaié are prepared by rubbing the leaves to release their potency, then placing them in cool water to steep. An apparently effective *chá* is also made by boiling together the crumpled leaves of macaié, macela, and artemiso (*Ambrosia artemisiaefolia*), the latter two members of the sunflower family. Another mixture employed to alleviate the painful symptoms of dysentery is a pleasant-tasting tea made from the leaves of cidreira and the lemon-scented capim santo (*Cymbopogon* spp.) (Fig. 37).

Infusions for treating intestinal upsets are also prepared from the roots of certain plants. Cipó escada (*Bauhinia* sp.), a thick liana with an unusual convoluted stem,[9] is one of the most sought-after forest products for the treatment of diarrhea. The roots of cipó escada are crushed and soaked in cool water. The onion-like, bulbous roots of cocinho are chopped into small pieces and stirred into cold water. A glass of the pink solution is taken daily until symptoms abate. The thickened roots of batata purga (*Operculina alata*) are pounded into a mash, toasted, mixed into hot water, then swallowed while still warm.

Batata purga is widely taken as a purgative in Brazil, the last thing one would want to take with undisciplined bowel movements. A settler explained that the herbaceous creeper is used in such cases because it cleans out the intestinal tract, thus expelling the offending microbes. A product from the tubers of another cultivar, manioc, is employed to produce the opposite effect. Tapioca is eaten mixed with vinegar, or the starchy nodules are stirred into a glass of sugared water and swallowed.

Tree barks are another important source of remedies for enteritis. Of the eight tree species used in this manner, six are found in the forest. The inner bark of cajá (*Spondias lutea*) is scraped and the shavings are placed in cool water. When the infusion is pink, sugar is added and the solution is swallowed. The astringent bark of anoira is scraped, stirred into water, and taken without

9. Hence the common name for the plant, which means "the staircase vine." Sections of *cipó escada* are occasionally sold to tourists in curio shops as inexpensive souvenirs of Amazonia, and they are sometimes used as a rustic decoration in homes of the region.

sugar. The outer barks of the towering jatobá (*Hymenaea* spp.), pariri (*Pouteria pariri*), mutamba (*Guazuma ulmifolia*), and the smaller preciosa (*Aniba canelilla*) are boiled separately to make teas to calm disturbed intestines. Preciosa tea is sweetened and its clean, rosy flavor is widely appreciated. Teas from the barks of the cultivars cashew and pau ferro are prepared without sugar.

Orange-peel tea is a common remedy for diarrhea, especially among southerners. Coils of orange rind are typically hung close to the stove to keep dry. The peels are boiled and served hot or cold, usually with sugar. The fruit of limão (*Citrus aurantifolia*), rumã, and unripe banana maçá are cut up and boiled to make sour-tasting brews. Banana stalks, especially of the mangara variety, are slashed to extract the watery sap. The collected liquid is then mixed with sugar before drinking. A salty decoction is made from the male flowers of papaya to reduce the frequency of bowel movements. Another apparently effective treatment is prepared by boiling a section of sassacaroba, a forest vine. The solution is imbibed when it cools. One colonist from Paraná relies on hot, unsweetened coffee for the same purpose. In most cases, though, the stimulant acts as a laxative.

Northeasterners are responsible for introducing at least three treatments for diarrhea and dysentery along the Transamazon. Coconut (*Cocos nucifera*) husks are cut into small pieces, boiled, and sweetened. The warm tea is prescribed particularly for children. Coconuts grace the sandy coast of the Northeast and adapt well to the freshwater environment of Amazonia. A dwarf variety is occasionally planted around homes along the highway. In another exotic remedy, a section is cut from one of the thick, fleshy leaves of erva babosa and eaten with a piece of bread. This treatment has not yet gained wide acceptance among colonists. The pungent yellow liquid that oozes from the cut leaf discourages experimentation. Another poorly disseminated remedy is prepared from the legume pau ferro. Two beans are removed from a pod and are put in cool water to steep. After about half an hour, the mild-tasting infusion is drunk.

Some of the plants used to treat intestinal complaints are probably pharmacologically active. Settlers are unlikely to employ so many plants in remedies unless they produce some beneficial effect. Almost all the remedies for diarrhea and dysentery are teas; at the very least, the replaced liquids would help the patient. The frequent use of sugar in the infusions provides an energy boost, especially welcome considering the enervating effects of enteritis. The addition of table salt in several teas helps to restore the body's electrolyte balance. The World Health Organization recommends a rehydration mixture of water, glucose, salt, sodium bicarbonate, and potassium chloride for people suffering from diarrhea or dysentery (Agarwal, 1979). The use of citrus fruits and their peels, which are rich in potassium, would also help an enteritis patient to recuperate. Although public health officials generally look askance at home remedies for illnesses, in the case of intestinal disorders they are probably less dangerous than the indiscriminate use of antibiotics purchased in drugstores.

In contrast to treatments for dysentery and diarrhea, few of the remedies for intestinal worms employ teas made from leaves. Only seven plants are used in this manner. Mastruz is by far the most common ingredient in treatments prepared at home to combat the parasites. The aromatic herb sprouts readily from seed and grows to about half a meter in height. It is a widely recognized vermifuge, particularly against hookworms (Mors and Rizzini, 1966:92; Wheelwright, 1974:188). After the leaves have been boiled in water, crushed garlic or castor bean oil is added to the liquid. The decoction is swallowed on an empty stomach for maximum effect. Within a few hours, the active ingredient ascariodole expels some of the helminths.

Sugarless brews are also made by boiling the foliage of papaya, mango, or sacatinga (*Solanum asperum*). Some settlers make *chá* from the leaves of chicory (*Cichorium intybus*) and add juice squeezed from mastruz or garlic (*Allium sativum*). A cool, refreshing mint tea is reputed to calm agitated intestinal worms, especially if scorched goat horn is powdered and added to the brew. Tea from the leaves of benjaminzeiro (*Ficus microcarpa*) is administered in a special manner. On the first day the *chá* is made from one leaf. On the second day two leaves are used in preparing the brew, until on the ninth day nine leaves are employed. After a three-day pause, the cycle is repeated.

Some of the remedies for intestinal worms clearly illustrate the influence of Old World concepts about disease. For example, goats are rare along the Transamazon, but they figure prominently in the diet and lore of Mediterranean peoples. The significance of the number nine in the benjaminzeiro treatment can also be traced to the Old World. In medieval Europe, for example, a salve to discourage nocturnal visits by goblins involved singing mass nine times over an herbal concoction placed on an altar (Moss and Cappannari, 1976). And in Greece a cure for the evil eye entails holding nine cloves in the right hand while making the sign of the cross (Dionisopoulos-Mass, 1976).

The roots of five plant species are also used to combat helminths. Northerners chop up a bulb of the orange-flowered cebola berrante, add the pieces to boiling water, and drink the infusion when it cools. In another remedy, southerners eat several raw onions, which are purchased in stores, since they do not grow in Amazonia. An onion may be sliced into sections and allowed to steep in a glass of cool water. The next day the unsavory solution is quickly swallowed. Colonists from all regions claim that garlic tea suppresses the activity of worms.[10] A tea is made from the roots of chicory, an herb also used as a condiment.

The barks of only two trees, both from the forest, are used in remedies for helminth infestations. A bitter-tasting brew is prepared from the outer bark of gameleira (*Ficus* spp.). The bark of andiroba-jaruba (*Andira inermis*) is pounded and boiled at sunset. In the early hours of the morning, the infected victim eats some hard brown sugar (*rapadura*), then half an hour later drinks a glass of the decoction. According to settlers, intestinal worms are especially fond of sugar; if some *rapadura* is eaten first, the parasites are actively feeding when the lethal brew arrives.

Most of the remedies for treating intestinal worms do not involve boiling leaves, roots, or barks. The juice of mastruz, for example, is taken pure in the morning, before breakfast. Mastruz has an unpleasant taste, so it is sometimes disguised by an ingredient such as milk. One remedy calls for blending mastruz extract with hot milk and sugar, then leaving the mixture outside

10. Garlic may be harmful to intestinal helminths, since it contains allicin, an antibiotic (Purseglove, 1975:53).

overnight so that it collects dew. Some settlers prefer to beat mastruz juice with egg whites and castor bean oil before drinking it. Mastruz is also pounded with garlic; the filtered liquid is swallowed promptly.

Ubiquitous papaya trees are also frequently used to prepare several worm remedies. Settlers gash the skin of green papaya fruits to collect the sticky sap, which is drunk with water. The white latex, a recognized vermicide (Mors and Rizzini, 1966 : 92), is also gathered from the top part of the trunk. The numerous black seeds of papaya are crunched and eaten with the fruit to expel worms. The seeds are also pounded and taken with milk or water. Squash (*Cucurbita* spp.) seeds are toasted and eaten in the morning upon rising. The baked seeds are also ground and mixed with milk or egg yolk. Pumpkin seeds are reportedly active against tapeworms (*Taenia* spp.), which can be acquired by eating poorly cooked beef or pork (Mors and Rizzini, 1966 : 94). Settlers from all the regions in Brazil claim that the seeds are effective against intestinal nematodes.

The pale yellow flowers of matapasti (*Cassia obtusifolia*) and passion fruit are boiled, sugared, and taken when cool. The foliage of melão São Caetano and guava is rubbed and left to steep in cool water before it is drunk. Cotton (*Gossypium* spp.) and mastruz leaves are dried, crushed into a powder, and mixed together with a banana for breakfast. The astringent juice of the common weed gervão verde is reportedly an effective, albeit unpopular, vermifuge. A piece of erva babosa leaf, eaten with a piece of bread, is also a remedy of last resort.

The abundant latex of gameleira, a proven vermicide (Mors and Rizzini, 1966 : 92), is drunk pure or stirred into coffee to disguise its disagreeable flavor. The following day, the infected settler swallows a spoonful of castor bean oil. The pale, viscous sap of mamuí is blended with milk before drinking. Both remedies are used mainly by northerners, since the trees are native to the forests of Amazonia.

The fruits or nuts of four plants are prepared to treat intestinal helminths. A *chá* is made from the green fruits of rumã, a bush cultivated in house gardens. Other vermifuges include swallowing the fresh beans of cacao (*Theobroma cacao*), or sucking on several sour limes. Nordestinos and peasants from Amazonia prepare a medicine for worms by pounding the nuts of babaçu palm. The resulting oil is left out overnight to collect dew before it is swallowed. One colonist from Paraná, where the palm is absent, has adopted the remedy.

The importance of dew in the babaçu oil cure for worms illustrates once again the influence of Old World ideas on the perception of disease along the Transamazon. In Hippocratic medicine, for example, dew distilled from morning mist is considered clean, soft, and healthful (Chadwick and Mann, 1950 : 93). Dew is also thought to be important in the helminth treatment involving mastruz juice, hot milk, and sugar. But not all colonists share a belief in the benign effects of dew in herbal medicine preparations. One settler, for example, attributed his recent case of malaria to walking in dew-coated grass before breakfast.

Stomachache is another common ailment along the Transamazon, especially among children. At least twenty-seven plants are used to treat gastric disorders, of which 78 percent are cultivars; second growth and the forest supply only three species each to the pharmacopoeia for treating the sickness. Some of the remedies are designed to reduce stomach acidity, whereas others apparently act as mild pain killers. Two plants are powerful emetics.

Most of the remedies for upset stomach are prepared by making warm or cool teas from foliage. The soothing, lemon-mint *chás* of cidreira and capim santo are most commonly prescribed for the complaint. Less pleasant, but apparently equally effective, brews are prepared by boiling the leaves of capim da saúde, elixir paregórigo, embaúba (*Cecropia* spp.), eucalyptus, folha santa (*Bryophyllum calycinum*), ficatil, guava, lozinaverde, macaié, papaya, quebra pedra (*Phyllanthus niruri*), or tokin (*Pluchea quitoc*). Mango leaves are also used to make a *chá* for calming the stomach; they contain turpentine and are used to make numerous domestic remedies in other parts of the basin (Prance and Silva, 1975 : 37). Leaves from losna (*Artemisia absinthium*), an herb introduced to Brazil from Europe (Cruz, 1965 : 572), are also brewed to soothe indigestion. Settlers with nausea sometimes prepare a *chá* of sete dor; within minutes they vomit and feel relieved.

Another quick-acting emetic is prepared from macela. The

small, white flowers of the composite are first boiled. When the decoction cools, ash and salt are added. One glass of the solution is usually sufficient. A tea made from dried lime peel and the roots of carrapicho de espinho (*Bidens bipinnata*) is taken afterwards as a calmative. The fresh leaves of bordo (*Coleus barbatus*), ficatil, or melão São Caetano are squeezed directly into cool water. The resulting drink also reputedly soothes tender stomachs. Northerners suck on a piece of quina bark if there are no appropriate cultivars available to alleviate stomach pain. Castor bean oil, prepared at home from bushes growing in the yard, is taken to aid digestion.

Remedies for malaria are based mostly on wild plants. Of the twenty-six species used to treat the disease, nine are forest trees and six are weeds. Malaria is endemic to all parts of Brazil except the extreme south. In each region, rural folk have learned to use wild plants to alleviate the high fever and chills associated with the sickness. Along the Transamazon, Paraenses have a near monopoly on the knowledge of forest and *capoeira* plants which can allegedly cure malaria, or at least mitigate the painful symptoms of the illness.

Most malaria remedies are prepared from barks and roots. The most procured barks for treating the disease are stripped from quina, of which there are at least three species along the highway (Appendix 4). None of the quinas employed by Transamazon settlers apparently have any real therapeutic value (Mors and Rizzini, 1966: 90). Quinine, an alkaloid lethal to *Plasmodium* parasites, is extracted from the bark of several species of *Cinchona* which are native to the forest-clad slopes of the Andes above 300 meters (Purseglove, 1974: 452). Other bitter teas are prepared from the barks of pau para tudo (*Simaba cedron*), gurantã, or caférana (*Picrolemma pseudocoffea*). In another decoction the bark of barrote is boiled with the pounded roots of pau para tudo. Some six liters of water are used; when half has boiled away, the brew is buried. After three days the malaria victim drinks a glass of the red infusion and pours the remainder over his body.

Only one forest species, janaúba (*Hymathantus sucuuba*), provides roots for treating malaria. The tree's fine surface roots are scraped into a glass of water; after steeping overnight, the astringent infusion is swallowed rapidly. Most of the folk remedies for malaria derived from roots are pulled from weeds, such as canapu (*Physalis angulata*), mangerioba (*Cleome aculeata*), picão (*Bidens bipinnata*), jambu (*Wulffia stenoglossa*), or fedegoso. The latter annuals are hard to find during the dry season, hence the importance of forest and cultivated plants in malaria treatments. A tea made from the roots of the cultivar quebra pedra (*Phyllanthus stipulatus*) is reputed to ameliorate the condition of malaria sufferers. Another brew for treating the disease is prepared from assafrão (*Curcuma* sp.).[11] The orange-yellow rhizomes of the perennial are boiled with sugar. The brew is taken when it is cool.

All but one of the teas made with leaves for malaria victims are prepared from domesticated plants. The exception, gervão verde *chá,* is drunk with an aspirin tablet. The foliage of passion fruit, the shade tree castanhola (*Terminalia catappa*), crajiru, or cotton is also boiled to make decoctions. In the case of cotton, the infusion is also used to wash the patient. The tea prepared by boiling the dry gourd of cabaçinha (*Luffa operculata*) is so bitter that it causes trembling when taken in large doses. Settlers drink the green juice of melão São Caetano in the morning before breakfast, or prepare an elixir of the plant with sugarcane alcohol (*cachaça*) as a base. Some colonists opt for the acrid oil extracted from andiroba (*Carapa guianensis*) seeds, or the juice of sour limes to combat malaria. One settler claims that when a red-hot iron poker is plunged into a glass of sugarcane syrup, the liquid acquires antimalarial properties. This idea stems from the belief that the syrup has a high iron content and can thus fortify the blood. The poker would impart additional quantities of the metal to the remedy.

Two domestic malaria treatments are prepared from black peppers. In one remedy a spoon of ground pepper is blended with two cut-up limes and three pieces of chopped garlic. The mixture is boiled with a little salt and taken twice a day, with an interval of two hours, until the recurrent fever subsides. In the second preparation nine kernels of pepper are boiled; then the

11. One colonist from Pará prepares a rich-tasting, finely ground flour from assafrão tubers for domestic consumption. It serves as a substitute for manioc flour at the table.

decoction is left to cool with the lid in place to secure its potency. Almost all the infusions for treating malaria are extremely bitter, a prerequisite for effectiveness, according to many settlers.

Remedies for fevers, other than those attributed to malaria, are very different from those prescribed for *Plasmodium* infections. In contrast to malaria treatments, the majority of plants used for fever remedies are cultivars. Only two of the thirteen plants used are wild species. Most home-made medications to lower body temperature are simple teas prepared from foliage, such as cidreira, erva mate (*Allamanda cathartica*),[12] eucalyptus, hortelão, lima (*Citrus medica*), macaié, quebra pedra (*Phyllanthus niruri*), or sabugueira. A cool, unsweetened tea is prepared from the pounded roots of chá preto (*Borreria verticillata*).

One colonist from Pará enthusiastically asserted that the latex from amapá (*Hancornia amapa*) quickly reduces fever. The sticky sap from the forest tree is beaten in water with a little sugar, then swallowed. Another reputedly effective febrifuge is prepared by frying the male flowers of papaya with sugar, then adding them to hot water. The concoction is ready for drinking when it cools. Juice from the leaves of cordão de frade is squeezed directly into a cup of hot coffee. The sweetened beverage is said to alleviate fever. To refresh the body and lower its temperature, some settlers boil the oily leaves of mucuracáa. The resulting warm solution is used for bathing.

Transamazon settlers choose from a pharmacopoeia of at least twenty-three plants to treat liver complaints. Brazilians attribute numerous illnesses to liver problems. The organ is perceived as an important regulator of the body's functions. Enteritis, for example, is frequently ascribed to a malfunctioning liver rather than to pathogenic bacteria, protozoa, or viruses, which are more common causes of dysentery and diarrhea. Many fevers are also thought to derive from disorders of the liver. A battery of products in drugstores, frequent commercials on television and the radio, as well as advertisements in the press, all directed to the welfare of the liver, underline the widespread concern for the fitness of the organ. The seeming obsession for the health of

12. Erva mate may have antibiotic properties, since a related species, *Allamanda violacea*, is known to contain an ingredient active against microbes (Rizzini and Mors, 1966:86).

the liver has some basis. Malaria, a major public health problem in many rural areas of Brazil, damages the organ, particularly during prolonged or repeated infections.

Of the twenty-three plants used to treat real or imagined liver disorders, 61 percent are cultivars, 35 percent come from second growth, and 4 percent are gathered in the forest. Most of the remedies are prepared by boiling leaves, as in the case of treatments for fevers, stomachache, and intestinal problems. The foliage of agrião (*Spilanthes acmella*), avocado, capeba, chá preto, ficatil, gervão verde, guava, jambu, lozinaverde, losna, macaco, quebra pedra (*Phyllanthus stipulatus*), tomato, or tokin is used in this manner. The teas are taken without sugar; as in the case of malaria treatments, bitterness is generally regarded as necessary if the medication is to be effective. Another sugarless brew is made from the leaves of amor crescido and jambu. For hepatitis victims, an infusion is prepared by boiling the leaves of crajiru and salsa (*Petroselinum sativum*).

Tart pineapples are eaten in large quantities by settlers who wish to detoxify their livers. Hard avocado seeds are scraped into water and boiled to prepare a tea with allegedly similar properties. The jenipapo (*Genipa americana*) treatment for distended livers is a ritual. On the first night one leaf is placed on the abdomen over the liver area and is secured in place with a bandage. On the second night two new leaves of the forest tree are pressed to the same place, and so on until on the ninth evening nine freshly picked leaves are used. Genipapo foliage is rich in mannitol (Prance and Silva, 1975:225); it is not clear, though, whether the alcoholic compound is beneficial to the liver, or if the organ can absorb the chemical from leaves placed on the skin surface. An astringent brew is prepared from the roots of fedegoso and picão (*Bidens bipinnata, B. pilosus*) to diminish the pain and tenderness of a swollen liver.

At least twenty-three plants are used by settlers to mitigate the symptoms of colds and influenza. Cultivars, with eighteen species, are particularly important in cold remedies. Second growth and the forest supply only three and two species respectively to the pharmacopoeia of cold treatments. One of the most common remedies used to relieve the discomfort of colds is prepared by boiling lime rinds. While the decoction is still warm, sugar and juice from several of the acidic fruits are added to it. Hot beverages made with the leaves of orange, lima, bergamot (*Citrus aurantium*), cidreira, or mint are also frequently prepared for the same purpose. Northerners, in particular, sometimes make a sweet, minty brew with poejú, whereas southerners and Nordestinos often resort to eucalyptus teas to combat colds. Most of the *chás* are served hot with generous portions of semirefined sugar, dark sugarcane syrup, or wild honey.[13]

Syrups for treating colds are prepared by simmering the leaves of malva (*Sida rhombifolia*) and malva do reino (*Salvia* sp., Fig. 37) with liberal quantities of sugar or honey. A lid is placed loosely on top of the pan to capture as much of the essential oil as possible. Another syrup, taken with milk in the morning, is made by boiling crushed cipó escada. The juice of mastruz is squeezed into a glass of milk for breakfast, but it is not clear how the vermifuge ameliorates colds. Cotton leaves are first heated in a pan, then the juice is squeezed out and swallowed pure. A tea made from the pods of the legume coronha (*Acacia farnesiana*), a tree cultivated for its exuberant blossoms, is reported by northeasterners to clear nasal passages blocked with mucous. Cold victims are sometimes bathed in a lavender-smelling solution prepared by boiling the leaves of tokin.

Garlic again finds a medicinal use in the treatment of colds. Several cloves are simmered in water, and the infusion is drunk pure while still hot, or mixed with alcohol, such as *cachaça*. To help render garlic's overpowering flavor more palatable, the brew is sometimes blended with ground pepper, coffee, or lime juice. Another decoction for colds is prepared by boiling the roots of fedegoso. Ginger (*Zingiber officinale*) rhizomes are pounded and boiled with dried lime peels and sugar; the resulting hot, spicy tea apparently facilitates breathing. South-

13. Honey is collected in the forest from native stingless bees. A fire is lit at the base of the tree, and the wood is chopped open with an axe or a machete. In second growth, honey from *Apis mellifera adansonii* is collected at night when the bees are relatively inactive and less likely to sting. The latter species, a Brazilian hybrid of the infamous African honey bee, has spread rapidly since it escaped from an apiary in São Paulo state in 1952 (Michener, 1975). I first observed feral populations of the species along the Estreito–Itaituba stretch of the highway in 1973 (material identified by H. Daly, Department of Entomology, University of California, Berkeley).

erners and northeasterners make a syrup to relieve the discomfort associated with colds and influenza by adding the crushed roots of carrapicho de ovelha (*Acanthospermum australe*) to sugar and hot water. Northerners boil the nodulous rhizomes of apií (*Dorstenia reniformis*) to prepare a syrup with similar properties. Paraenses make another syrup by simmering a piece of jatobá bark in water and sugar. Several spoonfuls of the concoction are taken daily.

There is no cure for the common cold, so colonists save a considerable amount ot time and money by resorting to a large selection of medicinal plants to help overcome the more severe symptoms. Colds are rarely responsible for hospital admissions, but the virus-related sickness is surprisingly common along the Transamazon. Colds are definitely not restricted to colder climates.

Transamazon colonists use at least fourteen plants, all cultivars, to relieve pain other than stomachache. A brew made from the roots of the cashew tree is reputed to be an effective painkiller, especially for teething babies. A tea prepared from crushed cotton leaves is considered a good general analgesic. Headache remedies include inhaling a powder obtained by grinding toasted seeds of alfavaca (*Ocimum minimum*) and drinking decoctions of avocado, erva mate, or folha santa leaves. A cool infusion for the same problem is prepared by squeezing juice from the leaves of bordo or cordão de frade into water. Another headache remedy is prepared by frying male papaya flowers with sugar, then adding the mixture to water.

Northeasterners and peasants from Amazonia employ two species of euphorbs in an attempt to mitigate head pains. Oil is extracted from the fruits of pião branco (*Jatropha curcas*) and is swallowed pure. It contains a toxic protein, curcin; in small doses the oil acts as a purgative, but in large amounts it is poisonous (Mors and Rizzini, 1966:27; Prance and Silva, 1975:107). Some settlers claim to obtain relief from headaches by placing a heated leaf of pião roxo (*Jatropha gossypifolia*) on their foreheads.

One housewife from Maranhão attributed her chronic head pains to her loss of hair. She apparently suffers from acute headaches when rats collect her long, black strands from the floor of the house and carry them to the rafters to line their nests. In an effort to halt her rapidly receding hairline, the housewife wound some locks of her hair round the tips of several branches of pião roxo growing in the yard. She hoped that the vigorous growth of the young leaves would rejuvenate her scalp and help restore her lost hair.

To alleviate earache with plant products, settlers crush the leaves of alfavaca, folha santa, or oriza and pour the liquid into the ear canal. Alfavaca juice is sometimes heated on a spoon with mineral oil before being placed into the offending ear. The canal is then stuffed with a piece of cloth or a wad of compacted leaves for several hours. Mint tea also allegedly soothes earache. To relieve sore eyes, colonists drink cidreira tea or put an alfavaca seed on the cornea.

The pharmacopoeia for treating other health problems, such as lesions, measles, and insomnia, is much more limited. Although fewer plants are employed in remedies for the other group of diseases, they are nevertheless frequently used. Minor wounds, bruises, coughs, and skin rashes are relatively common health complaints along the Transamazon.

Although the pharmaceutical value of many of the remedies may appear dubious, some of them, such as the sugared teas for treating diarrhea, are beneficial. Oil from pião fruits, taken to relieve constipation, is an efficient purgative (Mors and Rizzini, 1966 : 27). Cumaru bean oil, swallowed by settlers suffering from pneumonia, is known to moderate respiration and reduce pain (Pio Corrêa, 1931 : 476). The essential oil expressed from andiroba seeds and used by colonists to treat malaria, contains the alkaloid carapine, a febrifuge (Pio Corrêa, 1926 : 113). Even if a plant has no apparent medicinal value, it still serves a useful purpose. When a settler is ill and far from a drugstore or medical post, the fact that someone prepares a concoction for him is likely to bring some comfort, even if it is only psychological.

The supernatural and disease

A settler's perception of the causes of an illness is often at variance with explanations provided by conventional medicine. Notions about disease are frequently steeped in superstition and mysticism. In the minds of many colonists, sickness is not just caused by an organic problem, an invasion of the body by pathogenic organisms, improper food, or psychological stress. Supernatural forces also impinge on a person's well-being. The roots of such concepts extend into aboriginal, African, and European religions and mythology.

If conventional medicine is too expensive or ineffective, some colonists seek the services of a spirit healer (*curandeiro, pajé, benzedor*). *Curandeiros* live in Transamazon towns, *agrovilas*, or on farm lots along the highway. Some healers advertise their services with hand-pointed signs above their front door, but most are known by reputation. *Curandeiros* are good listeners. After the patient has described his health problem, the male or female healer consults his group of spirits (*linha*) to decipher the cause. The *curandeiro* usually prescribes herbal medicines, to be prepared at home or bought in a specialist store (*casa de umbanda*). Several *umbanda* shops serve a large number of urban and rural customers in Marabá, Altamira, and Itaituba. The stores sell an impressive array of charms, roots, barks, packaged and bottled herbal blends, and incense. Such preparations are designed to expel malevolent influences, refresh the body, and provide a tonic.

Spirit healers are reluctant to divulge their methods of treatment. They claim that they cannot remember the incantations recited when they consult with their patients, for the words are not their own: they are uttered by spirit allies. The formulas prescribed for remedies often require incantations to be effective, thereby necessitating a return visit. *Curandeiros* rarely set a fee for their services, since they attribute their powers to divine providence. Such gifts should not be used for profit. It is customary, however, to make a modest contribution, in the form of either cash or produce.

Spirit healers are not feared, as is the case with shamans in some Indian tribes, such as the Jivaro (Harner, 1973). *Curandeiros* do not see themselves as competitors to Christianity; many attribute their power ultimately to God. There is a great deal of syncretism between the spiritualism of *curandeiros* and the Catholic faith. Both belief systems rely a great deal on intermediaries to help solve personal problems. The Virgin Mary and saints may be called upon in addition to faith healers to alleviate a health disorder. *Curandeiros* are accessible, sympathetic, and generally respected for their benevolent works.

A *benzedora* who resides in *agrovila* Leonardo da Vinci has acquired minor fame in the vicinity of the community for her curative powers. She is a stocky housewife, well advanced in years. Her husband owns a lot nearby. In 1979 the young daughter of a colonist, who also lives in Leonardo da Vinci, suffered from a painful inflammation of her left leg. The mother first took her sick daughter to a drugstore in Altamira, but the medication sold to her was apparently ineffective. The mother then carried her girl to the *benzedora* in Leonardo da Vinci. The healer gently examined the child's leg and momentarily withdrew to her backyard to collect three sprigs of vassoura (*Scoparia dulcis*). The *benzedora* first swished one branch of the herbaceous weed on the left and right sides of the patient's swollen leg, then she repeated the motion with two sprigs, and finally with three. Each time, the old lady recited an unintelligible supplication. Within a couple of days, the edema had vanished and the girl was able to walk again. The healer received a plump chicken for her efforts.

The *benzedora*'s use of three sprigs illustrates the influence of Christianity in folk medicine. The first sprig invokes the Father, the second branch represents the Son, and the third symbolizes the curing power of the Holy Ghost. The number three also signifies the Trinity in folk remedies in the Old World. In Italy, for example, a cure for the evil eye entails taking a bowl of water, putting three drops of oil into it, then crossing oneself and reciting an incantation three times (Appel, 1976).

Young children are vulnerable to the evil eye (*quebranto, mau olho*). If a child is subjected to a great deal of admiration, he or she may become weak and feverish. A victim of *mau olho* is listless and has little or no appetite. Attractive infants, such as little girls with soft, blond hair, are especially prone to the sinister power of the evil eye. Adults, particularly strangers, are deemed responsible for the sudden deterioration of the child's health. People who have just returned from a tiring journey or a day's work in the field and play with a young girl are likely to trigger *quebranto*. Illicit sexual desire undoubtedly underlies the concept of *mau olho*. Lavish attention by outsiders toward young children is thus not always welcomed by the parents. Settlers procure a spirit healer to break the spell of the evil eye.

To ward off the harmful influence of *mau olho,* Transamazon colonists and peasants throughout the North plant pião roxo, pião branco, vassoura, or arruda in the yard. The concept of the evil eye can be traced to the Old World. In certain parts of India, for example, parents become apprehensive if a stranger praises a child; an attractive baby is especially susceptible to the dangers of the evil eye (Maloney, 1976). In Tunisia children are traditionally dressed in shabby clothes to discourage the attention of the evil eye (Teitelbaum, 1976). It is not surprising that European plants also figure prominently in folk remedies along the Transamazon. In ancient Greece arruda was widely acclaimed for its miraculous powers (Cruz, 1965 : 122); along the highway the cultivar serves to repel *mau olho*.

Evangelical Christians along the highway regard the beliefs in *quebranto* and spells with disdain. They are considered superstitious nonsense—or worse, courting the devil. Protestants usually opt for conventional medical treatment or appeal directly to the Almighty. The use of traditional home remedies involving pharmaceutical plants, such as orange peel tea, is acceptable, provided that the treatments do not include rituals, incantations, or images. Pentecostal sects account for a minority of settlers, so the use of medicinal plants with a supernatural connotation is widespread along the highway.

Although public health officials and most religious leaders look askance at spiritual healers, the latter nevertheless fill a need in pioneer communities, as well as urban areas in developing countries. Faced with almost two billion people scattered over wide areas and with a limited income, conventional medicine will not be able to reach significant numbers of the needy in the Third World. There are plenty of examples in developing countries where scarce public money is channeled into the construction of costly medical centers equipped with modern and sophisticated equipment. All too often, however, the well-to-do reap the benefits of such governmental largesse. Public health programs in the Third World need to be more closely tailored to the culture and purchasing power of the mass of peasants and urban poor.

chapter

The Transamazon and Regional Development

Many individuals have benefited from the Transamazon scheme. Government personnel on the highway receive a handsome salary bonus for working at a hardship post; several have purchased ranches and farms along the road and in the vicinity of Marabá, Altamira, and Itaituba. Most construction companies, hotels, restaurants, storekeepers, and landowners in the pre-existing towns have profited from the Transamazon. For the first time, several thousand peasants have titles to land that is rapidly increasing in value. Children can study in schools, albeit rudimentary ones, and families have access to free medical care, even if it is not always prompt. Some colonists, who arrived with few goods and little if any savings have managed to generate modest cash surpluses with which to improve their homes and purchase equipment.

Nevertheless, the Transamazon has not achieved many of its objectives. The rapid turnover of lots indicates that the project has not created a favorable environment for the establishment and growth of small-scale farms by formerly landless peasants. As of 1978, 19 percent of the lots in the Marabá area and 30 percent of the parcels in the Altamira region have been abandoned by their original owners, according to INCRA statistics. Of the 170 lots I visited in 1979, only 56 percent were occupied by their first owners. Officially, colonists are not allowed to sell their land. If they wish to leave, they are supposed to return the property to INCRA and take care of any outstanding bank debts. Furthermore, it is illegal for a person to own more than one lot.

In practice, a colonist in financial straits sometimes sells his land. He asks the buyer to pay off accumulated bank loans and to compensate him for buildings and crops on the lot. The buyer takes the papers to a registry office (*cartório*) in Marabá, Altimira, or Itaituba, to acquire a document designating him as procurator for the original owner. The buyer then occupies the land or installs a caretaker.

Successful colonists are thus able to acquire lots for their sons. If a settler has no male offspring of legal age, then the second lot is put in the name of a brother, or even of his wife, so long as the person can prove that he or she has an independent source of income. This formality is easy to satisfy; a teacher's salary or even a document claiming that the wife is a seamstress is sufficient. The purchaser of the lot does not need to reside on the Transamazon. Some colonists and outsiders have thus acquired as many as five lots.

Many factors are responsible for prying settlers off their land. Disappointing agricultural yields, a confusing credit system, administrative shortcomings, and disease have all contributed to the demise of new homesteads. The preponderance of a particular factor in the decision to abandon the lot varies from case to case. Another important reason why so many colonists have left the project is that selection procedures were apparently not very rigorous.

All INCRA colonists were supposed to have had some prior agricultural experience, but some individuals were able to circumvent this requirement. In 1972 I met a colonist in Coco Chato who had just arrived from Fortaleza. In the capital of Ceará, he worked as a taxi driver. He had never tilled land. In 1973 when I returned to the *agrovila,* he had sold out and left. A general lack of farm management skills has been a major drawback to agricultural productivity along the highway (Moran, 1979).

Peasants with large families were to be given high priority in INCRA's screening process. A rationale for this prerequisite was that offspring would help with farming chores. In practice, though, many colonists were bachelors. Few of the single men came with sufficient resources to hire labor. Most of the unmarried men came for speculative reasons. One bachelor who arrived in Nova Fronteira in 1972 sold his lot for a handsome price after two years. With the money, he bought a truck to haul cargo along the Transamazon.

The price of a 100-ha parcel of land along the Transamazon depends on soil type, crops, and location. Lots of *terra roxa* bordering the main axis of the highway with a perennial water course sell for about $35,000 (U.S.). Lots with sandy soil on side roads can be purchased for as little as $4,000. Sellers do not always invest their money wisely. Some purchase secondhand vehicles that soon break down or are demolished in accidents. Others drift to towns and cities to try and make a living by operating small stores. Few succeed, because of the numerous competitors. Many sellers revert to sharecropping, work as day laborers, or migrate to new settlement frontiers.

The least successful colonists are especially tempted to sell out. Entrepreneurs who buy the lots generally invest capital and bring machinery and workers to their new farms. Agricultural productivity is thus likely to increase along the highway, at least in the short term. But a major social problem remains unsolved. The project has failed to secure a home for a significant number of the landless.

Moran (1975, 1976) has correctly highlighted the superior ecological knowledge of northerners along the Transmazon. Although *caboclos* are certainly highly capable of feeding themselves in a rainforest environment, they are not necessarily wiser or more prosperous farmers. Northerners clear forest on steep slopes and destroy riparian vegetation in the same manner as Nordestinos and southerners. *Caboclos* are generally at a disadvantage in the cash-cropping, market-oriented agricultural system along the highway. The 1978 household income of northerners averaged only $1,640 (s = 1,417, n = 33), considerably less earnings than families from the South with a mean of $3,652 (s = 4,032, n = 52), the Northeast (mean = 4,040, s = 5,549, n = 44), the Center-West (mean = 3,706, s = 6,978, n = 18), and the Southeast (mean = 3,782, s = 2,770, n = 8). Most *caboclos* have little if any entrepreneurial skills; they are accustomed to a subsistence life or to working for a patron (*patrão*), particularly in extractive industries such as rubber or Brazil-nut gathering.

A brief history of four families at *agrovila* Nova Fronteira, two from Pará and the others from the South, will serve to illustrate the important factors that account for the success or failure of pioneers along the Transamazon. Bento was thirty-five when he arrived at the *agrovila* with his nineteen-year-old wife in December 1971. He was born in Pasto dos Bons in Maranhão, where he worked as a sharecropper until the age of twenty. For the next fifteen years Bento worked as a day laborer in various locations in Goias and Pará states. Before coming to the Transamazon, he collected Brazil nuts in the rainy season and looked for diamonds in the Tocantins River during the dry months. He had never owned any equipment or land; he was used to being grubstaked by a *patrão*.

Although Bento was one of the first to arrive at Nova Fronteira, he was assigned a lot of poor quality. The yellow latosol on his land produces meager yields. Since it is on an undulating side road, he has encountered difficulties in preparing and sending his rice crop to market. Bento enthusiastically embraced the idea of credit; he quickly piled up bank debts to clear his land and to purchase equipment, such as a power saw. Like many other settlers, he cleared far more land than he could effectively use. The chain blade of his power saw broke several times; the replacements, at $30 each, soon became prohibitively expensive. Bento soon fell into arrears at the bank. He could no longer afford to hire labor. His three children, born on the Transamazon, were too young to help.

In an effort to gain some income, the family moved to their lot and built a small wooden house. The *agrovila* home was rented out for $10 a month. Although the family had sufficient to eat, earnings were modest. In 1978 the family's income totaled $1,161. Under the burden of mounting financial obligations and constant offers to buy his property, Bento finally relented in 1980. The family packed their few belongings and moved to the shores of the Amazon near Santarém. Bento was hopeful that he could make a good living by farming and fishing on the floodplain of the silt-laden river.

João arrived with his wife and nine children at Nova Fronteira during the same month in 1971 as Bento. João, now forty-one, has spent his entire life within a 200-km radius of Altamira. He has sustained his family with subsistence agriculture on vacant land. With the arrival of the Transamazon, João quickly signed up for a lot of his own. He drew a 100-ha parcel of sharply dissected yellow latosol next to Bento's lot. João wanted to fill his lot with pasture grass and raise a herd of dairy cattle. With Banco do Brasil credit, he cleared 15 ha of forest in 1972 and planted rice and *Panicum maximum* seed. His *barbalha* rice crop failed. The few clumps of guinea grass were soon covered by second growth. He could not afford to hire labor, and his two eldest sons, twelve and ten years old, were unable to take sufficient time away from school to weed the lot, 4 km from the *agrovila*.

In 1974 João sold his land for the equivalent of $2,000 (U.S.). He now rents a house in Nova Fronteira and works on a piece-meal basis for other colonists, mainly cutting forest and planting crops. On weekends João supplements the family income by hunting; neighbors eagerly purchase portions of paca, white-lipped peccary, or deer for seventy cents per kilogram. His wife, Maria, contributes small sums sporadically by washing clothes for government employees in the *agrovila*.

Although João has lost his land, he seems relatively content. In 1978 the family earned $2,567, enough to cover subsistence needs. João prefers to walk with a "cool" head; he is now free of the worrisome bank debts. The family eats fresh game several times a week, and João is able to buy rice, manioc, and fruits from colonists at cheap prices. João and Maria expect their children to take care of them when they are older. Their eldest daughter, Antonia, is a maid in Altimira; she will probably marry soon. Lourenço, the oldest son at twenty, works as a mechanic in the same town. Celine, now nineteen, is married to a settler in the vicinity of *agrovila* Leonardo da Vinci. In 1970 Rosane became the common-law wife of a mechanic in Altamira, shortly after her thirteenth birthday.

Domingos drove his pickup truck into *agrovila* Nova Fronteira in July 1972. His wife, of German extraction, and nine children had accompanied him on the ten-day journey from Tenente Portela in Rio Grande do Sul. A chartered truck followed close behind carrying a rice-threshing machine, a wooden oxcart, and other belongings. Domingos had purchased a relatively level lot of *terra roxa* along the highway earlier in the year from a bachelor for $300. The *gaúcho,* of Italian descent, deposited $16,000 into a savings account in an Altamira bank, the proceeds from the sale of a 66-ha plot of land near the town of Tenente Portela.

Domingos arrived on the Transamazon with a great deal of agricultural experience, albeit in a temperate zone at 26° south latitude. In the South he belonged to the COTRIJUI co-op, grew soybeans and maize for market, and raised a small herd of cattle and pigs. The family decided to risk starting a new life in Amazonia because their steep and rocky plot could not be easily mechanized. Furthermore, land had become very expensive since the area was pioneered in the early 1950's; it would be difficult for any of his sons to farm their own lot in the future.

Domingos and his family have prospered on the Transamazon. Their lot is by the principal axis of the highway, so they are rarely cut off from the main market in Altamira. Most of the family worked hard on the lot from 6:30 in the morning until sunset every day of the week except Sunday. The land is located only 1 km from their home in the *agrovila.*

A diversified crop base and a relatively fertile soil have also contributed to the success of the *gaúcho* family in their new environment. By 1979 Domingos had 2 ha of cacao, 10 ha of bananas, and 30 ha of well-formed pasture. The 1978 income of $10,927 was derived from the sale of cattle (46%), cheese (9%), cacao beans (8%), eggs (7%), and rice (6%). The family has built a brick house at the entrance to Nova Fronteira, where they have installed a small general store and bar. Profits from the sale of drinks and general provisions account for a fifth of the family's income. On the weekly trip to town to buy merchandise, Domingos charges passengers $1.80 for the 80-km journey to Altamira. Freight and passenger fees, some 5 percent of the household income, more than pay for the gasoline costs.

The 100-ha lot belonging to Domingos has increased in value 117 times in eight years, but he has no intention of selling. Through careful management, cattle are likely to remain the mainstay of the family's income. The lush pasture grows on rich soil and is regularly weeded. Domingos has invested in fencing in order to rotate pastures. In this manner, the relatively flat pastures are unlikely to be overgrazed or become eroded.

Domingos has acquired four lots for his sons. Ismar, a twenty-four-year-old bachelor, is the owner of the adjacent parcels that formerly belonged to João and Bento. He already owns fifteen head of cattle and plans to expand the area of pasture to at least 100 ha on the two lots. Elido, twenty-seven years old and also single, cultivates a *terra roxa* parcel by the margin of the Transamazon. Vilmar occupies a recently purchased *terra roxa* plot close to the *agrovila*. The other three sons opted to study. The eldest, Olzeno, works as an agricultural extension agent in the territory of Roraima. Ildo is studying to be a lawyer in Manaus. Nilson is finishing high school in Belém and wants to go on to University.

Domingos has helped relatives become established in the vicinity of Nova Fronteira. A sister and a brother of Domingos's wife have moved from Rio Grande do Sul with their respective families to settle on lots within a 6-km radius of the community. The proximity of family is of immense psychological help, especially while adjusting to a new life. The various families help each other with labor, equipment, and the occasional loan.

Cassiano, a brother-in-law of Domingos, arrived at Nova Fronteira in August 1972, in a rented truck. Of Italian descent, Cassiano had spent most of his life as a farmer in the vicinity of Tenente Portela. During the five years previous to coming to the Transamazon, the family of nine children had lived in the region of Santo Antonio in Paraná. In the latter state, Cassiano cultivated a 3-ha plot of *terra roxa*, and as a member of SABADI, he sold most of the maize and soybean crop to the co-op. The family heard about the Transamazon scheme on the local radio and decided to leave for a piece of land thirty-three times as large at very reasonable terms. Cassiano arrived on the Transamazon with a total of $2,300 in savings.

Cassiano and his family soon improved their standard of living. They obtained a lot of *terra roxa* by the Transamazon and built a home there. Cassiano recognized the reddish soil as fertile *(terra gorda)*. The industrious family worked long hours in the fields and erected a warehouse to store crops. By 1977 Cassiano was able to buy a new tractor on credit, which enabled him to increase his effective planting area by pulling out tree stumps and by ploughing under weeds. In 1978 the household revenue totaled $5,589. Cacao beans, rice, and kidney beans were the most important sources of income for the family, accounting for 80 percent, 21 percent, and 5 percent respectively of the earnings for that year. Cassiano plans to greatly expand his 2-ha cacao plantation.

The family has suffered some severe setbacks in their new environment. A one-half-hectare plot of arabica coffee, containing 1,000 bushes of the *Mundo Novo* variety, has been abandoned to pests and second growth. The production of beans did not even satisfy domestic needs. One hectare of sugarcane remains unharvested after several years because of problems at the mill, 10 km away. Cassiano plans to destroy the cane field, a difficult and time-consuming task, so that he can plant bananas and cacao.

In 1978, 18 percent of the family income was spent on medical expenses. But health problems had a far more profound impact on the family than the statistic suggests. In August of that year, Carlos, the twenty-year-old son, was helping to clear forest on his father's lot when a tree fell in an unexpected direction; a branch pinned him to the ground and broke his ankle. He was first taken to a private clinic to have the leg set, then transferred to the Santo Agostinho hospital. After sixteen days of internment, the bone was not fusing properly and secondary infection had set in. Carlos was flown to Belém, where the ankle was reset. Two years later he still has not regained full use of that leg. A month after the mishap of Carlos, his mother, Vinilda, was returning home from town when the bus she was traveling in sped out of control while descending a hill. Vinilda and fifteen other passangers were pulled out of the wreckage in a gulley and taken to the FSESP hospital in Altamira. She suffered multiple lacerations and several broken bones. Although Vinilda was interned for only six days, she could hardly walk or do house chores for several months.

In spite of recent reverses, the family of Cassiano is relatively well-off, and they have no intention of moving. His eldest son, Versil, has acquired his own lot, also on *terra roxa*, only four kilometers away. His second oldest son, Jośe, has entered military service and may make a career in the army. Cassiano feels that the year-round growing season along the Transamazon is a great advantage. He is optimistic about the future.

The experience of the two families from the temperate South of Brazil indicate that neither a close familiarity with tropical plants nor prior exposure to a hot climate are necessary prerequisites for success in a pioneer rainforest environment. Large families with several older sons to help with agricultural tasks and entrepreneurial skills are more helpful than an intimate knowledge of forest resources. In the absence of a large family, it is necessary to have substantial working captial to hire labor on a permanent basis.

The timber industry

An important objective of the Transamazon scheme, that of providing access to natural resources, such as timber, has also met with mixed results. Most of the trees felled along the highway are burned in fields. The loss of lumber is not entirely a waste; the ashes supply nutrients for crops, and the strewn logs help check soil erosion. The heterogeneity of the forest is an obstacle to the lumber trade because the desirable species are usually widely scattered. The high cost of transporting boles to sawmills is another reason why the timber industry is poorly developed along the Transamazon. Diesel oil costs thirty cents a liter, and a heavily laden truck will travel only three or four kilometers on one liter of the fuel.

Only eight sawmills have been built along the Marabá–Itaituba stretch of the highway.[1] Most are small and privately owned,

1. Sawmills along the Marabá–Itaituba stretch of the Transamazon are located as follows: Itupiranga, at the end of the side road leading east from km 42 Marabá–Altamira; Serraria Monte Azul, at km 67 Marabá–Altamira; Pacajá, at km 280 Marabá–Altamira; Serraria IMPAR in Altamira; *agrópolis* Brasil Novo, km 46

and operate by diesel power. Sawdust and wood scraps, which could be used to fire boilers, litter the surroundings of the mills. The most valuable woods, such as mahogany *(Swietenia macrophylla)* and cedar *(Cedrela odorata)*, have been mostly logged out within a 15-km zone on either side of the Transamazon. Sawmills are now working chiefly with cumaru *(Dipteryx odorata)*, pau d'arco *(Tabebuia* spp.), tatajuba *(Bagassa guianensis)*, jatobá, orelha de macaco *(Enterolobium schomburgkii)*, jarana *(Holopyxidium jarana)*, sapucaia *(Lecythis usitata)*, and mata mata *(Eschweilera* sp.).

Colonists are offered very little for timber trees growing on their lots. The price paid to a settler ranges from $11 to $17 per standing tree, even for 50-meter-high canopy emergents. Only 8 of the 155 colonists interviewed claimed to have sold trees in 1978. The 8 settlers received an average of $166 (s = 156) each from the sale of boles, which accounted for 0.2 percent of the total income of the colonists sampled.

The Transamazon will help to provide access to 216,000 ha of forest in the Tocantins valley, which will be flooded when the Tucuruí dam closes in 1982. The government has opened up the area to large companies, which are expected to extract timber worth $1.5 billion. Some of the wood will be logged from Transamazon lots after the settlers have been removed. INCRA has not yet decided where the displaced colonists will be accommodated. The Transamazon will have to be rerouted between Marabá and Pacajá; the detour will open up new areas for exploitation by the lumber industry.

The timber trade along the Transamazon is hardly benefiting settlers. In some cases, it is likely to prove detrimental to the long-term interests of colonists. Although federal law prohibits the cutting down of Brazil-nut trees because of the valuable nuts, enforcement is lax. Some of the sawmills purchase the fine timber trees for as little as $14 each. Mill operators claim that they

---

Altamira–Itaituba, formerly run by INCRA but now operated by COTRIJUI; km 112 Altamira–Itaituba, operated by COTRIJUI; *rurópolis* Medicilandia at km 150 Itaituba–Altamira, run by INCRA; Serraria Itapacurazinho, km 25 of the Itaituba–Altamira section of the highway.

are allowed to remove a Brazil-nut tree if it is dead or dying. Colonists do not usually fell the trees, but they are often damaged when the fields burn (Fig. 24). A few dry or scorched leaves are sufficient to condemn a specimen of *Bertholletia excelsa*.

Brazil nuts are a far more important source of income for Transamazon colonists than timber, especially along the Marabá–Altamira stretch. The nuts, gathered from the forest floor, earned nearly four times as much income for settlers than the sale of wood. A mature *Bertholletia excelsa* can annually produce 100 liters of unshelled nuts, worth $28, twice as much as the trunk can be sold for. The trees only fruit from December to April; thereafter, settlers in financial difficulties may be tempted to sell one of their *castanheiras*. By so doing, settlers deprive themselves of a long-term source of income and an important dietary supplement. The nuts contain 15 percent protein (FAO, 1970).

The mining industry

The Transamazon has not created an important avenue for the extraction of rich mineral deposits. The Serra dos Carajás iron ore field is located only 140 km southwest from Marabá, but it has not been linked to the highway. It is one of the largest finds of the mineral; reserves are estimated at 17 billion tons with an iron content of at least 66 percent. The ore will be transported 900 km by rail to Itaqui, a deepwater port recently built near São Luis in Maranhão.[2] At Itaqui, the ore will be loaded into oceangoing vessels for export.

The highway has facilitated the flow of itinerant miners, mostly from Maranhão, to alluvial gold deposits in the Tapajós watershed. Several buses daily unload hundreds of the miners in Itaituba and Jacareacanga and at a small settlement that has

2. The Serra dos Carajás iron ore field was to be exploited by a joint venture between United States Steel Corporation and the Brazilian-owned Companhia Vale do Rio Doce. In 1976 United States Steel pulled out of the agreement, and the mining program has been delayed. A glut of iron ore on the world market was probably a major reason why United States Steel withdrew from the operation. Japanese companies are studying the possibility of joining Companhia Vale do Rio Doce at Serra dos Carajás.

sprung up at the border between the states of Pará and Amazonas. The recent steep rise of the price of the precious metal in international markets has spurred the movement of *garimpeiros* into Amazonia in search of a fortune. Most of the gold is flown, as contraband, in small air taxis to Santarém and then by larger aircraft to São Paulo and the Northeast.

Only one company, Mineração Taboca, transports minerals along the Transamazon. The firm is a subsidiary of Paranapanema, which built the Prainha–Humaitá portion of the highway.[3] Mineração Taboca has built a side road leading south from km 156 of the Humaitá–Prainha stretch of the Transamazon to extract cassiterite, containing at least 60 percent tin, from the 40,000-ha São Francisco field and the nearby Igarapé Preto deposit, which extends over 30,000 ha. The 1978 production from the fields reached 1,100 and 800 tons respectively, representing a quarter of Amazonia's tin ore supply for that year. The ore is washed, packed in 50-kg sacks, and transported by truck to São Paulo. The journey normally takes eight days; delays are frequent along the unasphalted stretches between the mines and Humaitá, and from Porto Velho to Cuiabá. A regularly scheduled bus takes workers on the 416-km trip between Humaitá and mining concessions.

Mining is thus only an important activity in the extreme western portion of the highway. The Transamazon does not slice across any major mineral deposits. The road is not paved with precious metals or priceless gems, as was depicted in advertisements and fanciful articles during the construction phase of the highway. Mining companies do not provide a significant souce of employment for Transamazon families. Settlers sometimes leave their lots for extended periods to pan for gold in the region of Jacareacanga or along the Cuiabá–Santarém highway. Few return with any significant wealth; most of the profits go to middlemen. In the meantime, agricultural productivity suffers.

3. Paranapanema owns several mines in the territory of Rondônia and adjacent areas of Amazonas state. The company accounted for 46 percent of the 8,000 tons of cassiterite mined in the Brazilian Amazon in 1978 (Anon., 1980b). Prior to 1970, the tin ore was extracted by itinerant miners; thereafter the government outlawed independant *garimpeiros* in cassiterite areas because they were allegedly using wasteful methods of extraction.

The cost and prospects of the Transamazon scheme

The substantial investment of federal funds in the Transamazon project has thus far brought few benefits. The Brazilian government spent $131 million just to build the highway (Moran, 1976:81). Since then considerable sums have been spent on infrastructure, salaries of government employees, equipment, and road repairs. The task of highway maintenance is contracted out to private companies under the supervision of DNER (Fig. 39). By 1975, the Transamazon scheme had cost the Brazilians about $300 million (Mahar, 1978:32). I estimate that the figure had swollen to at least $500 million by 1980. Some $65,000 has thus been spent for each family settled by INCRA.

The federal government never attempted to justify the Transamazon project with a cost-benefit analysis. The highway was a symbol of Brazil's self-confidence and optimism. Brazil won the world soccer cup in 1970 for the third time, and a Brazilian, Emerson Fittipaldi, was a superstar of the international formula-one automobile race track. The gross national product was growing at 11 percent a year, the highest rate in the world. Finally, the Transamazon was conceived in an era of cheap energy. Brazil paid only $1.74 for a barrel of crude oil in 1970.

The economic picture is now quite different. The growth of the national economy has slowed by half. Inflation, only 15 percent when the scheme was announced, is now in excess of 100 percent a year. The expansionist economic policies of the early 1970s may have to be trimmed. Brazil consumes 1.1 million barrels of crude oil a day and is forced to import 85 percent of her needs. The price of imported oil has increased many times in the decade since work began on the Transamazon. As of February 1980, the country had to pay an average of $28 per barrel of crude, and the price goes up every few months.[4]

In 1978 Brazil paid $4 billion for petroleum imports. By 1979 the cost had climbed to $7 billion. In 1980 the import bill for oil

4. The major suppliers of petroleum to Brazil are as follows: Iraq, 57%; Saudi Arabia, 18%; Kuwait, 7%; Iran, 5% (Anon., 1980c). The 1980 Iran-Iraq war produced a shortfall in petroleum supplies to Brazil, thus underlining the country's vulnerability as a major oil importer.

Figure 39. Regrading the Transamazon after the rainy season in 1974

rose to $12 billion and consumed 55 percent of export earnings.[5] With a 1980 foreign debt of $52 billion, approximately $470 per Brazilian citizen, the country can ill afford to embark on grandiose development schemes without maximizing the economic benefit for as large a segment of the population as possible.

The Transamazon settlement scheme has proved too costly to serve as a model for other developing regions. Even in Brazil, INCRA has not adopted the expensive and cumbersome *urbanismo-rural* pattern in other colonization projects. In Rondônia, for example, lot size and services are similar to those along the Transamazon, but there are no *agrovilas, agrópoli,* or *rurópoli*. In spite of the modifications in settlement plans, INCRA is still being criticized for the dubious economic performance of most of its colonization efforts (Wesche, 1978).

In response to the high cost and disappointing results of government-run colonization projects, emphasis has shifted to

5. Sources: *Bank of London and South America Review*, vol. 13 (7), p. 411, (1979); vol. 14 (4), p. 243, (1980); *The Economist*, 24 November 1979, p. 90; *Veja*, 26 December 1979, p. 156; *Veja*, 12 December 1979, p. 126.

settlement of pioneer areas of Amazonia by private companies, particularly in northern Mato Grosso. Near São Felix on the Xingu River, INCRA has sold 400,000 ha to Andrade Gutierrez, a construction company that has worked on the Northern Perimeter highway. The forested parcel, acquired for $1.25 a hectare, is to be subdivided into lots for small-scale farmers.[6] It remains to be seen how committed the firms are to implanting flourishing agricultural colonies. Tax incentives, mineral deposits, timber reserves, and land speculation may be motivating the interest of the companies in settlement projects.

It is a mistake to open up substantial areas of the interfluves of Amazonia for settlement by either the government or private concerns (Skillings and Tcheyan, 1979). The large influx of land-seekers has contributed little to the economic development of the region. Considering the potential dangers of regional or even global climatic change as a result of accelerated deforestation, as well as the problems of erosion and access to markets, most of the *terra firme* should remain under permanent plant cover.

The uplands of Amazonia are better left to parks, nature and forestry reserves, silviculture, mining, and Indian territories. The Amazon forest contains many potential drug plants and candidates for crop domestication that may be forever lost if the undisciplined land rush continues (Schultes and Swain, 1976; Myers, 1979). The North should not be viewed as a covenient depository for the excess population from other regions. If the problems of land reform in the Northeast were to be tackled with more vigor, then the outflow of people would be reduced. SUDENE has favored industrial projects, which have created few jobs. Irrigation schemes in the region have displaced more people than they have settled (Hall, 1978). A restructuring of priorities, with more emphasis on an equitable distribution of the land, as well as integrated agricultural development, would provide greater employment opportunities.

It seems unlikely that the flow of migrants to Amazonia will slow, at least in the short term. Powerful political and economic forces will surely continue to resist effective land reform. Even in the Amazon basin, government policies have mostly favored

6. *Veja*, 13 February 1980, p. 22.

the establishment of latifundia, principally for cattle raising by companies from São Paulo and multinational corporations. Between 1965 and 1977, for example, SUDAM approved fiscal incentives for the establishment of 355 ranches in the North, covering 7.8 million ha (Ianni, 1979:80). Many of the cattle operations have displaced preexisting settlers, but have offered them few employment opportunities. The projected permanent labor need for the approved livestock projects is only 17,119, an average of 48 persons per ranch. The expelled peasants generally move on to cut forest in seemingly unused areas, invade Indian reserves, or drift to the peripheral slums of urban centers.

Even if land was distributed more equitably in the Amazon and the Northeast, the current of migration to the North would still remain strong. In Paraná and Rio Grande do Sul, minifundia and the high cost of land are propelling a significant flow of peasants to Amazonia, especially to Rondônia and northern Mato Grosso. The flux of spontaneous settlers reaching Rondônia is not known with certainty, but it is estimated at approximately 10,000 families a year.[7] The focus of settlement has now shifted to southwest Amazonia, aided in part by the Cuiabá–Porto Velho highway and the relative abundance of fertile *terra roxa*. Vila Rondônia, a village of 1,200 inhabitants in 1970, grew to a thriving town of 160,000 within seven years.

To accommodate the continued stream of settlers into Amazonia, attention could be focused on the potential of floodplain areas for colonization. It is no accident that, historically, most of the region's population has been concentrated along rivers, especially the silt-laden water courses. Sternberg (1956) has documented the ecological advantages of the *várzea* for human settlement. The floodplains of the Amazon, Madeira, Purus, and Juruá offer particularly favorable sites for settlement because of the relatively fertile alluvial soils—which are annually replenished with nutrients during the floods—and the abundance of fish. Although the floodplains occupy less than 2 percent of the basin, they nevertheless cover some 64,000 sq. km, almost twice the size of the Netherlands (Sternberg, 1975).

The sinuous margin between the uplands and floodplain areas

7. *Veja*, 26 March 1980, p. 46.

(várzea) offers several advantages for agricultural colonization. Buildings can be erected along the upland bluff, thereby escaping the annual inundation. Perennial crops, such as manioc, bananas, pepper, and cacao, can be planted on *terra firme,* while annuals, such as rice, beans, squash, maize, sweet potato *(Ipomoea batatas),* and jute *(Corchorus* spp.), can be grown and harvested on the *várzea* during the low-water period. The yearly surging of the rivers over their floodplains destroys weeds and kills crop pests and pathogens.

As the waters recede settlers have access to a clean planting surface. Soil erosion is not a serious problem on the *várzea,* since the terrain is relatively flat. In the case of the Juruá and Purus, the rivers are constantly shifting their channels, thereby creating a broad expanse of oxbow lakes. Along meandering rivers, the division of the floodplain into individual lots is likely to create problems as some parcels are undermined by the restless water courses. Other plots are likely to be eventually stranded some distance from the river. In such areas, communally held property, as once practiced by the now extinct Indian tribes, would provide the necessary flexibility to compensate for the constantly shifting distribution of land and water.

The proximity of a perennial source of water is another important advantage of settlement along the edge between *terra firme* and the *várzea.* With a modest investment, unlimited supplies of treated water could be piped to market centers, thereby reducing the incidence of enteric diseases. Another compelling argument in favor of colonization on upland bluffs near rivers is the relatively low cost of water transportation. In the decade since construction began on the Transamazon, the cost of gasoline in Brazil, when compensated for inflation, has increased dramatically. In early 1981 Brazilians were paying the equivalent of over $3 a gallon for the product, one of the highest prices in the world.

Although the *várzea* offers a more suitable environment for colonization, an unrestrained land rush to the riverine areas of the basin could trigger serious ecological consequences. A massive, incessant flow of people onto the floodplains of Amazonia could jeopardize the productivity of fisheries. Several fish species, important to both commerce and subsistence, such as tambaquí *(Colossoma macropomum)* and pacu (species of *Metynnis, Mylossoma,* and *Myleus),* depend on fruits from floodplain forests for the bulk of their nourishment (Goulding, 1980; Smith, 1981). If extensive tracts of *várzea* forest are leveled for agriculture, the population of tambaquí, pacu, and other species are likely to decline. Fish are an important source of dietary protein in the regional diet. Large-scale alteration of floodplain vegetation could lead to widespread malnutrition.

Most state-organized colonization schemes in tropical South America have been unsuccessful (Nelson, 1973). Settlement, whether in floodplain areas or on *terra firme,* would most likely benefit from a minimum of bureaucratic planning and control. Government agencies could issue land titles, facilitate access to credit, and operate schools, medical posts, and hospitals. The marketing of produce should be left to private concerns or co-ops. One of the few successful planned settlement schemes in Brazil was organized by a private company in northern Paraná between 1925 and the 1950s (Katzman, 1978).

No blueprint for Amazon colonization schemes is offered here. Problems associated with the Transamazon effort have been discussed, and some broad suggestions for settlement in floodplain areas are offered. Proposed colonization zones need to be studied individually as to ecological and market conditions, as well as the cultural background of the settlers. Only general guidelines should be drawn up; let the people solve as many problems as possible by themselves. The Transamazon serves as an example of the pitfalls inherent in paternalistic schemes devised in offices far removed from the scene of implementation.

Appendix 1. Monthly Temperatures, Rainfall, and Relative Humidity for Marabá, 1973–1978

Month/ Year	Mean Temp. (°C)	Max. Temp. (°C)	Min. Temp. (°C)	Precip. (mm)	Max. P 24 Hrs. (mm)	Relative Humidity (%)
Jan.	26.2	33.3	20.1	223.3	47.5	85
Feb.	25.8	32.0	20.3	275.7	68.0	88
Mar.	25.9	33.0	20.9	284.6	53.5	90
Apr.	25.6	32.2	20.3	294.9	87.4	90
May	25.8	32.4	19.8	121.2	41.5	87
June	25.8	33.0	19.4	70.5	42.0	85
July	25.3	34.0	17.8	27.6	8.9	86
Aug.	25.9	36.0	16.0	16.6	7.5	80
Sept.	25.9	34.0	17.0	79.0	30.9	80
Oct.	25.8	34.2	18.0	144.2	25.0	83
Nov.	25.9	33.2	18.4	137.1	36.0	84
Dec.	24.7	32.2	17.4	300.3	76.0	88
1973	25.7			1,975.0		85
Jan.	24.3	32.4	16.7	230.9	63.0	91
Feb.	24.3	31.8	17.1	482.2	157.5	93
Mar.	24.2	32.3	17.8	486.0	111.7	94
Apr.	24.6	32.0	18.0	321.0	64.0	92
May	25.3	32.2	17.6	55.7	30.0	87
June	25.9	32.9	19.4	18.4	12.0	84
July	25.6	33.8	17.1	4.1	3.8	84
Aug.	26.3	35.1	18.4	4.1	3.5	84
Sept.	26.2	38.1	21.1	38.1	15.0	90
Oct.	26.1	33.9	18.5	70.8	27.0	88
Nov.	26.0	33.9	19.0	89.7	52.0	90
Dec.	25.1	32.3	18.5	221.0	39.0	92
1974	25.3			2,022.0		89
Jan.	26.0	33.1	—	386.6	124.7	95
Feb.	26.0	31.3	—	380.6	99.0	92
Mar.	26.2	31.1	—	466.0	140.6	95
Apr.	26.6	32.3	—	417.8	80.0	96
May	26.4	32.3	—	116.6	30.3	96
June	26.9	33.5	—	52.5	19.5	92
July	26.1	32.7	—	65.6	28.0	87
Aug.	27.7	33.9	—	11.9	11.9	83
Sept.	27.7	33.9	—	60.0	60.0	84
Oct.	26.0	33.9	—	127.4	70.0	83
Nov.	26.0	33.9	19.1	142.5	79.0	84
Dec.	25.6	32.5	19.1	161.2	62.2	92
1975	26.4			2,388.7		90

Appendix 1. Monthly Temperatures, Rainfall, and Relative Humidity for Marabá, 1973–1978 (continued)

Month/ Year	Mean Temp. (°C)	Max. Temp. (°C)	Min. Temp. (°C)	Precip. (mm)	Max. P 24 Hrs. (mm)	Relative Humidity (%)
Jan.	25.2	31.7	20.5	216.2	64.0	88
Feb.	25.1	32.1	20.5	382.4	62.6	90
Mar.	25.9	32.3	19.7	374.9	114.0	87
Apr.	25.9	32.1	20.6	271.3	100.7	88
May	26.2	33.1	20.6	96.4	82.4	85
June	25.5	33.4	18.5	2.2	2.2	75
July	25.8	34.1	18.6	11.6	9.4	74
Aug.	26.4	34.5	19.0	1.8	1.8	75
Sept.	26.4	34.7	20.1	27.2	10.4	79
Oct.	26.6	33.5	21.0	201.7	124.5	82
Nov.	25.6	32.8	19.6	189.2	63.5	84
Dec.	26.2	33.1	19.0	198.2	40.3	89
1976	25.9			1,973.1		83
Jan.	25.3	32.1	20.4	272.8	40.0	88
Feb.	25.2	32.3	20.1	453.5	104.7	89
Mar.	26.0	32.5	20.7	299.8	42.3	87
Apr.	26.0	33.6	21.7	458.3	102.0	87
May	26.0	33.1	19.5	166.2	39.2	86
June	26.1	32.5	20.4	28.8	7.2	83
July	26.1	34.1	19.2	39.7	33.0	79
Aug.	26.8	35.0	19.0	12.1	11.8	76
Sept.	27.0	34.3	19.0	33.3	17.6	—
Oct.	26.6	33.5	19.0	81.3	23.3	79
Nov.	26.7	33.5	18.7	60.2	26.0	78
Dec.	26.3	33.6	18.0	258.8	106.0	80
1977	26.1			2,164.8		
Jan.	25.8	33.2	20.0	422.2	140.7	83
Feb.	26.1	32.8	22.0	321.9	60.0	85
Mar.	25.8	32.6	21.0	364.0	64.2	84
Apr.	26.4	33.3	21.7	310.1	50.4	82
May	26.3	32.7	21.6	134.7	45.5	82
June	25.8	32.5	19.5	33.8	14.1	79
July	25.8	33.7	20.0	26.4	9.2	80
Aug.	26.3	35.2	19.0	0.0	0.0	80
Sept.	26.7	35.1	20.5	49.0	23.2	84
Oct.	26.3	33.5	21.0	87.5	27.8	83

Month/ Year	Mean Temp. (°C)	Max. Temp. (°C)	Min. Temp. (°C)	Precip. (mm)	Max. P 24 Hrs. (mm)	Relative Humidity (%)
Nov.	26.6	34.3	19.5	133.2	40.4	82
Dec.	25.5	32.6	20.0	215.3	57.9	85
1978	26.1			2,098.1		82

Source: Departamento Nacional de Meteorologia, Belém.

Appendix 2. Monthly Temperatures, Rainfall, and Relative Humidity for Altamira, 1973–1978

Month/ Year	Mean Temp. (°C)	Max. Temp. (°C)	Min. Temp. (°C)	Precip. (mm)	Max. P 24 Hrs. (mm)	Relative Humidity (%)
Jan.	25.8	32.2	21.9	220.8	27.4	85
Feb.	25.4	31.7	21.3	305.2	74.2	89
Mar.	25.4	31.5	21.8	336.8	76.0	90
Apr.	25.4	32.2	21.1	373.4	63.1	89
May	25.6	31.2	21.5	292.7	53.8	89
June	25.7	31.9	21.4	142.1	33.1	88
July	25.3	32.2	20.0	286.8	48.4	86
Aug.	25.8	33.2	19.8	26.0	9.4	83
Sept.	26.5	33.2	21.0	29.6	7.5	81
Oct.	26.4	33.6	20.9	183.7	73.5	81
Nov.	26.6	33.3	21.8	59.5	25.0	81
Dec.	25.3	32.7	20.3	267.5	70.5	86
1973	25.8			2,524.1		86
Jan.	25.1	31.3	20.6	306.6	70.0	88
Feb.	24.9	31.6	21.2	391.0	54.2	88
Mar.	24.6	30.8	20.5	682.9	107.0	90
Apr.	25.1	30.7	21.4	420.7	78.8	90
May	25.0	30.6	21.0	280.0	57.0	90
June	25.1	32.3	20.0	92.8	29.8	86
July	24.0	31.9	16.4	31.3	20.2	82
Aug.	25.6	33.1	19.4	20.3	12.0	84
Sept.	25.8	32.5	20.2	83.2	41.0	84
Oct.	26.2	33.4	20.4	72.0	26.0	82
Nov.	26.3	32.6	21.4	63.0	29.4	82
Dec.	25.4	31.5	19.6	232.4	90.0	86
1974	25.2			2,676.2		86
Jan.	25.0	31.5	20.5	417.3	113.0	88
Feb.	24.9	30.6	19.9	299.7	59.0	88
Mar.	25.0	31.1	21.1	395.6	45.4	88
Apr.	25.5	30.9	21.5	257.3	32.0	88
May	25.5	31.2	21.4	307.2	55.1	86
June	25.4	31.3	20.5	204.6	36.0	85
July	24.7	32.1	18.2	78.9	26.7	85
Aug.	25.7	32.6	17.7	27.4	8.2	82
Sept.	26.4	34.3	21.0	60.0	38.0	79
Oct.	26.4	33.6	20.2	44.9	15.3	80
Nov.	26.2	33.0	21.1	145.8	65.3	83
Dec.	25.7	32.5	20.8	170.4	46.5	84
1975	25.3			2,409.1		85

Month/ Year	Mean Temp. (°C)	Max. Temp. (°C)	Min. Temp. (°C)	Precip. (mm)	Max. P 24 Hrs. (mm)	Relative Humidity (%)
Jan.	25.0	31.8	20.7	317.2	59.6	86
Feb.	24.9	31.4	20.6	489.3	81.4	88
Mar.	25.6	31.9	21.1	375.9	59.5	88
Apr.	25.7	31.7	21.7	274.8	43.4	87
May	25.9	31.9	21.5	194.1	87.7	85
June	25.7	32.2	19.4	55.8	13.6	83
July	25.4	32.4	19.1	112.9	54.0	82
Aug.	26.0	32.9	18.9	10.8	4.7	80
Sept.	26.5	35.6	20.2	21.8	12.2	75
Oct.	26.8	33.8	21.9	63.5	30.6	78
Nov.	26.4	32.9	20.0	27.0	23.0	80
Dec.	26.4	32.7	20.6	177.8	86.0	82
1976	25.9			2,120.9		83
Jan.	25.2	31.5	21.7	466.2	84.2	87
Feb.	25.0	31.4	21.0	427.2	64.3	89
Mar.	25.3	31.1	21.4	500.1	61.1	89
Apr.	25.6	31.5	21.2	286.3	37.2	88
May	25.7	31.7	21.2	149.5	19.0	86
June	25.5	32.3	20.3	151.8	66.7	85
July	25.5	32.5	19.4	59.9	23.5	81
Aug.	26.3	34.1	19.4	34.2	24.9	79
Sept.	27.0	34.7	21.0	14.7	9.2	77
Oct.	27.1	34.1	21.1	26.9	11.3	78
Nov.	27.2	34.0	21.4	14.7	12.1	75
Dec.	26.6	33.3	21.9	139.0	39.0	80
1977	26.0			2,270.5		83
Jan.	25.5	32.0	21.5	378.7	46.9	88
Feb.	26.0	32.2	21.6	290.9	56.6	89
Mar.	25.4	32.1	21.1	404.0	86.4	88
Apr.	25.7	32.2	21.5	186.7	28.5	88
May	25.8	31.2	21.4	244.4	73.2	88
June	25.6	32.2	20.1	83.6	35.3	85
July	25.6	32.2	20.4	109.9	28.3	83
Aug.	25.5	34.0	18.5	51.2	35.3	80
Sept.	26.8	33.7	20.7	7.0	2.8	78
Oct.	26.6	34.2	20.4	91.7	36.4	78
Nov.	27.1	33.6	21.1	20.8	11.8	78
Dec.	26.2	33.1	21.2	240.3	84.0	85
1978	26.0			2,109.2		84

Source: Departamento Nacional de Meteorologia, Belém.

Appendix 3. Rice Yields along the Transamazon in 1978

Harvested Yield Kg/ha	Hectares Planted	Soil	Vegetation Cleared
3,538	3.9	Red podzolic	Forest
3,444	0.9	Terra roxa	Forest
3,077	13.0	Terra roxa	Forest
2,800	5.0	Terra roxa	Forest
2,778	1.8	Latosol	Forest
2,708	12.0	Terra roxa	Forest
2,702	14.8	Yellow latosol	Forest
2,592	2.7	Yellow latosol	2-yr. 2nd growth
2,520	5.0	Terra roxa	Forest
2,500	15.0	Terra roxa	Forest
2,500	3.6	Yellow latosol	Forest
2,500	0.6	Podzolic	Forest
2,500	0.9	Yellow latosol	Forest
2,392	6.0	Yellow latosol	Forest
2,389	4.5	Podzolic	4-yr. 2nd growth
2,375	0.8	Terra roxa	4-yr. 2nd growth
2,244	12.7	Yellow podzolic	Forest
2,222	45.0	Red latosol	1-yr. 2nd growth
2,222	1.8	Yellow podzolic	2-yr. 2nd growth
2,200	5.0	Red-yellow latosol	Forest
2,200	15.0	Latosol	Forest
2,143	7.0	Terra roxa	Forest
2,125	4.8	Yellow podzolic	2-yr. 2nd growth
2,115	13.0	Yellow latosol	Forest
2,000	3.6	Podzolic	3-yr. 2nd growth
2,000	2.0	Terra roxa	4-yr. 2nd growth
2,000	4.8	Yellow latosol	5-yr. 2nd growth
1,900	5.0	Terra roxa	Forest
1,875	4.8	Podzolic	Forest
1,832	11.0	Terra roxa	Forest
1,800	5.0	Terra roxa	Forest
1,800	4.0	Red-yellow podzolic	Forest
1,800	4.0	Yellow latosol	4-yr. 2nd growth
1,800	0.5	Terra roxa	1-yr. 2nd growth
1,770	6.1	Yellow latosol	5-yr. 2nd growth
1,765	8.5	Red-yellow podzolic	Forest
1,740	5.0	Terra roxa	Forest
1,667	3.6	Yellow latosol	Forest
1,667	1.8	Yellow latosol	6-yr. 2nd growth
1,656	16.0	Yellow latosol	Forest
1,620	5.0	Podzolic	10-yr. 2nd growth
1,600	10.0	Terra roxa	Forest
1,600	10.0	Yellow latosol	Forest

Harvested Yield Kg/ha	Hectares Planted	Soil	Vegetation Cleared
1,600	10.0	Pale latosol	Forest
1,559	1.7	Red-yellow podzolic	Forest
1,543	7.0	Brown loam	4-yr. 2nd growth
1,527	5.5	Yellow latosol	2-yr. 2nd growth
1,500	5.0	Terra roxa	2-yr. 2nd growth
1,500	8.0	Yellow podzolic	2-yr. 2nd growth
1,500	10.0	Terra roxa	Forest
1,500	15.0	Yellow latosol	Forest
1,500	0.6	Terra roxa	Forest
1,500	6.0	Red-yellow podzolic	Forest
1,458	2.4	Yellow latosol	1-yr. 2nd growth
1,445	20.0	Latosol	Forest
1,400	3.0	Podzolic	1-yr. 2nd growth
1,380	10.0	Terra roxa	Forest
1,375	4.8	Red-yellow podzolic	3-yr. 2nd growth
1,354	4.8	Red-brown grumosol	Forest
1,350	8.0	Podzolic	Forest
1,333	3.6	Yellow latosol	Forest
1,333	12.1	Yellow podzolic	Forest
1,319	9.1	Terra roxa	Forest
1,250	12.0	Yellow latosol	3-yr. 2nd growth
1,204	5.4	Yellow podozolic	3-yr. 2nd growth
1,200	5.0	Yellow latosol	2-yr. 2nd growth
1,200	5.0	Terra roxa	Forest
1,200	7.5	Podzolic	Forest
1,200	2.5	Red latosol	1-yr. 2nd growth
1,150	10.0	Yellow latosol	2-yr. 2nd growth
1,137	9.5	Terra roxa	Forest
1,125	6.0	Yellow latosol	Forest
1,110	15.0	Terra roxa	Forest
1,083	3.0	Terra roxa	3-yr. 2nd growth
1,080	10.0	Yellow latosol	2-yr. 2nd growth
1,033	1.5	Yellow latosol	3-yr. 2nd growth
1,000	8.0	Podzol	Forest
1,000	3.0	Yellow podzolic	3-yr. 2nd growth
1,000	10.0	Yellow podzolic	Forest
960	5.0	Yellow latosol	6-yr. 2nd growth
917	12.0	Yellow latosol	Forest
917	3.6	Yellow podzolic	1-yr. 2nd growth
911	14.0	Yellow latosol	Forest
908	22.0	Yellow latosol	1-yr. 2nd growth
900	5.0	Terra roxa	Forest
840	5.0	Yellow latosol	1-yr. 2nd growth

Appendix 3. Rice Yields along the Transamazon in 1978 (continued)

Harvested Yield Kg/ha	Hectares Planted	Soil	Vegetation Cleared
840	5.0	Red-yellow podozolic	Forest
833	0.6	Red latosol	3-yr. 2nd growth
720	5.0	Yellow latosol	2-yr. 2nd growth
700	3.0	Yellow latosol	2-yr. 2nd growth
700	5.0	Yellow latosol	Forest
600	15.0	Yellow latosol	3-yr. 2nd growth
547	64.0	Yellow latosol	Forest
515	48.5	Podzolic	5-yr. 2nd growth
480	1.5	Yellow podzolic	6-yr. 2nd growth
458	12.0	Yellow latosol	1-yr. 2nd growth
200	5.0	Terra roxa	Forest

Appendix 4. Plants Used for Medicinal Purposes along the Transamazon

Common name(s)	Scientific name(s)	Family	Habitat	For treatment of
Abacate	*Persea americana*	Lauraceae	Cultivated	Kidneys, liver, headache, dysentery
Abacaxi	*Ananas comosus*	Bromeliaceae	Cultivated	Liver intoxication, dysentery
Abóbra	*Cucurbita* spp.	Cucurbitaceae	Cultivated	Worms
Agrião	*Spilanthes acmella**	Compositae	2nd growth	Liver, constipation
Alfavaca, mangericão, favaca	*Ocimum minimum**	Labiatae	Cultivated	Irritated eyes, headache, earache, upset nerves
Algodão	*Gossypium* spp.	Malvaceae	Cultivated	Colds, sore throat, malaria, lesions, pain, worms
Alho	*Allium sativum*	Alliaceae	Cultivated	Coughs, colds, worms
Amapá	*Hancornia amapa*	Apocynaceae	Forest	Fever
Amor crescido	*Portulaca pilosa*	Portulacaceae	Cultivated	Liver
Amoreira	*Morus nigra*	Moraceae	2nd growth	Colds
Andiroba	*Carapa guianensis*	Meliaceae	Forest	Malaria
Andiroba-jaruba	*Andira inermis*	Leguminosae	Forest	Worms
Anica	*Pilea microphylla**	Urticaceae	Cultivated	Bruises
Anoira	?		Forest	Dysentery
Apií	*Dorstenia reniformis*	Moraceae	Cultivated	Colds
Arruda	*Ruta graveolens**	Rutaceae	Cultivated	Intestinal disorders
Artemiso	*Ambrosia artemisiaefolia**	Compositae	Cultivated	Dysentery
Assafrão	*Curcuma* sp.*	Zingiberaceae	Cultivated	Measles, malaria
Babaçu	*Orbygnia martiana*	Palmae	Forest, 2nd growth	Kidneys, worms
Banana	*Musa* spp.	Musaceae	Cultivated	Constipation, dysentery
Barrote	?		Forest	Malaria
Batata purga, batatão	*Operculina alata*	Convolvulaceae	Cultivated	Dysentery, worms
Benjaminzeiro	*Ficus microcarpa*	Moraceae	Cultivated	Worms

Appendix 4. Plants Used for Medicinal Purposes along the Transamazon (continued)

Common name(s)	Scientific name(s)	Family	Habitat	For treatment of
Bergamota, mixirica	*Citrus aurantium*	Rutaceae	Cultivated	Colds
Bom dia	*Vinca rosea* var. *alba**	Apocynaceae	Cultivated	Menstrual bleeding
Bordo, boldo	*Coleus barbatus**	Labiatae	Cultivated	Headache, upset stomach, dysentery
Cabaçinha	*Luffa operculata*	Cucurbitaceae	Cultivated	Bruises, malaria
Cacao	*Theobroma cacao*	Sterculiaceae	Cultivated	Worms
Café	*Coffea arabica*	Rubiaceae	Cultivated	Dysentery
Cafërana	*Picrolemma pseudocoffea*	Simarubiaceae	Forest	Malaria
Cajá	*Spondias lutea*	Anacardiaceae	Forest	Dysentery
Caju	*Anacardium occidentale*	Anacardiaceae	Cultivated	Wounds, skin rashes, pain, snake bite, dysentery
Cana	*Saccharum officinarum*	Gramineae	Cultivated	Malaria
Canapu	*Physalis angulata**	Solanaceae	2nd growth	Malaria, kidneys, skin rashes
Capeba	*Potomorphe peltata**	Piperaceae	2nd growth	Liver, dysentery
Capim da saúde	*Andropogon* sp.*	Gramineae	Cultivated	Stomachache
Capim santo	*Cymbopogon* spp.	Gramineae	Cultivated	Upset stomach, cough, dysentery
Carrapicho de ovelha	*Acanthospermum australe**	Compositae	Cultivated	Colds
Castanhola	*Terminalia catappa*	Combretaceae	Cultivated	Malaria
Cebola	*Allium cepa*	Alliaceae	Cultivated	Worms
Cebola berrante	*Hippeastrum* sp.*	Amaryllidaceae	Cultivated	Worms
Chá preto	*Borreria verticillata**	Rubiaceae	Cultivated	Fever, liver, wounds
Chambá	*Lantana* sp.*	Verbenaceae	Cultivated	Dysentery, worms, bruises
Chicora, chicória, chicoré	*Cichorium intybus*	Compositae	Cultivated	Worms
Cidreira	*Lantana canescens**	Verbenaceae	Cultivated	Stomachache, eyeache, insomnia, dysentery, colds, fever, heart problems

Cipó escada	*Bauhinia* sp.	Leguminosae	Forest	Amebic dysentery, colds, asthma
Cocinho, cebolinha	*Eleutherina plicata**	Iridaceae	Cultivated	Dysentery, diarrhea
Coco	*Cocos nucifera*	Palmae	Cultivated	Inflammations, dysentery
Cordão de frade	*Leonotis nepetaefolia**	Labiatae	Cultivated	Headache, fever
Copaíba	*Copaifera multijuga*	Leguminosae	Forest	Wounds
Coronha	*Acacia farnesiana*	Leguminosae	Cultivated	Colds, heart
Crajiru	*Arrabidea chica**	Bignoniaceae	Cultivated	Malaria, hepatitis
Cumaru	*Dipteryx odorata*	Leguminosae	Forest	Pneumonia
Elixir paregórigo, elixe parigo	*Piper cavalcantei**	Piperaceae	Cultivated	Stomachache, dysentery
Embaúba	*Cecropia* spp.	Moraceae	2nd growth	Stomachache
Erva babosa	*Aloë* sp.	Liliaceae	Cultivated	Dysentery, worms, bruises
Erva doce	*Pimpinella anisum*	Umbelliferae	Cultivated	Dysentery, nausea, coughs
Erva mate	*Allamanda cathartica**	Apocynaceae	Cultivated	Fever, headache, pain in urinary tract
Eucalipto	*Eucalyptus* spp.	Myrtaceae	Cultivated	Colds, coughs, fever, stomachache
Ficatil	?*	Amaranthaceae	Cultivated	Stomachache, liver
Ficatilha	?*	Compositae	Cultivated	Liver, dysentery
Fedegoso	*Cassia occidentalis**	Leguminosae	2nd growth	Malaria, liver, colds, snakebite
Folha santa, fortuna	*Bryophyllum calycinum**	Crassulariaceae	Cultivated	Stomachache, headache, earache, embedded thorns
Fumo	*Nicotiana tabacum*	Solanaceae	Cultivated	Lesions
Gameleira	*Ficus* spp.	Moraceae	Forest	Worms
Gengibre	*Zingiber officinale*	Zingiberaceae	Cultivated	Colds
Gervão verde	*Stachytarpheta cayennensis**	Verbenaceae	2nd growth	Liver, bruises, worms, malaria, dysentery
Goiabeira	*Psidium guajava*	Myrtaceae	Cultivated	Stomachache, liver, worms, dysentery
Gurantã, cuelheiro	?		Forest	Malaria

Appendix 4. Plants Used for Medicinal Purposes along the Transamazon (continued)

Common name(s)	Scientific name(s)	Family	Habitat	For treatment of
Hortelão, hortelã	*Mentha* sp.	Labiatae	Cultivated	Stomachache, earache, fever, colds, worms, sore throat
Jambu, jambuzinho	*Wulffia stenoglossa**	Compositae	2nd growth	Liver, malaria
Janaúba	*Hymathantus sucuuba*	Apocynaceae	Forest	Malaria
Jatobá	*Hymenaea* spp.	Leguminosae	Forest	Dysentery, colds
Jenipapo	*Genipa americana*	Rubiaceae	Forest	Liver
Laranjeira	*Citrus sinensis*	Rutaceae	Cultivated	Nerves, colds, dysentery
Lima	*Citrus medica*	Rutaceae	Cultivated	Fever, colds
Limão	*Citrus aurantifolia*	Rutaceae	Cultivated	Upset stomach, dysentery, worms, colds, malaria
Losna	*Artemisia absinthium**	Compositae	Cultivated	Upset stomach, nerves, liver
Lozinaverde	*Tessaria absinthioides**	Compositae	Cultivated	Liver, stomachache
Macaco	*Ilex macoucoua*	Aquifoliaceae	2nd growth	Liver, kidneys
Macaié, rubim	*Leonurus sibiricus**	Labiatae	Cultivated	Fever, stomachache, headache, dysentery, hemorrhoids
Macela	*Egletes viscosa**	Compositae	Cultivated	Dysentery, worms, upset stomach
Malva	*Sida rhombifolia*	Malvaceae	Cultivated	Colds
Malva do reino	*Salvia* sp.*	Labiatae	Cultivated	Colds, coughs
Mamão	*Carica papaya*	Caricaceae	Cultivated, 2nd growth	Upset stomach, dysentery, headache, fever, worms
Mamona	*Ricinus communis*	Euphorbiaceae	Cultivated	Stomachache
Mamuí	?		Forest	Worms
Mandioca	*Manihot esculenta*	Euphorbiaceae	Cultivated	Dysentery
Mangeira	*Mangifera indica*	Anacardiaceae	Cultivated	Upset stomach, worms
Mangerioba	*Cleome aculeata**	Capparidaceae	2nd growth	Malaria, snakebites
Maracujá	*Passiflora edulis*	Passifloraceae	Cultivated	Worms, dysentery, malaria
Mastruz, Santa Maria	*Chenopodium ambrosioides**	Chenopodiaceae	Cultivated	Worms, bruises, wounds, colds

Matapasti	*Cassia obtusifolia**	Leguminosae	2nd growth	Colds, worms
Melão São Caetano	*Momordica charantia**	Cucurbitaceae	Cultivated	Malaria, stiff neck, upset stomach, worms
Mucuracáa	*Petiveria alliacea**	Phytolacaceae	Cultivated	Fever
Mutamba	*Guazuma ulmifolia*	Sterculiaceae	Forest	Dysentery
Oriza	*Pogostemum patchuli**	Labiatae	Cultivated	Earache
Pariri, frutão	*Pouteria pariri*	Sapotaceae	Forest	Dysentery
Pau ferro	*Caesalpinia ferrea* var. *cearensis**	Leguminosae	Cultivated	Dysentery, coughs
Pau para tudo	*Simaba cedron*	Simarubiaceae	2nd growth	Malaria
Pega pinto	*Boerhaavia paniculata**	Nyctaginaceae	2nd growth	Rheumatism, edema
Pião branco	*Jatropha curcas*	Euphorbiaceae	Cultivated	Headache, constipation, wounds
Pião roxo	*Jatropha gossypifolia*	Euphorbiaceae	Cultivated	Headache, mouth sores
Picão, picão da praia,	*Bidens bipinnata**	Compositae	2nd growth	Malaria, liver, stomachache
carrapicho de espinho	*Bidens pilosus**	Compositae	2nd growth	Malaria, liver
Pimenta do reino	*Piper nigrum*	Piperaceae	Cultivated	Malaria
Poejú	*Mentha pulegium**	Labiatae	Cultivated	Colds
Preciosa	*Aniba canelilla*	Lauraceae	Forest	Dysentery
Quebra pedra	*Phyllanthus stipulatus**	Euphorbiaceae	Cultivated	Liver, amebic dysentery, malaria
	*Phyllanthus niruri**	Euphorbiaceae	2nd growth	Amebic dysentery, kidneys, stomachache
Quina, quiné	*Geissospermum sericeum*	Apocynaceae	Forest	Malaria, upset stomach
	Ogcodeia amara	Moraceae	Forest	Malaria, upset stomach
	Coutarea hexandra	Rubiaceae	Forest	Malaria, upset stomach
Rumã	*Cuphea* sp.*	Lythraceae	Cultivated	Dysentery, worms
Sabugueira	*Sambucus japonica**	Caprifoliaceae	Cultivated	Measles, fever
Sacatinga	*Solanum asperum**	Solanaceae	2nd growth	Worms

Appendix 4. Plants Used for Medicinal Purposes along the Transamazon (continued)

Common name(s)	Scientific name(s)	Family	Habitat	For treatment of
Salsa	*Petroselinum sativum*	Umbelliferae	Cultivated	Hepatitis, kidneys
Sassacaroba	?		Forest	Dysentery
Serraião	*Eupatorium* sp.*	Compositae	Cultivated	Dysentery
Sete dor	?*	Verbenaceae	Cultivated	Dysentery, upset stomach
Tamanco de Nossa Senhora	*Alternanthera amoena**	Amaranthaceae	Cultivated	Excessive menstrual bleeding
Tokin, pitokó, quitoko	*Pluchea quitoc**	Compositae	Cultivated	Stomachache, liver, colds
Tomate	*Lycopersicon esculentum*	Solanaceae	Cultivated	Liver
Trevo	*Alternanthera bettzikiona**	Amaranthaceae	Cultivated	Irregular heartbeats
Tuna	*Opuntia tuna*	Cactaceae	Cultivated	Embedded splinters
Vassoura	*Scoparia dulcis**	Scrophulariaceae	2nd growth	Edema
Vinagreira	*Hibiscus sabdariffa**	Malvaceae	Cultivated	Worms

*Denotes specimens collected and deposited in the herbariums of INPA, Manaus, and the Museu Goeldi, Belém. Worms refers to intestinal helminths.

Bibliography

Ab' Sáber, A. N.

1966a. O domínio morfoclimático Amazônico. Instituto de Geografia, Universidade de São Paulo, *Geomorfologia* 1.

1966b. Superfícies aplainadas e terraços na Amazônia. Instituto de Geografia, Universidade de São Paulo, *Geomorfologia* 4.

1970a. Uma revisão do Quaternário Paulista: do presente para o passado. *Revista Brasileira de Geografia* 31(4):1–51.

1970b. Províncias geológicas e domínios morfoclimáticos no Brasil. Instituto de Geografia, Universidade de São Paulo, *Geomorfologia* 20.

1973. A organização natural das paisagens inter e subtropicais brasileiras. Instituto de Geografia, Universidade de São Paulo, *Geomorfologia* 41.

1977. Espaços ocupados pela expansão dos climas secos na América do sul, por ocasião dos períodos glaciais Quaternários. Instituto de Geografia, Universidade de São Paulo, *Paleoclimas* 3.

Absy, M.L.

1979. A palynological study of Holocene sediments in the Amazon basin. Ph.D dissertation, University of Amsterdam.

Absy, M.L., and T. Van der Hammen

1976. Some palaeoecological data from Rondônia, southern part of the Amazon basin. *Acta Amazonica* 6(3):293–299.

Adams, C. D.
1972. *The Flowering Plants of Jamaica*. University of West Indies Press, Mona.

Agarwal, A.
1979. A cure for a killer—but how to deliver it? *Nature* 278(5703): 389–391.

Almeida, F. B., and P. Machado
1971. Sôbre a infecção do *Panstrongylus geniculatus* pelo *Trypanosoma cruzi* em Manaus, Amazonas, Brasil. *Acta Amazonica* 1(2): 71–75.

Almeida, F. B., and J. A. Mello
1978. Sobre a ocorrência da moléstia de Chagas no Estado do Amazonas, Brasil. *Acta Amazonica* 8(4):595–599.

Alvares-Afonso, F. M.
1979. O cacau na Amazônia. Comissão Executiva do Plano da Lavoura Cacaueira, *Boletim Técnico* 66:3–36.

Alvim, P.
1977a. The balance between conservation and utilization in the humid tropics with special reference to Amazonian Brazil. Pp. 347–352 in G. T. Prance (ed.), *Extinction is Forever*. New York Botanical Garden, Bronx.
1977b. Cacao. Pp. 279–313 in P. Alvim, and T. Kozlowski (eds.), *Ecophysiology of Tropical Crops*. Academic Press, New York.
1978. Perspectivas de produção agrícola na região amazônica. *Interciencia* 3(4):243–251.

Anderson, A.
1972. Farming the Amazon: the devastation technique. *Saturday Review*, 30 September, pp. 61–64.

Anon.
1977. Report from the Evandro Chagas Institute, FSESP, Brazilian Ministry of Health, Belém, Brazil: 1. Yellow fever in Pará state, 1977. *Arthropod-Borne Virus Information Exchange* 33:27–28.
1980a. Brazil. *Bank of London and South America Review* 14(1):15.
1980b. Estimulo aos empresários. *Amazônia* 5(49):12–15.
1980c. Brazil. *Bank of London and South America Review* 14(2):64.

Ansari, N. (ed.)
1973. *Epidemiology and Control of Schistosomiasis (Bilharziasis)*. University Park Press, Baltimore.

Appel. W.
1976. The myth of jettatura. Pp. 16–27 in C. Maloney (ed.), *The Evil Eye*. Columbia University Press, New York.

Ascoli, W., M. A. Guzman, N. S. Scrimshaw, and J. E. Gordon

1967. Nutrition and infection field study in Guatemalan villages, 1959–1964. *Archives of Environmental Health* 15:439–449.

Aubréville, A.

1961. *Étude Écologique des Principales Formations Végétales du Brésil et Contribution à la Connaissance des Forêts de l'Amazonie Brésilienne.* Centre de Technique Forestier Tropical, Nogent-sur-Marne.

Azevedo, M. C., and R. C. Maroja

1956. Inquérito parasitológico entre crianças, realizado nos municípios de Ponta de Pedras e Souré-Pará. *Revista do Serviço Especial de Saúde Pública* 8(2):469–478.

Azevedo, T.

1979. The "chapel" as symbol: Italian colonization in southern Brazil. Pp. 86–95 in M. Margolis and W. Carter (eds.), *Brazil, Anthropological Perspectives: Essays in Honor of Charles Wagley.* Columbia University Press, New York.

Barbosa, F. S.

1972. Natural infection with *Schistosoma mansoni* in small mammals trapped in the course of a schistosomiasis control project in Brazil. *J. Parasitology* 58(2):405–407.

Barbosa, F. S., J. E. Dobbin, and M. V. Coelho

1953. Infestão natural de *Rattus rattus frugivorus* por *Schistosoma mansoni* em Pernambuco. *Publicações Avulsas do Instituto Aggeu Magalhães* 2(4): 43–46.

Barbosa, O., and J. R. Andrade Ramos

1959. Território do Rio Branco (aspectos principais da geomorfologia, da geologia e das possibilidades minerais de sua zona setentrional). Departamento Nacional da Produção Mineral, *Boletim* 196:1–46.

Barker, W. H.

1975. Perspectives on acute enteric disease epidemiology and control. *Bulletin of the Pan American Health Organization* 9(2): 148–155.

Barrett, S. W.

1980. Conservation in Amazonia. *Biological Conservation* 18:209–235.

Barrett, T. V., R. Hoff, K. E. Mott, F. Guedes, and I. Sherlock

1979. An outbreak of acute Chagas's disease in the São Francisco valley region of Bahia, Brazil: Triatomine vectors and animal reservoirs of *Trypanosoma cruzi. Transactions of the Royal Society of Tropical Medicine and Hygiene* 73(6):703–709.

Béhar, M.

1975. The role of feeding and nutrition in the pathogeny and prevention of diarrheic processes. *Bulletin of the Pan American Health Organization* 19(1):1–9.

Berg, C. C.

1978. Espécies de *Cecropia* da Amazonia brasileira. *Acta Amazonica* 8(2):149–182.

Bigarella, J. J.

1971. Variações climáticas no Quaternário superior do Brasil e sua datação radio-métrica pelo método do Carbono 14. Instituto de Geografia, Universidade de São Paulo, *Paleoclimas* 1.

Black, G. A., T. H. Dobzhansky, and C. Pavan

1950. Some attempts to estimate species diversity and population density of trees in Amazonian forests. *Botanical Gazette* 111(4): 413–425.

BNB

1967. *Mandioca: Aspectos da Cultura e da Indústria*. Banco do Nordeste do Brasil, Fortaleza.

1971. *Aspectos Industriais da Mandioca no Nordeste*. Banco do Nordeste do Brasil, Fortaleza.

Bordas, E., W. G. Downs, and L. Navarro

1953. Inactivation of DDT deposits on mud surfaces. *Bulletin of the World Health Organization* 9(1):39–57.

Box, E. D., Q. T. Box, and D. Young

1963. Chloroquine-resistant *Plasmodium falciparum* from Porto Velho, Brazil. *American Journal of Tropical Medicine and Hygiene* 12(3):300–304.

Braun, E. H., and J. R. Ramos

1959. Estudo agrogeológico dos campos Puciari-Humaitá, Estado do Amazonas e Território Federal de Rondônia. *Revista Brasileira de Geografia* 21(4):443–497.

Brazil

1976. *Programa de Pólos Agropecuários e Agrominerais da Amazônia: POLAMAZÔNIA*. Ministério do Interior, Brasília.

Britto, R., and E. Cardoso

1973. *A Febre Amarela no Pará*. SUDAM, Belém.

Brown, K. S.

1977. Centros de evolução, refúgios Quaternários e conservação de patrimônios genéticos na região neotropical: Padrões de diferenciação em Ithomiinae (Lepidoptera: Nymphalidae). *Acta Amazonica* 7(1):75–137.

Brown, K. S., P. M. Sheppard, J. R. Turner

1974. Quaternary refugia in tropical America: Evidence from race formation in *Heliconius* butterflies. *Proceedings of the Royal Society* 187:369–378.

Brown, L. R.
1978. *The Twenty Ninth Day*. Norton, New York.
Bruce-Chwatt, L. J.
1970. Global review of malaria control and eradication by attack on the vector. *Miscellaneous Publications of the Entomological Society of America* 7(1):7–23.
Bunker, S. G.
1979. Power structures and exhange between government agencies in the expansion of the agricultural sector. *Studies in Comparative International Development* 14(1):56–76.
1980. Forces of destruction in Amazonia. *Environment* 22(7):14–20, 34–43.
Bustamante, F. M.
1957. Distribuição geográfica e periodicidade estacional da malária no Brasil e sua relação com os fatores climáticos. Situação atual do problema. *Revista Brasileira de Malariologia e Doenças Tropicais* 9(2):181–189.
1959. Considerações sôbre certos problemas especiais relacionados com a erradicação da malária no Brasil. *Revista Brasileira de Malariologia e Doenças Tropiciais* 11(1):9–17.
Butt, A. J.
1970. Land use and social organization of tropical forest peoples of the Guianas. Pp. 33–49 in J. P. Garlick and R. W. Keay (eds.), *Human Ecology in the Tropics*. Pergamon Press, London.
Butzer, K. W.
1980. Adaptation to global environmental change. *Professional Geographer* 32(3):269–278.
Camargo, M. N., and I. C. Falesi
1975. Soils of the central plateau and Transamazonic highway of Brasil. Pp. 25–45 in E. Bornemisza, and A. Alvarado (eds.), *Soil Management in Tropical America*. North Carolina State University Press, Raleigh.
Carneiro, R. L.
1961. Slash-and-burn cultivation among the Kuikuru and its implications for cultural development in the Amazon basin. Pp. 47–67 in J. Wilbert (ed.), *The Evolution of Horticultural Systems in Native South America*. Caracas. No. 2.
Causey, O. R., and O. M. Maroja
1959. Isolation of yellow fever virus from man and mosquitoes in the Amazon region of Brazil. *American Journal of Tropical Medicine and Hygiene* 8(3):368–371.
Causey, O. R., M. P. Deane, O. Costa, and L. M. Deane
1945. Studies on the incidence and transmission of filaria, *Wuchere-*

ria bancrofti, in Belém, Brazil. *American Journal of Hygiene* 41(2): 143–149.

Causey, O. R., O. Costa, and C. E. Causey
1947. Incidência de parasitos intestinais do homem em Belém, Pará e visinhanças. *Revista do Serviço Especial de Saúde Pública* 1(2): 221–233.

Cavalcante, P. B.
1974. Frutas comestíveis da Amazônia:11. *Publicações Avulsas do Museu Goeldi* 27:1–77.

Caviedes, C. N.
1975. El Niño 1972: Its climatic, ecological, human, and economic implications. *Geographical Review* 65(4):493–509.

Chadwick, J., and W. N. Mann
1950. *The Medical Works of Hippocrates*. Blackwell Scientific Publications, Oxford.

Charlwood, J. D.
1979. Estudos sobre a biologia e hábitos alimentares de *Culex quinquefasciatus* Say de Manaus, Amazonas, Brasil. *Acta Amazonica* 9(2):271–278.

Charlwood, J. D., and N. D. Paraluppi
1978. O uso de caixas excito-repelentes com *Anopheles darlingi* Root, *A. nuneztovari* Gabaldon e *Culex pipiens quinquefasciatus* Say obtidos em áreas perto de Manaus, Amazonas. *Acta Amazonica* 8(4):605–611.

Chatfield, C.
1954. Food composition tables—minerals and vitamins. Food and Agricultural Organization, *Nutritional Studies* 11:1–117.

Clark, A.
1936. Report on the effects of certain poisons contained in foodplants of West Africa upon the health of the native races. *Journal of Tropical Medicine and Hygiene* 39(23):269–276.

Clarke, W. C.
1967. The Ndwimba basin, Bismarck mountains, New Guinea: Place and people. Ph.D dissertation, University of California, Berkeley.

Coene, R.
1956. Agricultural settlement schemes in the Belgian Congo. *Tropical Agriculture* 33(1):1–12.

Colinvaux, P.
1979. The ice-age Amazon. *Nature* 278(5703):399–400.

Colwell, E. J., R. L. Hickman, and S. Kosakal
1972. Tetracycline treatment of chloroquine-resistant falciparum

malaria in Thailand. *Journal of the American Medical Association* 220(5):684–686.

Comer, R. D., M. D. Young, J. A. Porter, J. R. Gauld,and W. Merritt
1968. Chloroquine resistance in *Plasmodium falciparum* malaria on the Pacific coast of Colombia. *American Journal of Tropical Medicine and Hygiene* 17(6):795–799.

Conklin, H. C.
1954. An ethnoecological approach to shifting agriculture. *Transactions of the New York Academy of Sciences* 17(2):133–142.

Conly, G. N.
1975. The impact of malaria on economic development: A case study. *Scientific Publication of the Pan American Health Organization* 297:1–117.

Cooper, C., P. de Petris, J. Ehleringer, R. Fisher, S. Hurlbert, S. Schneider, and J. Zieman
1974. Impacts of regional changes on climate and aquatic systems. Pp. 183–224 in E. Farnworth and F. Golley (eds.), *Fragile Ecosystems*. Springer-Verlag, New York.

Costa, J. M.
1979. Amazônia: Recursos naturais, tecnologia e desenvolvimento (Contribuição para o debate). Pp. 37–88 in J. M. Costa (ed.), *Amazônia: Desenvolvimento e Ocupação*. IPEA, Rio.

Costa, O. R., M. C. Azevedo, and R. Maroja
1955. Inquérito parasitológico entre crianças, realizado em seis municípios da zona Bragantina, Estado do Pará, em 1950. *Revista do Serviço Especial de Saúde Pública* 8(1):231–256.

Cowgill, U. M.
1960. Soil fertility, population, and the ancient Maya. *Proceedings of the National Academy of Sciences* 46(8):1009–1011.

Croat, T. B.
1972. The role of overpopulation and agricultural methods in the destruction of tropical ecosystems. *Bioscience* 22(8)465–467.

Cruz, G. L.
1965. *Livro Verde das Plantas Medicinais e Industriais do Brasil*. Velloso, Belo Horizonte. 2 vols.

Cunha, E.
1976. *Rebellion in the Backlands*. University of Chicago Press, Chicago.

Damuth, J. E., and R. W. Fairbridge
1970. Equatorial Atlantic deep-sea arkosic sands and ice-age aridity in tropical South America. *Bulletin of the Geological Society of America* 81(1):189–206.

Dasmann, R. F.
1975. *The Conservation Alternative*. Wiley, New York.
Davidson, B. R.
1972. *The Northern Myth*. Melbourne University Press, Melbourne. 3rd ed.
Deane, L. M.
1947. Observações sôbre a malária na Amazônia brasileira. *Revista do Serviço Especial de Saúde Pública* 1(1):3–59.
Deane, L. M., O. R. Causey,and M. P. Deane
1946. An illustrated key by adult female characteristics for the identification of thirty-five species of anophelini from the Northeast and Amazon regions of Brazil, with notes on the malaria vectors. *Monograph Series of the American Journal of Hygiene* 18:1–18.
1948. Notas sôbre a distribuição e a biologia dos anofelinos das regiões Nordestina e Amazônia do Brasil. *Revista do Serviço Especial de Saúde Pública* 1(4):827–965.
Deane, L. M., J. F. Ledo, E. S. Freire, V. A. Sutter, J. Cotrim, and G. C. Andrade
1949. Contrôle da malária na Amazônia pela aplicação domiciliar de DDT e sua avaliação pela determinação do índice de transmissão. *Anais do Sétimo Congresso Brasileiro de Higiene*. Vol. 1, pp. 455–464.
Denevan, W. M.
1973. Development and the imminent demise of the Amazon rain forest. *Professional Geographer* 25(2):130–135.
De Schlippe. P.
1956. *Shifting Cultivation in Africa: The Zande System of Agriculture*. Routledge and Kegan Paul, London.
Dias, L. C., F. D. Avila-Pires, and A. C. Pinto
1978. Parasitological and ecological aspects of schistosomiasis mansoni in the valley of the Paraíba do Sul river (São Paulo state, Brazil) 1. Natural infection of small mammals with *Schistosoma mansoni*. *Transactions of the Royal Society of Tropical Medicine and Hygiene* 72(5):496–500.
Dionisopoulos-Mass, R.
1976. The evil eye and bewitchment in a peasant village. Pp. 42–62 in C. Maloney (ed.), *The Evil Eye*. Columbia University Press, New York.
DNPM
1974a. *Projeto RADAM*. Ministério das Minas e Energia, Departamento Nacional de Produção Mineral, Brasília, vol. 5.

1974b. *Projeto RADAM*. Ministério das Minas e Energia, Departamento Nacional de Produção Mineral, Brasília, vol. 4.

Douglas, I.

1969. The efficiency of humid tropical denudation systems. *Transactions of the Institute of British Geographers* 46:1–16.

Ducke, A., and G. Black

1953. Phytogeographical notes on the Brazilian Amazon. *Anais da Academia Brasileira de Ciências* 25(1):1–46.

Dunn, F. L.

1972. Intestinal parasitism in Malayan aborigines. *Bulletin of the World Health Organization* 46:99–113.

Edgcomb, J. H., and C. M. Johnson

1970. Natural infection of *Rattus rattus* by *Trypanosoma cruzi* in Panama. *American Journal of Tropical Medicine and Hygiene* 19(5): 767–769.

Eisenmann, E.

1961. Favorite foods of neotropical birds: Flying termites and *Cecropia* catkins. *Auk* 78:636–638.

Elliott, R.

1972. The influence of vector behavior on malaria transmission. *American Journal of Tropical Medicine and Hygiene* 21(5):755–763.

Fairbridge, R. W.

1976. Shellfish-eating preceramic Indians in coastal Brazil. *Science* 191 (4225):353–359.

Falesi, I.

1972. Solos da rodovia Transamazônica. *Boletim Técnico do Instituto de Pesquisa Agropecuária do Norte* 55:1–196.

FAO

1970. Amino-acid content of foods. Food and Agricultural Organization, *Nutritional Studies* 24:1–285.

1973. Report of the ICP mission to Brazil: Agro-industrial potential of legal Amazonia. Food and Agricultural Organization, DDI: G/73/53, mimeo.

Fearnside, P. M.

1978. Estimation of carrying capacity for human populations in a part of the Transamazon highway colonization area of Brazil. Ph.D dissertation, University of Michigan, Ann Arbor.

1979. Cattle yield prediction for the Transamazon highway of Brazil. *Interciencia* 4(4):220–226.

1980. Black pepper yield prediction for the Transamazon highway of Brazil. *Turrialba* 30(1):35–42.

1981. *Carrying Capacity for Human Populations: Colonization of the Bra-*

zilian Rain Forest. Burgess Publishing Company, Minneapolis.

Ferraroni, J. J., and H. V. Dourado
1977. Uso da minociclina endovenosa no tratamento da malária por *Plasmodium falciparum*. *Acta Amazonica* 7(2):263–272.

Ferraroni, J. J., and J. Hayes
1979. Drug-resistant falciparum malaria among the Mayongong Indians in the Brazilian Amazon. *American Journal of Tropical Medicine and Hygiene* 28(5):909–911.

Ferraroni, J. J., J.C. Fonseca, and M. J. Ferraroni
1978. Malária por *P. falciparum* na Amazônia: Tratamento com a associação de sulfadoxina e pirimetamina por via parenteral. *Rev. Bras. Clin. Terap.* 7(5):301–305.

Ferri, M.
1973. A vegetação de cerrados brasileiros. Pp. 287–362 in E. Warming and M. Ferri, *Lagoa Santa e a Vegetação de Cerrados Brasileiros*, Editôra da Universidade de São Paulo, São Paulo.

Fittkau, E. J.
1967. On the ecology of Amazonian rain-forest streams. *Atas do Simpósio sôbre a Biota Amazônica*, vol. 3, pp. 97–108.

Flohn, H.
1969. *Climate and Weather*. McGraw-Hill, New York.

Fogh, S., S. Jepsen, B. H. Kean, J. Marr, P. Dubose, and J. McCroan
1978. Chloroquine-resistant *P. falciparum* in Kenya and Tanzania. *Morbidity and Mortality Weekly Report* 27:463–464.

Forattini, O. P., E. O. Rocha e Silva, O. A. Ferreira, E. X. Rabello, and D. G. Pattoli
1971. Aspectos ecológicos da tripanossomose americana 111: Dispersão local de triatomíneos, com especial referência ao *Triatoma sordida*. *Revista de Saúde Pública* 5(2):193–205.

Foster, R.
1967. Schistosomiasis on an irrigated estate in East Africa: 111. Effects of asymptomatic infection on health and industrial efficiency. *Journal of Tropical Medicine and Hygiene* 70(8):185–195.

Fraiha, H.
1968. Reinfestação do Brasil pelo *Aedes aegypti*. Considerações sôbre o risco de urbanização do virus da febre amarela silvestre na região reinfestada. *Revista do Instituto de Medicina Tropical de São Paulo* 10(5):289–294.
1977. *Panorama Atual das Parasitoses na Amazônia*. SUDAM, Belém.

Franco, S. R.
1967. Incidência de parasitos intestinais em escolares de Lábrea, Amazonas, Brasil. *Atas do Simpósio sôbre a Biota Amazônica*, vol. 6, pp. 99–102.

Freeland, W. J., and D. Janzen
1974. Strategies in herbivory by mammals: The role of plant secondary compounds. *American Naturalist* 108:269–289.

Freeman, J. D.
1955. *Iban Agriculture*. Colonial Research Studies, No. 18. London.

Freitas, C. A.
1972. Situação atual da esquistossomose no Brasil. *Revista Brasileira de Malariologia e Doenças Tropicais* 24(1–4):3–63.

Gabaldon, A.
1972. Difficulties confronting malaria eradication. *American Journal of Tropical Medicine and Hygiene* 21(5):634–639.

Galvão, S.
1968. Esquistossomose em Belém do Pará. *Revista Brasileira de Malariologia e Doenças Tropicais* 20:215–223.

García-Martin, G.
1972. Status of malaria eradication in the Americas. *American Journal of Tropical Medicine and Hygiene* 21(5):617–633.

Gentry, A. H., and J. Lopez-Parodi
1980. Deforestation and increased flooding of the Upper Amazon. *Science* 210:1354–1356.

Getz, L. L., P. C. Prather, and H. M. Platt
1975. Schistosomiasis in South America 1. Current status in Brazil. *The Biologist* 57(4):143–165.

Giglioli, G.
1938. Breeding habits of *Anopheles darlingii*: Natural factors which limit the distribution of this species and of malaria. *Agricultural Journal of British Guiana* 9(4):197–206.
1952. Eradication of *Anopheles darlingii* from inhabited areas of British Guiana by DDT residual spraying. *Journal of the National Malaria Society* 10(2):142–161.
1963. Ecological change as a factor in renewed malaria transmission in an eradicated area. *Bulletin of the World Health Organization* 29(2):131–145.
1968. Malaria in the American Indian. *Scientific Publication of the Pan American Health Organization* 165:104–113.

Gonçalves, C. R.
1957. Observações sôbre as saúvas da Amazônia. *Revista da Sociedade Brasileira de Agronomia* 12(3-4):43–52.
1967. As formigas cortadeiras da Amazônia, dos gêneros *Atta* Fabr. e *Acromyrmex* Mayr (Hym., Formicidae). *Atas do Simpósio sôbre a Biota Amazônica* 5:181–202.

Goodland, R. J., and H. S. Irwin
1975. *Amazon Jungle: Green Hell to Red Desert?* Elsevier, Amsterdam.

Gordon, J. E., M. A. Guzmán, W. Ascoli, and N. S. Scrimshaw.
1964. Acute diarrhoeal disease in less developed countries. *Bulletin of the World Health Organization* 31:9–20.

Goulding, M.
1980. *The Fishes and the Forest*. University of California Press, Berkeley.

Greenberg, B.
1965. Flies and disease. *Scientific American* 213(1):92–99.

Greenland, D. J., and P. H. Nye
1959. Increases in the carbon and nitrogen contents of tropical soils under natural fallows. *Journal of Soil Science* 10(2):284–299.

Guardiola-Rotger, A., E. F. Gonzales, A. Munoz, and E. Kauber.
1964. Studies on diarrheal diseases 11. Survey on the incidence of enteric organisms in the pediatric population of two isolated communities in Puerto Rico. *American Journal of Tropical Medicine and Hygiene* 13(3):417–424.

Guevara, S., and A. Gómez-Pompa
1972. Seeds from surface soils in a tropical region of Veracruz, Mexico. *Journal of the Arnold Arboretum* 53(3):312–335.

Haffer, J.
1969. Speciation in Amazonian forest birds. *Science* 165:131–137.

Hall, A. L.
1978. *Drought and Irrigation in North-East Brazil*. Cambridge University Press, Cambridge.

Hammond, A. L.
1977. Remote sensing: Brazil explores its Amazon wilderness. *Science* 196:513–515.

Harner, M. J.
1973. *The Jívaro: People of the Sacred Waterfalls*. Anchor Press/Doubleday, New York.

Hayes, J., and D. C. Charlwood
1977. O *Anopheles darlingi* evita o DDT numa área de malária resistente a drogas. *Acta Amazonica* 7(2):289.
1979. Dinâmica estacional de uma população de *Anopheles darlingi*, numa área endêmica de malária no Amazonas. *Acta Amazonica* 9(1):79–86.

Hayes, J., and J. J. Ferraroni
1978. Ocorrência de malária numa estrada recém-construída no Amazonas. *Acta Amazonica* 8(3):397–407.

Heinsdijk, D.
1958. Forest inventory in the Amazon valley (region between rio Tocantins and rios Guamá and Capim). Food and Agricultural

Organization, Expanded Technical Assistance Program, *Report* 992.

Hiraoka, M.
1980. Settlement and development of the Upper Amazon: The east Bolivian example. *Journal of Developing Areas* 14:327–347.

Hubert, L. F., A. F. Krueger, and J. S. Winston
1969. The double intertropical convergence zone—fact or fiction? *Journal of the Atmospheric Sciences* 26(4):771–773.

Hueck, K.
1972. *As Florestas da América do Sul*. Editôra da Universidade de Brasília, Brasília.

Hughes, C. C., and J. M. Hunter
1972. The role of technological development in promoting disease in Africa. Pp. 69–101 in M. T. Farvar and J. P. Milton (eds.), *The Careless Technology*. Natural History Press, New York.

Hunter, G. W., W. W. Frye, and J. C. Swartzwelder
1966. *A Manual of Tropical Medicine*. Saunders, Philadelphia. 4th ed.

Hunter, J. M.
1966. River blindness in Nangodi, Northern Ghana: A hypothesis of cyclical advance and retreat. *Geographical Review* 56:398–416.

Ianni, O.
1978. *A Luta Pela Terra*. Vozes, Petropolis.
1979. *Ditadura e Agricultura*. Civilização Brasileira, Rio.

IBGE
1978. *Anuário Estatístico do Brasil*. Instituto Brasileiro de Geografia e Estatístico, Rio.

IDESP
1970. Evolução e características da pecuária no Estado do Pará. Instituto de Desenvolvimento Econômico-Social do Pará, Belém. Mimeo.
1977a. *Diagnóstico do Município de Marabá*. Instituto do Desenvolvimento Econômico-Social do Pará, Belém.
1977b. *Diagnóstico do Município de Altamira*. Instituto do Desenvolvimento Econômico-Social do Pará, Belém.
1977c. *Diagnóstico do Município de Itaituba*. Instituto do Desenvolvimento Econômico-Social do Pará, Belém.

INCRA
1972a. *O Programa de Integração Nacional e a Colonização na Amazônia*. Ministério de Agricultura, Brasília.
1972b. *Altamira 1*. Ministério de Agricultura, Brasília.
1973a. *Urbanismo Rural*. Ministério de Agricultura, Brasília.
1973b. *Amazônia: Terra à Venda*. Ministério de Agricultura, Brasília.

n.d. *Uma Nova Marcha Rumo ao Norte*. Ministério de Agricultura, Brasília.

IPEAN

1974. Solos da rodovia Transamazônica: Trecho Itaituba-Rio Branco. Instituto de Pesquisa Agropecuária do Norte, Belém, Relatório Preliminar. Mimeo.

Jahoda, J. C., and D. L. O'Hearn

1975. The reluctant Amazon basin. *Environment* 17(7):16–30.

James, M., and R. Harwood

1970. *Herms's Medical Entomology*. MacMillan, New York.

Janzen, D. H.

1969. Birds and the Ant x Acacia interaction in Central America, with notes on birds and other Myrmecophytes. *Condor* 71(3):240–256.

1974. Tropical blackwater rivers, animals and mast fruiting by Dipterocarpaceae. *Biotropica* 6:69–103.

Jennings, D. L.

1970. Cassava in East Africa. Pp. 64–65 in D. L. Plucknett (ed.), *Tropical Root and Tuber Crops Tomorrow: Proceedings of the 2nd International Symposium on Tropical Root and Tuber Crops*. Hawaii. Vol. 1.

Joachim, A. W., and S. Kandiah

1948. The effect of shifting (chena) cultivation and subsequent regeneration of vegetation on soil composition and structure. *Tropical Agriculturist* 54(1):3–11.

Jobin, W. R., F. F. Ferguson, and L. A. Berrios-Duran

1973. Effects of *Marisa cornuarietis* on populations of *Biomphalaria glabrata* in farm ponds of Puerto Rico. *American Journal of Tropical Medicine and Hygiene* 22(2):278–284.

Journaux, M. A.

1975a. Geomorphologie des bordures de l'Amazonie Brésilienne: Le modele des versants; essai d'evolution paleoclimatique. *Bull. Assoc. Géogr. Franc.* 422–423:5–19.

1975b. Recherches géomorphologiques en Amazonie Brésilienne. *Bulletin de la Centre de Géomorphologie de Caen* 20:1–55.

Jurion, F., and J. Henry

1969. *Can Primitive Farming Be Modernized*? O.N.R.D./INEAC, Brussels.

Katzman, M. T.

1978. Colonization as an approach to regional development: northern Paraná, Brazil. *Economic Development and Cultural Change* 26(4):709–724.

Kellman, M. C.
1969. Some environmental components of shifting cultivation in upland Mindanao. *Journal of Tropical Geography* 28:40–56.
1974. The viable weed seed content of some tropical agricultural soils. *Journal of Applied Ecology* 11(2):669–678.

Kohlhepp, G.
1976. Planung und Heutige Situation Staatlicher Kleinbäuerlicher Kolonisationsprojekte an der Transamazônica. *Geographische Zeitschrift* 64(3):171–211.

Kumm, H. W.
1949. Estudos da febre amarela silvestre no Brasil durante os dez últimos anos. *Anais do Sétimo Congresso Brasileiro de Higiene.* Vol. 1, pp. 20–28.
1950. Seasonal variations in rainfall: Prevalence of *Haemagogus* and incidence of jungle yellow fever in Brazil and Colombia. *Transactions of the Royal Society of Tropical Medicine and Hygiene* 43(6):673–682.

Lacaz, C., R. G. Baruzzi, and W. Siqueira
1972. *Introdução à Geografia Médica do Brasil*. Editora Blucher, São Paulo.

Lainson, R., and J. J. Shaw
1978. Epidemiology and ecology of leishmaniasis in Latin-America. *Nature* 273 (5664):595–600.

Lainson, R., J. J. Shaw, R. D. Ward, and H. Fraiha
1973. Leishmaniasis in Brazil: 1X. Considerations on the *Leishmania braziliensis* complex:—Importance of the sandflies of the genus *Psychodopygus* (Mangabeira) in the transmission of *l. braziliensis braziliensis* in north Brazil. *Transactions of the Royal Society of Tropical Medicine and Hygiene* 67(2):184–196.

Lainson, R., R. D. Ward, and J. J. Shaw
1976. Cutaneous leishmaniasis in north Brazil: *Lutzomyia anduzei* as a major vector. *Transactions of the Royal Society of Tropical Medicine and Hygiene* 70(2):171–172.

Lainson, R., J. J. Shaw, R. D. Ward, P. Ready and R. Naiff
1979. Leishmaniasis in Brazil: XIII. Isolation of *Leishmania* from armadillos (*Dasypus novemcinctus*), and observations on the epidemiology of cutaneous leishmaniasis in north Pará state. *Transactions of the Royal Society of Tropical Medicine and Hygiene* 73(2):239–242.

Lainson, R., J. J. Shaw, H. Fraiha, M. Miles, and C. Draper
1979. Chagas's disease in the Amazon basin: I. *Trypanosoma cruzi* infections in sylvatic mammals, triatomine bugs and man in

the state of Pará, north Brazil. *Transactions of the Royal Society of Tropical Medicine and Hygiene* 73(2):193–204.

Lal, R.
1974. Soil erosion and shifting agriculture. Food and Agricultural Organization, *Soils Bulletin* 24:48–71.

Leck, C.
1972. Observations of birds at *Cecropia* trees in Puerto Rico. *Wilson Bulletin* 84(4):498–500.

LeCointe, P.
1922. La culture et la préparation du manioc en Amazonie. *Revue de Botanique Appliquée et d'Agriculture Coloniale* 2(11):331–337.

Leung, W., and M. Flores
1961. *Food Composition Tables for Use in Latin America*. INCAP-ICNND, Bethesda, Md.

Lovejoy, T. E.
1973. The Transamazonica: Highway to extinction? *Frontiers* 37(3):18–23.

Lowenstein, F. W.
1963. Nutrition and health of school children in a Brazilian Amazon town. *Journal of Tropical Pediatrics and African Child Health* 8(4):88–96.

Lynn Smith, T.
1972. *Brazil: People and Institutions*. Louisiana State University Press, Baton Rouge.

McGaughey, C. A.
1951. Hydrocyanic acid poisoning in nutrias caused by cassava (*Manihot utilissima* Pohl). *British Veterinary Journal* 107(6): 279–280.

Machado, W., and C. Martins
1951. Un foco autóctone de schistossomose no Pará. *O Hospital* 39:289–290.

McKelvey, T., A. Lunde, R. Vanreenen, E. Williams, H. Moore, M. Thomas, D. Worsley, and I. Crawford
1971. Chloroquine-resistant falciparum malaria among British service personnel in west Malaysia and Singapore. *Transactions of the Royal Society of Tropical Medicine and Hygiene* 65(3):286–304.

Maestri, M., and R. Barros
1977. Coffee. Pp. 249–278 in P. T. Alvim and T. T. Kozlowski (eds.), *Ecophysiology of Tropical Crops*. Academic Press, New York.

Mahar, D. J.
1978. *Desenvolvimento Econômico da Amazônia: Uma Análise das Políticas Governamentais*. IPEA, Rio.

Maloney, C.
1976. Don't say "pretty baby" lest you zap it with your eye—the evil eye in south Asia. Pp. 102–148 in C. Maloney (ed.), *The Evil Eye*, Columbia University Press, New York.
Marcgrave, J.
1942. *História Natural do Brasil*. Imprensa Oficial do Estado, São Paulo.
Margolis, M.
1979. Seduced and abandoned: Agricultural frontiers in Brazil and the United States. Pp. 160–179 in M. Margolis and W. Carter (eds.), *Brazil, Anthropological Perspectives: Essays in Honor of Charles Wagley*. Columbia University Press, New York.
Maroja, R. C.
1953. Incidência de esquistossomose em Fordlândia, município de Itaituba, Estado do Pará. *Revista do Serviço Especial de Saúde Pública* 6(1):211–218.
Marshall, C. F.
1980. Coffee in 1979: The effect of the Bogotá group. *Bank of London and South America Review* 14(1):3.
Meade, M.
1976. Land development and human health in west Malaysia. *Annals of the Association of American Geographers* 66:428–439.
Mein, R. M., and P. N. Rosado
1948. Experiência com novos medicamentos contra a malária no programa da Amazônia. *Revista do Serviço Especial de Saúde Pública* 1(4):1059–1091.
Michener, C. D.
1975. The Brazilian bee problem. *Annual Review of Entomology* 20:399–416.
Miracle, M. P.
1973. The Congo basin as a habitat for man. Pp. 335–344 in B. J. Meggers, E. S. Ayensu, and W. D. Ducksworth (eds.), *Tropical Forest Ecosystems in Africa and South America: A Comparative Review*. Smithsonian Institution Press, Washington, D.C.
Modenar, T.
1972. On the road. *Saturday Review*, 30 September, pp. 65–67.
Molion, L. C.
1975. A climatic study of the energy and moisture fluxes of the Amazonas basin with considerations of deforestation effects. Ph.D dissertation, University of Wisconsin, Madison.
Montoril Filho, M., J. J. Ferraroni, and D. Montoril
1978. Diagnóstico sócio-parasito-sanitário da cidade de Nova

Olinda do Norte, Amazonas. *Acta Amazonica* 8(1):91–98.

Moody, K.

1974. Weeds and shifting cultivation. Food and Agricultural Organization, *Soils Bulletin* 24:155–166.

Moore, D. V., and J. E. Lanier

1961. Observations on two *Plasmodium falciparum* infections with an abnormal response to chloroquine. *American Journal of Tropical Medicine and Hygiene* 10(1):5–9.

Moraes, M. A.

1972. A esquistossomose na Amazônia, Brasil. *Revista da Universidade Federal do Pará* 2(2):197–219.

1974. Onchocerciasis in Brazil. *Scientific Publication of the Pan American Health Organization* 298:122–128.

Moraes, M. A., H. Fraiha, and G. M. Chaves

1973. Onchocerciasis in Brazil. *Bulletin of the Pan American Health Organization* 7(4):50–56.

Moran, E. F.

1975. Pioneer farmers of the Transamazon highway: Adaptation and agricultural production in the lowland tropics. Ph.D dissertation, University of Florida, Gainesville.

1976. *Agricultural Development in the Transamazon Highway*. Latin American Studies Working Papers, Indiana University, Bloomington.

1979. Criteria for choosing successful homesteaders in Brazil. *Research in Economic Anthropology* 2:339–359.

1981. *Developing the Amazon*. Indiana University Press, Bloomington.

Morley, T.

1975. The South American distribution of the Memecyleae (Melastomaceae) in relation to the Guiana area and to the question of forest refuges in Amazonia. *Phytologia* 31(3):279–296.

Mors, W. B., and C. T. Rizzini

1966. *Useful Plants of Brazil*. Holden-Day, San Francisco.

Moss, L. W., and S. C. Cappannari

1976. Mal'occhio, ayin ha ra, oculus fascinus, judenblick: The evil eye hovers above. Pp. 1–15 in C. Maloney (ed.), *The Evil Eye*. Columbia University Press, New York.

Moss, R. P.

1969. The ecological background to land-use studies in tropical Africa, with special reference to the west. Pp. 385–407 in M. F. Thomas and G. Whittington (eds.), *Environment and Land Use in Africa*. Methuen, London.

Müller, P.
1973. *The Dispersal Centres of Terrestrial Vertebrates in the Neotropical Realm.* Junk, The Hague.

Myers, N.
1979. *The Sinking Ark.* Pergamon Press, Oxford.
1980. The present status and future prospects of tropical moist forests. *Environmental Conservation* 7(2):101–114.

Nájera-Morrondo, J. A.
1979. A suggested approach to malaria control and to the methodology applicable in different epidemiologic situations, based on experience in the Americas. *Bulletin of the Pan American Health Organization* 13(3):223–234.

Nelson, M.
1973. *The Development of Tropical Lands: Policy Issues in Latin America.* Johns Hopkins University Press, Baltimore.

Newton, K.
1960. Shifting cultivation and crop rotations in the tropics. *Papua and New Guinea Agricultural Journal* 13(3):81–118.

Norgaard, R. B.
1981. Sociosystem and ecosystem coevolution in the Amazon. *Journal of Environmental Economics and Management* 8(2).

Normanha, E. S., and A. S. Pereira
1950. Aspectos agronômicos da cultura da mandioca (*Manihot utilissima* Pohl). *Bragantia* 10(7):179–202.

Nye, P. H., and D. J. Greenland
1960. The soil under shifting cultivation. *Technical Communication of the Commonwealth Bureau of Soils* 51:1–153.

Oberg K.
1953. Indian tribes of northern Mato Grosso. Smithsonian Institution, Institute of Social Anthropology. *Publication* 15, pp. 1–144.

Oliver-González, J., and F. F. Ferguson
1959. Probable biological control of schistosomiasis mansoni in a Puerto Rican watershed. *American Journal of Tropical Medicine and Hygiene* 8(1):56–59.

Olson, S. L., and K. E. Blum
1968. Notes on avian dispersal of plants in Panama. *Ecology* 49(3):565–566.

Paula, R. D.
1972. A rodovia Belém-Brasília e os fazedores de desertos e a Transamazônica?, e as outras? *A Amazônia Brasileira em Foco* 6:78–95.

Paulini, E.
1974. Control of schistosomiasis (bilharziasis) in Brazil, past, present, and future. *Pest Articles and News Summaries* 20(3):265–274.
Pawley, W. H.
1971. In the year 2070. *Ceres* 4(4):22–27.
Pechnik, E., I. Mattoso, J. Chaves, and P. Borgas
1947. Possibilidade de aplicação do buriti e tucumã na indústria alimentar. *Arquivos Brasileiros de Nutrição* 4(1):33–37.
Pereira, O. D.
1971. *A Transamazônica: Prós e Contras*. Editôra Civilização Brasileira, Rio. 2nd ed.
Pimentel, L.
1974. A Transamazônica e o problema da integração social. *A Amazônia Brasileira em Foco* 9:24–54.
Pimienta, M. J.
1958. Modifications climatiques et subsidence récente affectant le glacis sud du bassin de l'Amazone (Rio Tocantis). *Comptes Rendus de la Académie des Sciences* 246(15):2268–2271.
Pine, R. H.
1973. Mammals (exclusive of bats) of Belém, Pará, Brazil. *Acta Amazonica* 3(2):47–79.
Pinheiro, F. P., G. Bensabath, A. Andrade, Z. Lins, H. Fraiha, A. Tang, R. Lainson, J. J. Shaw, and M. Azevedo
1974. Infectious diseases along Brazil's Trans-Amazon highway: Surveillance and Research. *Bulletin of the Pan American Health Organization* 8(2):111–121.
Pinheiro, F. P., G. Bensabath, D. Costa, O. Maroja, Z. Lins, and A. Andrade
1974. Hemorrhagic Syndrome of Altamira. *Lancet* 1(7859):639–642.
Pinheiro, F. P., G. Bensabath, A. Travassos da Rosa, R. Lainson, J. J. Shaw, R. D. Ward, H. Fraiha, M. Moraes, Z. Gueiros, Z. Lins, and R. Mendes
1977. Public health hazards among workers along the Trans-Amazon highway. *Journal of Occupational Medicine* 19(7):490–497.
Pinheiro, F. P., A. Travassos da Rosa, J. Travassos da Rosa, R. Freitas, W. Mello, and J. LeDuc
1978. Epidemias simultaneas de Mayaro e febre amarela em Belterra, Pará. *Boletim Epidemiologico* 10(16):146–152.
Pinheiro, F. P., A. Travassos da Rosa, M. Moraes, J. Almeida Neto, S. Camargo, and J. Filgueiras

1978. An epidemic of yellow fever in central Brazil. *American Journal of Tropical Medicine and Hygiene* 27(1):125–132.

Pinheiro, M., M. C. Marzochi, R. Giugliano, and L. Giugliano
1977. Enteroparasitoses em uma comunidade fechada. I—Estudo do solo como elo de transmissão em um orfanato de Manaus, Amazonas, Brasil. *Acta Amazonica* 7(4):503–506.

Pinotti, M.
1951a. The biological basis for the campaign against the malaria vectors of Brazil. *Transactions of the Royal Society of Tropical Medicine and Hygiene* 44(6):663–682.
1951b. The nation-wide malaria eradication program in Brazil. *Journal of the National Malaria Society* 10(2):162–182.

Pinto, L. F.
1973. A rodovia Perimetral Norte: Uma nova Transamazônica. Instituto de Geografia, Universidade de São Paulo, *Geografia e Planejamento* 10.

Pio Corrêa, M.
1926. *Diccionario das Plantas Uteis do Brasil e das Exoticas Cultivadas.* Imprensa Nacional, Rio. Vol. 1.
1931. *Diccionario das Plantas Uteis do Brasil e das Exoticas Cultivadas.* Imprensa Nacional, Rio. Vol. 2.

Pires, J.
1974. Tipos de vegetação da Amazônia. *Brasil Florestal* 5(17):48–58.

Piza, J., A. Silva Ramos, C. Brandão, and C. Figueiredo
1959. A esquistossomose no vale do Paraíba (Estado de São Paulo, Brasil). *Revista do Instituto Adolfo Lutz* 19:97–143.

Platt, B. S.
1962. Tables of representative values of foods commonly used in tropical countries. Medical Research Council, London. *Special Report Series* 302.

Popenoe, H.
1957. The influence of the shifting cultivation cycle on soil properties in Central America. *Proceedings of the 9th Pacific Science Congress* 7:72–77.

Potter, G. L., H. W. Ellsaesser, M. C. MacCracken, and F. M. Luther
1975. Possible climatic impact of tropical deforestation. *Nature* 258(5537):697–698.

Prance, G. T.
1973. Phytogeographic support for the theory of Pleistocene forest refuges in the Amazon basin, based on evidence from distribution patterns in Caryocaraceae, Chrysobalanaceae, Dichapetalaceae and Lecythidaceae. *Acta Amazonica* 3(3):5–28.

Prance, G. T., and H. Schubart
1978. Notes on the vegetation of Amazonia I. A preliminary note on the origin of the open white sand campinas of the lower rio Negro. *Brittonia* 30(1):60–63.

Prance, G. T. and M. F. Silva
1975. *Árvores de Manaus*. INPA, Manaus.

Prance, G. T., W. A. Rodrigues, and M. F. Silva
1976. Inventário florestal de um hectare de mata de terra firme km 30 da estrada Manaus-Itacoatiara. *Acta Amazonica* 6(1):9–35.

Prothero, R. M.
1965. *Migrants and Malaria in Africa*. University of Pittsburgh Press, Pittsburgh.

Purseglove, J. W.
1974. *Tropical Crops: Dicotyledons*. Wiley, New York.
1975. *Tropical Crops: Monocotyledons*. Wiley, New York.

Radke, M. G., L. S. Ritchie, and F. F. Ferguson
1961. Demonstrated control of *Australorbis glabratus* by *Marisa cornuarietis* under field conditions in Puerto Rico. *American Journal of Tropical Medicine and Hygiene* 10(3):370–373.

Ranzani, G.
1978. Alguns solos da Transamazônica na região de Marabá. *Acta Amazonica* 8(3):333–355.

Rassi, E., N. Lacerda, J. A. Guaimaraes, M. A. Vulcano, J. R. Perez, and A. Ramirez
1975. Preliminary report on a new vector of onchocerciasis in the Americas: *Simulium amazonicum* (Goeldi, Lutz 1910 and 1917). *Bulletin of the Pan American Health Organization* 9(1):10–12.

Rassi, E., N. Lacerda, and J. Guaimaraes
1976. Estudio de una zona de oncocerciasis en Brasil: Encuesta realizada en residentes locales. *Boletín de la Oficina Sanitaria Panamericana* 80(4):288–301.

Reis, A. F.
1960. *A Amazônia e a Cobiça Internacional*. Editôra Nacional, São Paulo.

Renjifo, S., and J. De Zulueta
1952. Five years' observations of rural malaria in eastern Colombia. *American Journal of Tropical Medicine and Hygiene* 1(4):598–611.

Rodrigues, D. C.
1961. Casos de malaria por *Plasmodium falciparum* resistentes ao tratamento pela cloroquina. *Arquivos de Higiene e Saúde Pública* 31(89):231–235.

Rosenberg, R., and N. Maheswary
1977. Chloroquine resistant *Plasmodium falciparum* in Bangladesh.

Transactions of the Royal Society of Tropical Medicine and Hygiene 70(5/6):533.

Sakamoto, T.
1960. Rock weathering on 'terras firmes' and deposition on the 'varzeas' in the Amazon. University of Tokyo, *Journal of the Faculty of Sciences* 22(2):155–216.

Salati, E., J. Marques, and L. Molion
1978. Origem e distribuição das chuvas na Amazônia. *Interciencia* 3(4):200–205.

Sanchez, P. A. (ed.)
1973. A review of soils research in tropical Latin America. *Technical Bulletin of the North Carolina Agricultural Experimental Station* 219:1–197.

Sanchez, P. A., and M. A. Nurēna
1972. Upland rice improvement under shifting cultivation systems in the Amazon basin of Peru. *Technical Bulletin of the North Carolina Agricultural Experimental Station* 210:1–20.

Scaff, L. M.
1979. Contribuição à biografia de Adolpho Ducke. *Ciência e Cultura* 31(5):565–572.

Scaff, L. M., and Z. M. Gueiros
1967. Prevalência e contrôle da filariose no Pará: Estado atual. *Revista Brasileira de Malariologia e Doenças Tropicias* 19(2):245–252.

Schalie, H.
1972. World Health Organization project Egypt 10: A case history of a schistosomiasis control project. Pp. 116–153 in M. T. Farvar and J. P. Milton (eds.), *The Careless Technology*. Natural History Press, New York.

Schmidt, S.
1965. Fases evolutivas da luta antipalúdica na região Amazônica. Primeiros trabalhos realizados no campo sôbre a resistência do *P. falciparum* às drogas cloroquinadas. *Revista Brasileira de Malariologia e Doenças Tropicais* 17(2/3):179–209.

Schultes, R. E., and T. Swain
1976. The plant kingdom: A virgin field for new biodynamic constituents. Pp. 134–171 in N. J. Fina (ed.), *The Recent Chemistry of Natural Products, Including Tobacco: Proceedings of the Second Philip Morris Science Symposium*. New York.

Schwaner, T. D., and C. F. Dixon
1974. Helminthiasis as a measure of cultural change in the Amazon basin. *Biotropica* 6(1):32–37.

Scott, G. A.
1974. Effects of shifting cultivation in the Gran Pajonal, eastern

Peru. *Proceedings of the Association of American Geographers* 6:58–61.

Scrimshaw, N. S., J. O. Morales, A. Salazar, and C. P. Loomis
1953. Some aspects of the community development project, rural area, Turrialba, Costa Rica. *American Journal of Tropical Medicine and Hygiene* 2(4):583–592.

Sefer, E.
1959. Pragas que ocorrem no Estado do Pará atacando produtos armazenados. *Boletim da Inspetoria Regional de Fomento Agrícola no Pará* 9:23–35.

Shaw, J. J., R. Lainson, and H. Fraiha
1969. Considerações sôbre a epidemiologia dos primeiros casos autóctones de Doença de Chagas registrados em Belém, Pará, Brasil. *Revista de Saúde Pública* 3(2):153–157.

Shiff, C. J.
1972. The impact of agricultural development on aquatic systems and its effect on the epidemiology of schistosomes in Rhodesia. Pp. 102–108 in M. Farvar and J. Milton (eds.), *The Careless Technology*. Natural History Press, New York.

Silva, J. R., P. F. Almeida Lopes, L. F. Ferreira, R. Morteo, and J. B. Naveira
1961. Resistência do *P. falciparum* à ação da cloroquina. *O Hospital* 60(5):43–58.

Silva Lima, E. J., J. L. Fernandes, E. Griner, E. R. Machado, and S. Brisolla
1978. Projeto Cotrijuí-Norte. *Arquitetura* 20:48–59.

Singer, R., and I. Araujo
1979. Litter decomposition and ectomycorrhiza in Amazonian forests. *Acta Amazonica* 9(1):25–41.

Sioli, H.
1953. Schistosomiasis and limnology in the Amazon region. *American Journal of Tropical Medicine and Hygiene.* 2:700–707.

Skillings, R. F., and N. O. Tcheyan
1979. Economic development prospects of the Amazon region of Brazil. Center of Brazilian Studies, Johns Hopkins University. *Occasional Papers Series* 9.

Skutch, A. F.
1980. Arils as food of tropical American birds. *Condor* 82:31–42.

Smith, N. J.
1973. House sparrows *(Passer domesticus)* in the Amazon. *Condor* 75:242–243.
1974. Agouti and babassu. *Oryx* 12(5):581–582.

1976a. Transamazon highway: A cultural-ecological analysis of settlement in the humid tropics. Ph.D dissertation, University of California, Berkeley.

1976b. Brazil's Transamazon highway settlement scheme: Agrovilas, agropoli and ruropoli. *Proceedings of the Association of American Geographers* 8:129–132.

1976c. Utilization of game along Brazil's Transamazon highway. *Acta Amazonica* 6(4):455–466.

1978. Agricultural productivity along Brazil's Transamazon highway. *Agro-Ecosystems* 4:415–432.

1980a. Anthrosols and human carrying capacity in Amazonia. *Annals of the Association of American Geographers* 70(4):553–566.

1980b. Further advances of house sparrows *(Passer domesticus)* into the Brazilian Amazon. *Condor* 82:109–111.

1981. *Man, Fishes, and the Amazon.* Columbia University Press, New York.

Sombroek, W. G.

1966. *Amazon Soils: A Reconnaissance of the Soils of the Brazilian Amazon Region.* Center for Agricultural Publications and Documentation, Wageningen.

Spencer, J. E.

1966. *Shifting Cultivation in Southeastern Asia.* University of California Press, Berkeley.

Sternberg, H. O'R.

1956. *A Água e o Homem na Várzea do Careiro.* Universidade do Brasil, Rio.

1975. The Amazon River of Brazil. *Erdkundliches Wissen* 40.

Teitelbaum, J. M.

1976. The leer and the loom—social controls on handloom weavers. Pp. 63–75 in C. Maloney (ed.), *The Evil Eye.* Columbia University Press, New York.

Thomas, M. F.

1969. Geomorphology and land classification in tropical Africa. Pp. 103–145 in M. F. Thomas and G. Whittington (eds.), *Environment and Land Use in Africa.* Methuen, London.

1974. *Tropical Geomorphology.* Wiley, New York.

Tricart, J.

1974. Existence de périodes sèches au Quaternaire en Amazonie et dans les régions voisines. *Revue de Géomorphologie Dynamique* 23:145–158.

1975. Influences des oscillations climatiques récentes sur le modèle en Amazonie orientale (region de Santarém) d'après les images radar latéral. *Zeitschrift für Geomorphologie* 19(2):140–163.

Tripathy, K., F. Gonzălez, H. Lotero, and O. Bolanos
1971. Effects of *Ascaris* infection on human nutrition. *American Journal of Tropical Medicine and Hygiene* 20(2):212–218.
Turner, F. J.
1928. *The Frontier in American History*. Holt, New York.
Van der Hammen, T.
1974. The Pleistocene changes of vegetation and climate in tropical South America. *Journal of Biogeography* 1(1):3–26.
Vanzolini, P. E.
1963. Problemas faunísticos do cerrado. *Simpósio sôbre o Cerrado*, Editôra da Universidade de São Paulo. Pp. 307–321.
1970. Zoologia sistemática, geografia e a origem das espécies. Instituto de Geografia, Universidade de São Paulo, *Série Teses e Monografias* 3.
Vargas, A., and A. C. Sá
1949. As variações de densidade e dispersão do *A. darlingi*: Suas relações com a malaria. *Anais do Sétimo Congresso Brasileiro de Higiene*. Vol. 1, pp. 385–394.
Vázquez-Yanes, C., A. Orozco, G. François, and L. Trejo
1975. Observations on seed dispersal by bats in a tropical humid region in Veracruz, Mexico. *Biotropica* 7(2):73–76.
Venkatachalam, P. S., and V. N. Patwardhan
1953. The role of *Ascaris lumbricoides* in the nutrition of the host: Effect of ascariasis on digestion of protein. *Transactions of the Royal Society of Tropical Medicine and Hygiene* 47(2):169–175.
Villa Nova, N., E. Salati, and E. Matsui
1976. Estimativa de evapotranspiração na bacia Amazônica. *Acta Amazonica* 6(2):215–228.
Ward, R. D., and H. Fraiha
1977. *Lutzomyia umbratilis* a new species of sandfly from Brazil (Diptera: Psychodidae). *Journal of Medical Entomology* 14:313–317.
Weber, N. A.
1947. Lower Orinoco river fungus-growing ants (Hymenoptera: Formicidae, Attini). *Boletin de Entomologia Venezolana* 6:143–161.
Wesche, R.
1974. Planned rainforest family farming on Brazil's Transamazonic highway. *Revista Geografica* 81:105–114.
1978. A moderna ocupação agrícola em Rondônia. *Revista Brasileira de Geografia* 40(3/4):233–247.
Wheelwright, E. G.
1974. *Medicinal Plants and Their History*. Dover Publications, New York.

Wood, C. H., and M. Schmink
1978. Blaming the victim: Small farmer production in an Amazonian colonization project. Pp. 77–93 in E. F. Moran (ed.), *Changing Agricultural Systems in Latin America.* Special issue of the *Journal of Third World Studies.* Williamsburg, Va.
Woodall, J. P.
1967. Virus research in Amazonia. *Atas do Simpósio sôbre a Biota Amazônica.* Vol. 6, pp. 31–63.
Woodwell, G.
1978. The carbon dioxide question. *Scientific American* 238(1):34–43.
Wozniewicz, W.
1974. The Amazonian highway system. Pp. 291–314 in C. Wagley (ed.), *Man in the Amazon.* University of Florida Press, Gainesville.
Wright, C. A.
1970. The ecology of African schistosomiasis. Pp. 67–80 in P. J. Garlick and R. W. Keay (eds.), *Human Ecology in the Tropics.* Pergamon Press, London.
Wright, J. W., R. F. Fritz, and J. Haworth
1972. Changing concepts of vector control in malaria eradication. *Annual Review of Entomology* 17:75–102.
Young, M. D., and D. V. Moore
1961. Chloroquine resistance in *Plasmodium falciparum. American Journal of Tropical Medicine and Hygiene* 10(3):317–320.
Young, M. D., P. G. Contacos, J. E. Stitcher, and J. W. Millar
1963. Drug resistance in *Plasmodium falciparum* from Thailand. *American Journal of Tropical Medicine and Hygiene* 12(3):305–314.
Zonneveld, J. I.
1975. Some problems of tropical geomorphology. *Zeitschrift für Geomorphologie* 19(4):377–392.

Index

Designer: Al Burkhardt
Compositor: Interactive Composition Corporation

Text: 10/12 Palatino
Display: Palatino

www.ingramcontent.com/pod-product-compliance
Lightning Source LLC
Chambersburg PA
CBHW031124270326
41929CB00011B/1483

9780520314306